THE DEVIL'S MATRIX

This World of Lies, Deceptions, Illusions & Distractions

James A. Watkins

CONTENTS

In The Beginning

"Evolution destroys utterly, and finally, the very reason Jesus' earthly life was supposedly made necessary. Destroy Adam and Eve and the original sin, and in the rubble, you will find the sorry remains of the Son of God. If Jesus was not the redeemer who died for our sins, and this is what Evolution means, then Christianity is nothing." So says *American Atheist* magazine.

If the account of the Creation in Genesis is not valid—in particular, the story of Adam and Eve—then Jesus cannot be our Savior. He said Adam was a real person and the first human being. If the Bible is wrong about the origin of Man, it must also be wrong about Man's ultimate end. The Theory of Evolution has already convinced millions of people that Genesis is not true. And that is the purpose of Evolution, a theory of satanic origin.

More and more, science confirms that the Universe appears to be designed. Discovery after discovery shows us this. A design naturally implies a Designer, a Designer with intent, who actualized all of this. And purposefulness is always the invention of the intellect, the thought, of a conscious person. The foundation of all reality is information, and information only comes from an intelligent mind. It indeed is apparent that Divine Intelligence created this Cosmos.

We know from experience that nothing is ever created by itself. Creative persons first formulate what they want to create— they conceive first and realize last. To create anything is to give of yourself; what you create reveals part of you. Therefore, we can expect that the Creation will show part of the Creator; Creation bears His signature. Arno Penzias, Nobel Prize winner for Physics, agrees, "The best data we have are exactly what I would have predicted, had I nothing to go on but the five books of Moses, the Psalms, and the Bible as a whole."

Now, the Darwinian idea, as taught by the Devil's minions, is that a pool of mineral water somehow, all by itself and entirely by accident, invented the genetic instructions to form every kind of living creature we see today. According to Genesis, inorganic matter cannot turn into living beings without God's power. Unless God says so, life does not emerge from inorganic materials.

Evolution cannot tell us how life began; it cannot tell us why we exist. Much of what scientists say today about the origin of life is not based on science at all but on the ideology of Atheism. Real science cannot say that God did not create the Universe. And it cannot say that Man was not specially designed by God as the Crown of His Creation. Science agrees with Genesis that Man had a beginning at some point, and so did the Universe. Science has lately come round to the truth that the fundamental information of living things cannot be reduced to energy or matter.

Andrew Parker, Research Director at the Natural History Museum in London, is an evolutionary biologist. He does not profess to believe in God. But he was inspired to take a look at Genesis 1 after several people wrote to him who suggested that his research on the origin of the eye seemed to echo the statement, "Let there be light."

Parker was amazed by what he found: "Without expecting to find anything, I discovered a series of parallels between the creation story on the Bible's first page and the modern, scientific account of life's history. This, at least, made me think. The congruence was almost exact. The more detail is examined, the more convincing and remarkable I believe the parallels become. Could it be that the creation account on page one of Genesis was written as it is because that is how the sequence of events really happened? Here, then, is the Genesis Enigma: The opening page of Genesis is scientifically accurate but was written long before science was known. How did the writer of this page come to write this creation account? I must admit, rather nervously as a scientist, averse to entertaining such an idea, that the evidence that the writer of the opening page of the Bible was divinely inspired is strong. I have never before encountered such powerful impartial evidence that the Bible is the product of divine inspiration."

You are more important than the Cosmos in which you find yourself. Look at how fine-tuned the Universe is to support life on Earth. It is evident that Earth is uniquely designed to be our home. It seems created for a purpose: To be inhabited by human beings.

Scientists once claimed that the Universe had always been here and would always be here. Their motive for making this claim was to prove that Genesis got it wrong. When other scientists determined the Universe, in fact, had a beginning and will one day end, that evidence was fought against for decades by the scientists entrenched in positions of power because they were afraid to admit anything that might make Genesis look to be true.

There is not much argument among scholars about the history presented in the Bible after Genesis 11, after the appearance of Abraham. We have archaeological evidence of biblical history after Genesis 11. It is Genesis chapters 4-11 that raise objections because of the Cosmos they make real.

When you read how God made Adam and Eve, notice how intimate it was. God fashioned Adam from the dust of the ground with His own hands (as it were) and breathed into the first man's nostrils the Breath of Life. Think of how that differs from the account given by diabolical Darwinism that our ancestors were apes. Man brought low indeed.

Adam and Eve were created from the beginning with the powerful gift of language, being able to communicate with each other and their Creator. That contradicts the Devil's lie that early Man could only grunt as an ape and language developed gradually.

Also of note is that Adam is called by God to work. In other words, work is ordained from on high. Since work is divinely ordained, naturally, the Devil says otherwise. He would teach us that work is a curse and a burden—not a calling or vocation. And since those who follow his doctrines see work as only something to be endured to survive, they will seek to avoid it.

One of the Devil's lies, as relayed by Feminism, is that God is anti-woman in the Bible. On the contrary, God created Eve to help Adam and be his companion for life. Made out of his very flesh, she was to be at his side. Without her, his life was empty and lonely. They completed each other.

It was the later demonic myths of pagans that demeaned womanhood. In Greek mythology, for instance, the first woman was created to *punish* man, to deceive him, torment him, and fill his life with pain, suffering, and sorrow. Her name was Pandora.

God presents woman as a sacred being. As Matthew Rueger writes, "Her womb is considered the seat of life from which comes beings created in the image of God. Life is sacred, and the place where life is formed is to be treated as sacred space."

Adam needed a mate, similar to him, but different from him. For one difference, God decided to give men twenty times more testosterone. Women have natural strengths, abilities, and gifts that men do not. The very fact that they are complementary is key to the survival of the human race. That is a core reality of our being.

Men are designed by their Maker to cherish and protect their mates, as they unite in purpose and love. Women are designed by their Maker to be 'the mother of all living.' As Martin Luther attested, "By nature, woman has been created to bear children. Therefore she has breasts."

Women are made to be mothers; men are made to be fathers. There is nothing more normal and natural than one man and one woman united in marriage. It should be evident to everyone that masculinity and femininity are part of God's design for us. The main reason God made human beings male and female was for reproduction, to "be fruitful and multiply." The power to create new life—what a gift!

As Maggie Gallagher wrote, "Sex makes babies. Society needs babies. Babies deserve mothers and fathers." Sex should be done in private, but what it produces is public. New life causes public celebrations. Promiscuous sex causes public disease. Rape causes public fear. Dr. Russell Moore had this to say: "Marriage isn't just a registering of *this is my special someone*. Marriage is about connecting the generations in the past, mother and father together, and connecting this union and this couple with generations that are to come."

The Serpent persuaded the first woman and man to follow their own will instead of the will of their Creator. The chief aim of the Evil One was then, and remains today, to tempt men and women to sin, i.e., to be immoral. He promotes lust of the flesh and pride. Note the etymology of the word 'evil' as something that wells up from underneath, as in, from our lower nature. It wells up to rebel against our higher nature and take its place if we permit it.

Sin entered the world when Adam and Eve disobeyed God and instead obeyed Satan. Along with sin came death. Afterward, in a great lesson for us, Adam does not confess his sin and repent and ask for forgiveness. He blames Eve and blames God. Instead of manning up, he tries to blame others for what he did.

After the Fall, God allowed Satan to remain on Earth to play the ultimate villain in the human drama. Of course, the *Satanic Bible* teaches a different story: "Satan represents man as nothing more than another animal, sometimes better, but more often worse than those who walk on four paws because he has become the most vicious animal of all."

Our culture loves to paint our ancestors as cavemen, ugly idiots, vastly inferior to us. That is the opposite of the truth. Adam and Eve were the most beautiful and intelligent human beings ever. It has been all downhill from there.

The first couple walked and talked with God every day. They lived in paradise, the Garden of Eden. They could do anything they wanted except for just one thing. That single prohibition was given to see if, given free will, they would or would not honor and obey their Creator.

Satan entered the scene, and the Fall followed. He had been observing them and waited for just the right moment to put the thought into Eve's mind, "This tree we are supposed to stay away from sure is gorgeous. I wonder why its fruit is forbidden?" The Serpent sows doubt in her mind about what God said, and what He meant by what He said—which was quite clear.

God commanded Adam to guard Eden against intruders, which could only mean evil spirits since there were no other people around. Satan gained dominion over Earth through the disobedience of Eve and Adam, of whom he was consumed with jealousy. Cain killed Abel, and Man was found to be as he is. I AM delivered the Hebrews out of abject slavery, and they repaid Him by making the Golden Calf. I AM came to Earth in the flesh, and men murdered Him.

All people knew God in the beginning. But they turned away from their Creator, preferring what they thought were their own ideas— which were, in reality, suggestions whispered into the minds of men and women by dark spiritual forces that secretly seethed with hatred toward humankind.

It is a diabolical lie that monotheism (the belief in one God) evolved from polytheism (the belief in many gods). The truth is the other way round. At the beginning of the human race, everybody knew there was only one Eternal Creator. Men enthroned demons as their gods because they wanted to join in the rebellion, to sin and have their sins approved. The Devil created the idea and put it into men's heads to dishonor their Father by worshipping evil spirits as gods—the more, the merrier. But never fear, for God has under His command an enormous army of warrior angels that send righteous messages to men and women. They fight for God's People when we come under demonic attack.

God designed the family to pass down faith in Him, and the worship of Him, from one generation to the next. Fathers are to teach their children about Him. The descendants of Adam's son Seth, Abel's replacement, proclaimed the One True God, and from Seth's line came Noah.

Cain married either one of his sisters or nieces; named the world's first city for his son Enoch; and formed a godless society that prospered. It invented politics and weapons.

The *Book of Enoch* claims that demons taught the human race how to do astrology and perform sorcery, how to make jewelry to ornament themselves, create and apply makeup (cosmetics), and to pervert natural sexuality via sodomy and other perversions. Thus men and women lived lives of rampant sexual immorality, practiced sexual deviancies, and were steeped in violence. That made God sad and angry. The Great Flood was His response.

There is not much more critical to your worldview, the lens through which you perceive everything else, than what you believe about the origin of the human race. Jesus tells us, "Have you not heard that He who created human beings, in the beginning, made them male and female. Therefore a man shall leave his father and his mother and hold fast to his wife, and the two shall become one flesh."

That teaches us that human beings are precious, and marriage is sacred. Century after century—until recently, in fact—this lesson has provided the very foundation of Western Civilization. In Genesis, God affirms that Man is made from molecules, from the Dust of the Earth. Still, human life is more than chemistry because Man only became a living spiritual being after God breathed the Breath of Life into the nostrils of Adam and Eve.

A Tale of Two Revolutions

In 2016, our Declaration of Independence—the most successful political document ever written—celebrated its 240th birthday. No other nation has been governed by its founding documents for as long as America. No country in 1776 elected its leaders or allowed private ownership of land by persons from all classes. There had never been a government of the people, for the people, and by the people. The intellectuals of Europe predicted it couldn't endure for more than a few years.

John Locke was a philosopher who much influenced the Founding Fathers. Locke believed in building a government upon the transcendent, timeless principles of Natural Law. He wrote: "The Law of Nature stands as an eternal rule for all men, legislators, and others. The rules that they make for other men's actions must be conformable to the Law of Nature, i.e., to the will of God. Laws made by humans must be made according to the general laws of Nature, and without contradiction to any positive law of Scripture, otherwise, they are ill-made."

The Declaration of Independence is based on the principles of the Holy Bible, which so permeated the atmosphere of the Founders; it was like water to fish. The biblical worldview saturated the hearts and the minds of virtually all Americans of the founding era. The Bible also heavily influenced the Constitution.

The University of Houston conducted an independent study to determine what were the most prominent influences on the minds of the men who drafted the Declaration of Independence and the Constitution. Its researchers wanted to see what our Founding Fathers read and quoted. They collected 15,000 records, and from those, found 3,154 quotes. It took the team ten years to document the source of each citation. The most quoted source was the Holy Bible, cited four times more than the next most used reference.

Many people conflate the American War of Independence and the French Revolution, but the two are opposites in spirit. The French saw the Church as their enemy; Christianity guided the Americans.

All but four of the fifty-six men who signed the Declaration of Independence, and all thirty-nine who signed the Constitution, were devout Christians. They founded a nation on the morals and values of Christianity. Our children are not told this today in government schools.

The United States Capitol was used for church services by the founding generation. As late as 1868, the largest Christian congregation in America still met at the U.S. Capitol. Carved into the stone of the Washington Monument are the words, Laus Deo! In English: Praise be to God!

It was not until 1947 that our courts began to restrict the open expression of our Christian faith by citizens and government. Since then, the godless Left has worked through courts to eliminate our First Amendment Right to the Free Exercise of Religion. In the 1960s, the social engineers who serve the Evil One banned God, the Bible, and prayer from our nation's schools, where all three had played an essential role for 300 years.

The foundation of America rests firmly on the idea that individual rights are not granted by government but are gifts from God that a *just* government is bound to recognize and protect. As Richard John Neuhaus has said of the founders: "The American experiment would advance the universal purposes of God in history." It is this very American experiment that the Left hates.

The Founding Fathers assumed that churches and families would mediate against state power. The state today presumes to take over the functions and authorities of church and family. The Founders believed in obedience to the sacred order, but progressives today believe nothing is sacred.

The foundations of freedom are being destroyed from the top down—by cultural elites. They have changed life, liberty, and the pursuit of happiness into freedom to transgress and the happiness of transgressing. Felicity does not lie in rebellion against God. Blessedness comes from right living—in accordance with your created nature. Joy is not freedom from the truth.

The very idea of creating a Constitution derived from the Founding Father's deep familiarity with the Covenants of the Bible. From this same source, they acquired their beliefs in individual rights, Providence, and an eternal reality beyond our temporal world. Since the time of the men who wrote the First Amendment, witnesses in court or before Congress have taken an oath to swear to God that they will tell the truth. The first act of America's first Congress was to ask a minister to open with prayer and to lead Congress in the reading of four chapters of the Bible. The same men who wrote the Bill of Rights appropriated federal funds to pay Christian chaplains to pray at the opening of all congressional sessions, a practice that has continued to this day.

George Washington called the American Revolution the Great Experiment. In his Farewell Address, he stated, "Of all the dispositions and habits which lead to political prosperity, religion and morality are indispensable supports. In vain would that any man claim the tribute of patriotism, who should labor to subvert these great pillars of human happiness."

This nation represents the pinnacle of human achievement. It proved that a free people could govern themselves. At the founding of America, the transfer of power from one regime to the next was rarely orderly, as it has been under our system. The United States was the first republic since Rome. It is a fragile thing.

The most significant change in America since its founding has been the change in attitude toward religious faith. Most Americans do not know what our Founding Fathers believed and how critical the Christian faith was to the founding of our nation and the freedoms we enjoy today. To the Founders, religious belief is indispensable to liberty. Samuel Adams said, "While the People are virtuous they cannot be subdued; but when once they lose their Virtue they will be ready to surrender their Liberties to the first external or internal Invader."

The Declaration of Independence claims that God grants our right to Life, Liberty, and the Pursuit of Happiness to us—not men or governments. James Madison declared that the finished Constitution was a product of "the finger of that Almighty Hand." "We have staked our future upon the capacity of each and all of us to govern ourselves, to sustain ourselves, according to the Ten Commandments of God. The belief in a God all-powerful, wise, and good, is essential to the moral order of the world and the happiness of man," wrote Madison.

The results of the American Experiment have been profound. The freedoms of our young nation began slowly spreading around the globe in the 19th Century. The success of our free-market capitalism gave birth to 200 years of incredible inventions, and spectacular advancements in technology and science.

The quality of life and the wealth that Americans enjoy today are the direct results of our founding philosophy. With only 5 percent of the world's population, the United States has created more wealth than the rest of the world combined; fed more people around the globe; led the planet in innovations that benefit humankind, and provided more foreign aid and relief to other peoples than the rest of the entire planet.

It is no accident that In God We Trust is the national motto of the United States. "Our Constitution was made only for a moral and religious people. It is wholly inadequate to the government of any other," John Adams pronounced.

Benjamin Franklin believed that the writing of our founding documents had been "influenced, guided, and governed by that omnipotent, omnipresent, and beneficent Ruler, in Whom all inferior spirits live, and move, and have their being." "I believe in one God, the Creator of the Universe. That He governs it by His Providence. That He ought to be worshipped," proclaimed Franklin. "From the day of our Declaration of Independence, the American people were bound by the laws of God, and the laws of the Gospel, which they nearly all acknowledge as the rules of their conduct," affirmed John Quincy Adams.

The Fathers of America believed they were part of a Manifest Destiny of divine design, and that America would prove to be a blessing for all of humankind. "I always consider the settlement of America with reverence and wonder, as the opening of a grand scene and design in Providence, for the illumination of the ignorant and the emancipation of the slavish part of mankind all over the earth," decreed John Adams.

In 1777, Congress, facing a national shortage of "Bibles for our schools, and families, and the public worship of God in our churches," announced that they "desired to have a Bible printed under their care & by their encouragement." Therefore, Congress ordered 20,000 copies of the Bible, paid for at government expense.

The 1783 Treaty of Paris, which officially ended the American War of Independence, and established America as an independent nation, begins "In the name of the most holy and undivided Trinity." In 1789, while framing the First Amendment, Congress passed the first federal law touching education. It declared "Religion, morality, and knowledge, being necessary to good government and the happiness of mankind, schools and the means of education shall forever be encouraged."

Everyone involved in the establishment of the United States knew its success depended on virtue in its citizenry because of the nearly unbridled freedom that the American Constitution allowed the citizens of the new nation. Americans faced few legal restrictions on their freedom of action. Self-government means citizens will govern their own conduct. As Benjamin Franklin said, "Only a virtuous people are capable of freedom. As nations become more corrupt and vicious, they have more need of masters."

Franklin loved the idea of small government. However, he recognized that only "A virtuous and laborious people may be governed cheaply." The constitutions of each of the 50 states, either in the preamble or body, explicitly recognize or express gratitude to God.

America's first Presidential Inauguration incorporated seven specific religious activities. They included the use of the Bible to administer the oath; affirming the spiritual nature of the oath by the adding the prayer "So help me God!"; inaugural prayers offered by the President; religious content in the inaugural address; civil leaders calling the people to worship and acknowledge God; church services attended en masse by Congress as an official part of congressional activities; and clergy-led inaugural prayers. Every subsequent President before Obama has replicated these activities in whole or part.

Americans were exceptionally honest and law-abiding. Criminals were looked upon as enemies of the human race. Marriage was the bedrock institution of American society. Americans considered marriage to be far more than a civil contract. It was a covenant. Marriage was the principal source of American virtue; as the promoter of hard work, proper education of children, the morals of the next generation, public peace and order, and as the most potent restrainer of public vice.

In 1835, German author Francis Grund wrote, "No government could be established on the same principle as that of the United States, with a different code of morals. The American Constitution is remarkable for its simplicity. However, it can only suffice a people habitually correct in their actions, such as the domestic habits of the Americans, their religious devotion, and their high respect for morality."

In 1853, the United States Senate declared that the Founding Fathers "Had no fear or jealousy of religion itself, nor did they wish to see us an irreligious people. They did not intend to spread over all the public authorities and the whole public action of the nation the dead and revolting spectacle of atheistic apathy."

Inside the United States Capitol, the declaration In God We Trust is prominently displayed in both the House and Senate Chambers. In 1854, the House of Representatives declared, "Religion must be considered as the foundation on which the whole structure rests. Christianity, in its general principles, is the great conservative element on which we must rely for the purity and permanence of free institutions."

In 1870, the Federal Government made Christmas an official national holiday. Christmas celebrates the birth of Christ, an event described by the U.S. Supreme Court as "acknowledged in the Western World for 20 centuries, and in this country by the people, the Executive Branch, Congress, and the courts for two centuries."

President John Adams declared, "As the safety and prosperity of nations ultimately and essentially depend on the protection and the blessing of Almighty God, the national acknowledgment of this truth is an indispensable duty which the people owe to Him."

President Andrew Jackson asserted that the Bible "Is the rock on which our Republic rests."

President Abraham Lincoln affirmed that the Bible `is the best gift God has given to men. But for it, we could not know right from wrong."

President William McKinley announced, "Our faith teaches us that there is no safer reliance than upon the God of our fathers, Who has so singularly favored the American people in every national trial and Who will not forsake us so long as we obey His commandments and walk humbly in His footsteps."

President Teddy Roosevelt stated, `The Decalogue and the Golden Rule must stand as the foundation of every successful effort to better either our social or political life."

President Woodrow Wilson proclaimed, "America was born to exemplify that devotion to the elements of righteousness which are derived from the revelations of Holy Scripture."

President Herbert Hoover declared, "American life is built, and can alone survive, upon the fundamental philosophy announced by the Savior nineteen centuries ago."

President Franklin D. Roosevelt not only led the nation in a six-minute prayer during D-Day on June 6, 1944, but also stressed that "If we do not prepare to give all that we have and all that we are to preserve Christian civilization in our land, we shall go to destruction." The U.S. government issued 17 million Bibles to its troops during World War Two.

President Harry S. Truman maintained, "The fundamental basis of this nation's law was given to Moses. The fundamental basis of our Bill of Rights comes from the teachings we get from Exodus and St. Matthew, from Isaiah and St. Paul." Truman also told a group touring Washington, DC, "You will see, as you make your rounds, that this nation was established by men who believed in God. You will see the evidence of this deep religious faith."

President Dwight D. Eisenhower insisted, "Without God, there could be no American form of government, nor an American way of life. Recognition of the Supreme Being is the first, the most basic expression of Americanism. Thus, the founding fathers of America saw it, and thus with God's help, it will continue to be," in a declaration later repeated by President Gerald Ford.

President John F. Kennedy acknowledged, "The rights of man come not from the generosity of the state but from the hand of God."

All sessions of the Supreme Court begin with the Court's Marshall announcing, "God save the United States and this honorable court." The Supreme Court has confirmed throughout our nation's history that the United States is "a Christian country," "a Christian nation," "a Christian people," "a religious people whose institutions presuppose a Supreme Being," and that "we cannot read into the Bill of Rights a philosophy of hostility to religion."

John Jay, an author of the Federalist Papers and original Justice of the Supreme Court, urged, "The most effectual means of securing the continuance of our civil and religious liberties is always to remember with reverence and gratitude the Source from which they flow." Justice James Wilson, a signer of the Constitution, declared, "Human law must ultimately rest its authority upon the authority of that law which is Divine. Far from being rivals or enemies, religion and law are twin sisters, friends, and mutual assistants."

James Madison summed it up well: "We have staked the whole future of American civilization, not upon the power of government, far from it. We have staked the future of all of our political institutions upon the capacity of each and all of us to govern ourselves, to control ourselves, to sustain ourselves according to the Ten Commandments of God."

The Founding Fathers based our government system on the First Commandment, "Thou shalt have no other gods before me." They understood that man was created to serve God, not the state. Since man is in God's image, a government should help secure man's God-endowed rights. They instituted a system of representative government with clear limits upon what the government could do. Those limits were carefully and meticulously delineated to ensure freedom.

To the Fathers, the government's goal is to be a servant of Mankind, never the master of it. The framers of our Constitution advocated that people govern themselves under God's laws. The government should never have the power to deprive individuals of rights that the Constitution stated were "endowed by their Creator."

When we reject the objective truths revealed to us by God, and lose the ability to make sound moral judgments, we forfeit what is most precious to human beings: our spiritual dimension. We squander the good sense and the will to recognize right from wrong, good from evil. A lack of religious training leaves a void to be filled by diversion. Misery and corruption will result from the lack of a moral compass.

In 1846, the Supreme Court decision in the *City of Charleston v. Benjamin* included these words: "Christianity is part of the common law of the land, with the liberty of conscience to all. It has always been so recognized. The observance of Sunday is one of the usages of the common law recognized by our U.S. and state Governments. It is the foundation of those morals and manners upon which our society is formed; it is their basis. Remove it, and they would fall. Morality has grown upon the basis of Christianity."

In 1931, the Supreme Court declared that Americans are Christian people who quite graciously allow non-Christians liberty of conscience. The court affirmed, "We are a Christian people, according to one another, the equal right of religious freedom and acknowledging with reverence the duty of obedience to God's will."

In *Zorach v. Clausen* (1952), the court claimed that America not only allows the free exercise of religion but that its various government levels were entirely right to join forces vigorously with the Church. The ruling reads, "The First Amendment does not say that there shall be a separation of Church and State in every and all respects. Otherwise, the state and religion would be aliens to each other—hostile, suspicious, and even unfriendly. We are a religious people whose institutions presuppose a Supreme Being. When the state encourages religious instruction or cooperates with religious authorities, it follows the best of our traditions."

By 1960, America had become the most prosperous, best educated, most free, creative, inventive, innovative, and generous nation of all time. Free market economics provided the foundation. The list of achievements by Americans in our first 200 years staggers the mind. The average lifespan doubled in America. American accomplishments affected people worldwide as we shared our inventions, and our political and economic ideas were emulated. We have only been able to help so many because of our attainments as a people. Where would the world be without America?

Now, we have lost our way. We punish the producers and reward the lazy. We created an entitlement mentality and victim mentality. Half of our national budget is now transfer payments from taxpayers to dependents of the state. Our country is plagued by massive sins, massive debts, and an idolatrous celebrity culture as we entertain ourselves to death.

America was founded on Anglo-Saxon principles: All people in positions of power were to be elected; all decisions require the consent of the people; law comes from Natural Law, which comes from the Almighty. Individuals, families, and local communities should solve their own problems. County or state governments can deal with difficulties of too broad a scope for them to handle. The federal government is the last resort.

We owe a duty to God, family, and country. Four crimes were considered an offense against everybody: Treason, cowardice, desertion, and homosexual acts. Federal powers are to be *few and defined*, according to James Madison. The powers of each state are to be *numerous and indefinite*. The idea: To keep as much power as close to the people as possible. It was considered immoral for one generation to pass on its debts to the next. The government, Jefferson said, "is unauthorized to saddle posterity with our debts, and we are morally bound to pay them ourselves."

Virtue must be learned, and therefore it must be taught—cultivated in homes, churches, and schools. Americans became the first free people in history. Education was to inculcate the Christian faith, Christian morals, and general knowledge.

Seven states of the original thirteen had official state religions when the Constitution was written. The First Amendment constrained the federal government from taking the side of any denomination. "The whole power over the subject of religion is left exclusively to the state governments," declared Supreme Court Justice Joseph Story in 1858.

Government welfare blunts the motivation to work for a living, encourages laziness, and makes you dependent and weak—you lose your job skills as you sit around. They atrophy much like a muscle not exercised. Temporary help is OK. A person should help himself, then turn to family, then to church, then the community, then to the county, and finally the state. Under no circumstances should the Feds be involved in charity. For it there is no *constitutional authority*.

God revealed Divine Law to Man. No government should contradict God's Law—only protect it. The divine pattern of law for human happiness includes reverence toward God and acknowledgment of His supremacy over all things. Marriage is sacred; adultery wrong; human life sacred; no lies; no stealing; do not covet; work for what you want; no murder; be honest in your dealings; support law and order; keep the peace; honor and obey parents; honor the elderly; cherish women, and men must protect, feed, clothe, and shelter their women and children. Help the helpless—the disabled person, the injured, the sick, the widow, the orphan. Do not participate in vice or promote it. Be morally upright, not filthy, nasty, and evil—support personal and public standards of decency.

America set the standard for the rest of the world. Religion and morality were deemed necessary for good government and the happiness of Mankind. Morality is a standard of behavior that distinguishes right from wrong. Religion is the foundation of morality: A fundamental system of beliefs concerning man's origin and his relationship to the cosmic universe and his relationship with his fellow man.

Liberty & Religion—Faith and Freedom united—produced Harmony & Order. America was founded on religious principles and Christian values. No law would be made opposed to Christian morals. The Founders even approved of church meetings in public buildings.

The non-denominational 'Five Fundamental Points' were taught in public schools:
1) Recognize and worship our Creator, who made all things.
2) The Creator revealed a moral code for a happy life, not for His sake but our sakes.
3) We will be held responsible for our actions by our Creator.
4) Man lives beyond the grave.
5) We will all face Judgment Day and eternal rewards or punishment.

It wasn't like they prayed all day in the public schools. They might recite the Lord's Prayer or say a generic prayer (voluntary for students) such as this one named in the Supreme Court case that imprudently got prayer kicked out of our schools: Almighty God, we acknowledge our dependence on Thee, and we beg Thy blessings upon us, our parents, our teachers, and our country.

In the 1925 *Gitlow Case*, the Supreme Court, for the first time, granted the federal government supremacy over the rights of heretofore-sovereign states. Then in 1940, the *Chartwell Case* was used against religious liberty. In 1947, the *Emerson Case* broke down the wall by asserting federal court power to dictate what states could do regarding religious questions. In 1948, the *McCollum Case* said kids couldn't be taught religion. And so here we are full of sexual perversions; addicted to narcotics, pornography, and violence; infested by filthy habits and manners and language; with the family in the toilet. As Daniel Webster had predicted: "If we and our posterity reject religious instruction and authority, violate the rules of eternal justice, trifle with the injunctions of morality, no man can tell how a sudden catastrophe may overwhelm us."

Unlike its American opposite, the French Revolution was about the 'de-Christianization' of France. The goal was to destroy Christianity and replace it with a religion of the state, which the French revolutionaries called the Cult of Reason. "For humanity's sake," bankers, scholars, gentlepersons, and merchants, along with their wives and children, were dragged from their homes and murdered.

The godless revolutionaries went on a rampage. They would demolish beautiful churches and magnificent monasteries that were centuries old; smash Christian paintings, statues, sculptures, and stained glass windows; open tombs of saints to despoil their skeletons; shred sacred books; ruin relics; desecrate altars; and slaughter priests and nuns. "Christianity has been struck down once and for all," proudly wrote Joseph Fouche, Minister of Police during the revolution.

Christians were banned from becoming teachers, Christian worship services outlawed, necklaces with crosses prohibited. A prostitute christened the Goddess of Reason was enthroned on the altar of Notre Dame Cathedral in Paris. Christians were beheaded, disemboweled, and impaled; women's breasts cut off, bodies defiled, and severed heads carried around on pikes. Christianity was banished from funerals and marriages; Christian names abolished. It was "the dream of the ACLU come true," says Ann Coulter.

None of that bears any similarity to the American War of Independence. There was no mass slaughter *for the people* in the American Revolution, no rabid mobs, no demonic hatred. The symbol of the American Revolution is the Liberty Bell; for the French Revolution, it is the guillotine (the national razor). Six hundred thousand people died, and 145,000 left the country, in what the French revolutionaries called 'the Terror.' In the American War of Independence, fewer than 20,000 died all told.

All but four of the men who signed the American Declaration were orthodox Trinitarian Christians, what liberals today would call 'extreme fundamentalists.' All but one of the signers of the Declaration of Independence died peacefully as old men; all of the leading French revolutionaries died violent deaths soon after their revolt. The American revolutionaries were like today's Tea Party; the French revolutionaries are like today's leftists who spout hatred, destroy property, and commit violence every time they get together.

All leftist revolutionaries since have followed in the footsteps of the French Revolution, with their atheism, mob violence, concentration camps, re-education programs, and killing fields. Lenin, Stalin, Mao, Kim IL Sung, Pol Pot, and Fidel Castro were all monstrous psychopaths, and the American Left exuberantly endorsed all of them.

The New York Times glorified Chairman Mao as he systematically murdered 78 million people, and celebrated the Ayatollah Khomeini's takeover of Iran as a "model of humane governance." *The Los Angeles Times* thought America should emulate the socialist slavery that is North Korea. *The Washington Post* backed the Khmer Rouge, who killed a quarter of the population of Cambodia. Years after those last mass murders, famous leftist Noam Chomsky still glorified Pol Pot for his "constructive achievements."

No matter how many people leftists slaughter, they continue to believe in godless totalitarianism. They are OK with mass killing because they dehumanize any persons who disagree with their plots. The most bloodthirsty people are those claiming to be righting past wrongs.

The French Revolution marked the first attempt of modern men to destroy Christianity and impose Atheism on a nation-state's citizens. Over a hundred years later, the communists of the Soviet Union would carry that ball forward with particular ferocity. Totalitarians see the Christian faith as the obstacle to their goal of creating, through massive bloodshed, an atheist utopia.

One Satanist who played a big part in the French Revolution, and declared himself "the personal enemy of Jesus Christ," was Anarchasis Cloots. He ordered the slaughter of imprisoned priests, abolished all Christian Holy Days (holidays), and even got rid of Sunday. By the time Lucifer finished with France, it lay in ruins.

But first, because of food shortages, depopulation was deemed the answer—mass extermination. Every revolution headed by the godless claims the same thing: We stand for the poor and oppressed, whose life we will make so much better. But they never do. Life always gets worse for everybody under their regimes, with more famine, suffering, torture, starvation, and state-sanctioned murder.

Great Men Who Served Satan

Life is a spiritual battle for the souls of men and women. On one side of this battle, God is the ultimate source of reality, law, salvation, and truth; on the other, Man is the source of all those things. A worldview with Man as god will inevitably produce a society that is sick and depraved. Just look at the history of the world, and you must admit Man makes for a lousy god. But Man as god is precisely what the Left demands so they can dispense with God's standards of good and evil and replace them with: Whatever produces pleasure is good; whatever causes pain is bad.

If all that God declares evil is called good by men, the only things left to call evil are good people—God's People. That is precisely what the servants of Satan do. Let us look at the brilliant men who acted as mouthpieces for Lucifer, who served as his instruments to lead man astray, to guide our thinking away from eternal truths, and to breed hostility in us towards our Father.

Niccolo Machiavelli (1469-1527), in his book *The Prince*, put forth the idea that political rulers must *pretend to be religious* so they will be trusted to rule justly. His advice is only appropriate for men who do not believe in God, since he recommends wickedness as a way of life. The basic idea is that evil deeds, high crimes, and unspeakable abominations are admirable as long as they serve a larger purpose. We can easily see that this philosophy is part and parcel of today's Democrat Party in America.

The Prince has long been a favorite book of atheists, including, for example, Vladimir Lenin. Machiavelli rejected the Christian faith and so dismissed the very idea that any action might be intrinsically evil. He considered Christianity an obstacle to progress, and sprinkled his book with what has been called "carefully crafted blasphemies."

The man who carried the ball forward, for those who want to rid this world of the Christian concept that God the Creator has revealed absolute moral laws to us, was Thomas Hobbes (1588-1679). Some consider Hobbes the 'Father of Psychology.' His significant contribution was to redefine what is real and what is not, with the 'not' including everything that cannot be 'proved' by the senses.

The first modern intellectual, and the most influential, was Jean-Jacques Rousseau (1712-1778). Rousseau did not believe in love. He did believe in sex. But he also surmised that release from pent-up passions could be gotten just as easily from a man, child, animal, or old sock, as from a woman.

Rousseau taught that marriage was unnatural and artificial. 'Free love' was the answer—an idea the hippies made their philosophy of living. It was strange for a man to have any ties with any particular woman since they all had the single part a man needed. Rousseau only had to convince women that indiscriminate sex was a good thing for them, too. We could then get rid of the idea that marriage was the proper place for sex and that there was some connection between having sex and having children. That is unbridled hedonism—the Playboy Philosophy, the Cosmo Girl—explicitly created to rebel against Christianity.

To Rousseau, the first man who said, "this is mine," led to the downfall of the human race, and all crimes and wars since. But ownership of property is not unique to humanity: Every animal is territorial.

Rousseau set in motion the ideas that caused the French Revolution, the movers and shakers of which considered him 'the teacher of mankind.' You can trace 'progressive' education, social engineering, and the cult of environmentalism straight back to Rousseau, as well as socialism, fascism, communism, and progressivism.

Self-pity and ingratitude were his two most prominent traits. He declared that happiness was "never to have to do anything I don't wish to do." He admonished his friends, "If you cause me the least annoyance, you will never see me again."

According to Rousseau, the first humans were the opposite of Adam and Eve. In his imaginings, our first parents and their descendants, for a least a few generations, lived only for pure sensations, and satisfied their animal appetites at will. There was no such thing as families, marriage, or sexual fidelity. No one owned anything, so there could be no theft. Claiming anything, even a wife or husband or child or home, as one's own, was the root of all human misery—an idea later latched onto by Karl Marx.

According to this philosophy, individual persons are not to blame for their actions—society is to blame. Does this sound familiar? Though celebrated as a great man then and now, Rousseau was a demented masochist and a chronic masturbator, which he said enabled him to subject all women to his sexual whims and give him pleasure without their consent (through fantasizing about them while abusing himself).

He was an admitted liar, thief, and coward. He shocked acquaintances by the contemptuous way he treated his wife and children. Rousseau loved animals more than people and called children 'an inconvenience.' What is most disturbing is that Rousseau was considered the preeminent teacher of how to raise children but never took any interest in his own five, none of which he ever even named, and all of whom were immediately upon being born dropped at an orphanage where he knew conditions were so horrible that two-thirds of the babies died before reaching their first birthday; only 14 percent lived to age seven; usually, those few who did survive to adulthood became vagrant beggars.

Rousseau appears to have been a complete sociopath. He preached that the state must raise all children and form their minds, an idea with which totalitarians everywhere have since utilized. Rousseau believed that the state should be in charge of every aspect of human activity—including what we think, because, "Those who control a people's opinions control its actions." The Almighty State will cure all the ills of humankind!

He proposed that men should merely satisfy whatever urges they may feel, without the ball and chains of love, marriage, family, society, or morality. That way, "men could be considered neither good nor evil, and had neither vices nor virtues." In this way, Man could be 'natural,' that is, he could live only for today with no thoughts beyond the moment.

To sum up, Rousseau (who invented the Noble Savage myth) thought Primitive Man was superior to civilized man, and taught a replacement Garden of Eden story, not based on any evidence but on what he wished to be true.

For Rousseau, sex was devoid of love and only an animal act. That goes against God's purposes, in which sexual intercourse is an act of love between a husband and wife who together create a family that is the natural essence of society. In Rousseau's teachings, any sexual act will do; conjugal love is unnatural; paternal love is nothing but a social construct; romantic love itself is meaningless; marriage is nonsensical; the distinction between men and women artificial; and the only thing that is real is sexual desire.

Next, we come to Adam Weishaupt (1748-1830), considered the founder of the Illuminati. However, it is possible he only revised, updated, and codified an already existing philosophy. The Illuminati seems to be present in Spain in the 15th century under the name Alumbrados (the Illuminated). It featured sexual rituals and taught that no sexual acts were sinful for its members, although they might be for non-members. If you joined, you could participate in the orgies without guilt, shame, or the need for God to forgive you.

Back in the 12th century, the Italian Joachim of Flora, who looked forward to a 'New Age' of enlightened men who needed no church, had founded a group of 'Illuminated Ones.' Further back, the Islamic Order of the Assassins, dating to A.D. 1080, smoked a lot of hash and murdered many people. For them, murder was a mystical experience, and some believe they were part of the Illuminati.

Anyway, Adam Weishaupt was once a Christian genius widely respected as a professor of law. We can learn a lot from his recruitment by the dark side.

While he had grown up a Christian, he also much admired Rousseau and his diabolical writings. In Weishaupt's twenties, a mysterious person known as Kolmer apprenticed him into Satanism. Soon after that, Weishaupt was persuaded by intellectual 'friends' to become a progressive liberal to match his political views with his anti-Christian immorality. Then, his brother's wife seduced him. When she became pregnant due to this illicit affair, Weishaupt found an abortionist to kill the fruits of their union. Now an adulterer and accomplice in the murder of his baby, he entirely turned his back on Jesus.

Germany had long been considered the earthly headquarters of Satanism before Weishaupt presented the founding document of the Illuminati May 1st, 1776. Notice that ever since, May 1st has been the major holiday among revolutionary organizations, especially for communists, fascists, socialists, and unionists.

The Illuminati was secret. Its 2,000 original members used 'nicknames,' the term deriving from the Devil, who was referred to as 'Old Nick.' When first joining, a man had to be anti-Church at the least. The novice would gradually convert to full-blown atheism or face expulsion. The insiders were all-out Devil worshipers but did not share this fact with all members.

Within a decade or two, many Christian men would join the Illuminati. Weishaupt allowed this to expand his sphere of influence in society. He employed a strategy first to convert Christians to Deism, and then to Pantheism, followed by atheism, and finally Satan worship. Anyone who resisted one of these steps had his progress halted in the organization, ruled not to be a candidate to move up. In this way, the bold and ruthless were separated, those men willing to set aside their religion, morality, and patriotism.

Part of the plan was the 'liberation' of women so that they would hand out sex like candy to men. The Illuminati even invented a new abortion potion to encourage free love. The strategy included deluding women into believing that they were being mistreated by men to sow discord between the sexes, and encouraging women to act like men.

The existence, ideas, and aims of the Illuminati had to be kept secret. As Weishaupt wrote, "The great strength of our Order lies in its concealment: let it never appear in any place in its own name but always covered by another name." Voltaire advised lying to the public: "The opposite of what is said and promised can be done afterward. That is of no consequence."

Every prominent leftist since has used that very strategy to disguise what they are really up to and to gain support from what they call their Useful Idiots. Useful Idiots are people whom leftists lie to by feeding them half-truths and promising them a great future in order to gain their political support. Karl Marx was undoubtedly in touch with Illuminists, if not writing on orders from them.

Alessandro Cagliostro, the famous magician, astrologer, and Satanist, had been initiated into the Illuminati and was used to foment the French Revolution. France was the first target to topple all governments and churches and institute official atheism and communism. Cagliostro instigated the Affair of the Necklace that began the downfall of King Louis XVI and his wife, Marie Antoinette. Satanist Aleister Crowley would much later claim to be Cagliostro reincarnated.

The motto of the Illuminati, Death is an Eternal Sleep, was plastered all over France's cemeteries by the Satanist Anaxagoras Chaumette, who also had a penchant for sex with boys. The slogan mocks Christianity with its promise of Eternal Life. Adolf Hitler would later declare that the spirit animating the Nazis was the same spirit that inspired the French Revolution.

The same year the United States declared independence, the Illuminati appears in Europe. It aimed to rule the world. The plan to reach that goal was to abolish all nation-states, religion, private property, marriage, and the family.

The Father of American Geography, Jedediah Morse, whose son would invent Morse Code, vehemently warned his fellow Americans of the presence of the Illuminati in our country as 1800 approached. Future U. S. President John Quincy Adams also sounded an alarm about the Illuminati working to undermine America, as did the President of Harvard. The President of Yale, Timothy Dwight, an honorable man if there ever was one, wrote extensively about the threat.

In 1826, Captain William Morgan was working on a book exposing the Illuminati in America when he was put in prison on trumped-up charges to stop him from publishing his expose'. He was subsequently kidnapped from the jail and murdered.

George Washington famously wrote, "It was not my intention to doubt that, the Doctrines of the Illuminati, and principles of Jacobinism had not spread in the United States. On the contrary, no one is more truly satisfied of this fact than I am. The idea that I meant to convey was that I did not believe that the Lodges of Free Masons in this Country had, as Societies, endeavored to propagate the diabolical tenets of the first, or pernicious principles of the latter."

Another supposed Illuminatus was the American Albert Pike (1809-1891), a man revered by Freemasons. He bragged about being an occultist and hosted many a wild séance in his home. Pike is quoted as saying his deity was Lucifer. He despised God, whom he criticized as a cruel, barbarous being that hated humankind and stood against science. Pike also believed that ancient Gnosticism was the worship of Lucifer by another name.

According to the famous poet who grew up in it, John Gould Fletcher, evil spirits haunted the mansion built by Albert Pike. Fletcher wrote a poem about his childhood home, *Ghosts of an Old House*.

It is believed that Clinton Roosevelt helped empower the Illuminati in America in the 1850s. In one of his books, he avowed: "There is no God. If there be a God, he is a malicious and vengeful being who created us for misery." That, my friends, is Luciferian dogma.

Because the Rothschilds, Karl Marx, the Warburgs, and countless other international bankers and political agitators were Jews, the phony *Protocols of the Elders of Zion* – the best selling book in the Muslim world today - stoked fears of a Jewish plot to take over the world. In reality, the plot of the Illuminati to rule the world, and the documents proving it, were probably discovered by anti-Semitic Russians. They then altered the materials to make it *seem like* a Jewish plot. It is not a Jewish plot. There are Jews and non-Jews embroiled in it. Jews are prominently and disproportionally represented, yes, but plenty of Goys are also involved.

Let us go back a bit and take a look at Georg W. F. Hegel (1770-1831), who invented a philosophy that formed the foundation of both the communism of Karl Marx and the socialism of Adolf Hitler. To Hegel, the state is almighty and has no morality that it is bound to obey or uphold because there is no such thing as Absolute Truth. Anyone, or better, any country, can make up its own truth. Since he was an exceedingly famous intellectual, his influence helped it become fashionable to reject the truth, morality, and even God.

The very roots of communism, socialism and Secular Humanism grow from the soil of deep resentment against the Christian world and Christ Himself. These sister ideologies rest on a common foundation of the philosophy of Positivism, the brainchild of Auguste Comte (1798-1857). Comte propounded that he would change the world because Positivism would "for the first time supply complete satisfaction to all the tendencies of the many-sided nature of man."

He meant that men and women need an object of worship because religious devotion is at the core of our nature. Comte's solution is a new Religion of Man to concentrate our feelings, thoughts, and actions around Humanity, as a substitute for God. Then, a "Statue of Humanity will have as its pedestal the Altar of God." With God eliminated, Man will be the new Supreme Being.

Auguste Comte regularly expressed bitter contempt towards the Gospel, and continually criticized its doctrines. He exhibited a particularly belligerent hatred for Jesus, for whom he wished "total exclusion" from the Earth. Since Christianity exalts the individual, it must go to make way for collectivism. Comte describes Jesus as, "That person who contributed nothing to mankind, essentially a charlatan." He even proposed a replacement for the Christian Trinity: Space, Earth, and Humanity.

Now, Comte knew that "No society can maintain itself without a priesthood of some kind." So he propounded that we need a priesthood of humanity, which would be an organized priesthood of scientists, exercising "a new spiritual power capable of replacing the clergy utilizing education." Social science must reorganize all of society. So, Sociology was to create a new Religion of Humanity, which would involve deciding political issues using science only, and making politics the object of religious devotion. The same faith that was formerly devoted to God, with no private precinct reserved for the self, must be transferred to the new religion.

Comte also affirmed that the entire notion of 'individual rights' comes from belief in God. He intended to make that a thing of the past because "It is as false as it is immoral." Only the collective has any rights, not any person.

Man had now become *an object* for science to study. By scrutinizing men and women, "social engineers could transform society." Sociology would be applied to manipulate men, women, and especially children.

The first big idea was eugenics, to hasten the evolution of man by directing his reproduction, preventing procreation by undesirables through sterilization, abortion, or infanticide; and to utilize select breeders to create a superior race. The next big idea was propaganda, to exploit the underlying psychology of men, women, and children, to imprison their minds, to put their minds in a matrix affixed from above—well, from men given power over you, but in reality a matrix from below.

Comte, the 'Father of Socialism,' offered Christian Europe a new god to worship—the human race. He was an atheist but intensely religious—devoted to his new Religion of Man with himself as High Priest. The problem with Christianity, Comte thought, was that it is based on the individual—you are saved or not saved all by yourself. No one else can choose salvation for you, and you cannot choose it for anyone else. In actuality, Comte knew almost nothing about the Gospel or the Bible, yet he presented himself as an authority on them.

He believed that scientific experts should organize and manage the world. He coined the word 'sociology' for the science he proposed for these wizards. To read his later writings are to read the words of a madman, inventing fables and illusions and starting to believe them himself. He is the grandfather of those leftists today who demand that the public square be scrubbed clean of Christianity.

"Let there be no doubt about the fact that the servants of Humanity are ousting the servants of God, root, and branch, from all control of public affairs, as incapable of really concerning themselves with such affairs and understanding them properly." ~ Auguste Comte

Turning briefly to America, we take a quick peek at Nathaniel Hawthorne (1804-1864). Even as a young man, he was firm in his militant atheism, rejecting the Church, denying Jesus, and mocking preachers while ridiculing their sermons.

Throughout his adult life, Hawthorne was nefariously obsessed with evil spirits. He sought out witches, wizards, mediums, and necromancers. From his diabolical writings, one can sense that the man was in league with the Devil. He never condemns Satan or witchcraft but paints God's People has horrible, bloodthirsty men.

A master at making Christians appear to be hypocritical, Hawthorne excuses adultery, homosexual behaviors, incest, and black magic. The central thesis of his work is to discredit the Christian faith, get rid of the concept of sin, and make God's Law look ridiculous.

You would be hard-pressed to name a book that has done more to separate America from its Christian heritage than Hawthorne's *The Scarlet Letter*. Widely read in every government school system, it has profound effects on young minds. It teaches them that those in rebellion against God are the heroes, and those who love God are villains. Hawthorne's inspiration for his writings came from a most wicked demon, which he did not deny.

The anti-Christian progressives, as noted by Henri De Lubac, "often preserved many values that were Christian in origin; but, having cut these values off from their source, they were powerless to maintain them in their full strength or even in their authentic integrity. Spirit, reason, liberty, truth, brotherhood, justice: these great things, without which there is no true humanity, were instituted by Christianity, and quickly become unreal when no longer seen as radiating from God, when faith in the living God no longer provides their vital substance."

Charles Darwin Made A Monkey Out Of Me

The Theory of Evolution was not altogether new. Ancient pagans in India, Egypt, and Polynesia believed the whole world evolved from an egg. Charles Darwin (1809-1882) concluded that all life forms were engaged in a struggle for survival, which meant the contest to reproduce. As observed in nature, such a battle naturally produces winners and losers. Of course, there is no morality or religion in nature or among animals. To Darwin, purely physical forces explain the whole story of the Cosmos and will shape the future. As pertains to living creatures, this would be brute force.

Many thinkers realized pretty quickly what becomes of the human race if everybody becomes a Darwinist. Man would lack any sense of spirituality and morality. Now before this, there was no battle between religion and science. After Darwin, there was, with Darwinists insisting that everything happened by pure chance and Christians arguing that our lives have meaning, human beings have a purpose, and so does the Cosmos.

Charles Darwin suffered from a cornucopia of psychological and physical ailments. Among them were depression, insomnia, hallucinations, vertigo, heart palpitations, muscle twitches, tremors, colic, nocturnal flatulence, nervous exhaustion, skin blisters, sensations of loss of consciousness, tinnitus, shortness of breath, chronic headaches, bloating, constant cramps, spasms, dizziness, vomiting, trembling, fainting spells, uncontrollable shaking spells, anxiety, double vision, nausea, shortness of breath, inordinate fear of death, and agoraphobia. In his own testimony, he was virtually incapacitated as a consequence of mental illness by the time he was twenty-eight-years-old.

Besides all that, Darwin was a twisted, strange man, and a sadist. His favorite thing was to kill birds by smashing their heads with his hammer. As a young man, he loved to kill animals just for the sheer delight of killing them. He also admitted that he enjoyed torturing animals. As a child, he beat puppies, as he wrote, "simply from enjoying the sense of power."

You must decide whom you believe about the world in which you find yourself: the most beautiful person who ever lived, Christ Jesus, or this man Charles Darwin, who bore the marks of demon possession, such as psychosis. Darwin himself wondered if his writings were "the cause of the main part of the ills which my flesh is heir to."

Darwin's tutor was Satan, who knew that if a person were led to believe in the Theory of Evolution, it would, in his mind and heart, torpedo confidence in Biblical Creation as revealed in Genesis. That would sabotage belief in the Fall of Mankind, and therefore in Yahweh's plan of redemption through the Cross. Thus, in one masterstroke, Lucifer could do away with the foundational historical facts that point to the verity of man's rebellion against his Maker, and our desperate need for salvation.

Anyone who teaches the Theory of Evolution could be considered a priest of a terrible satanic religious system. You see, the Prince of Darkness intended it to be a religion. That is because it was ingeniously devised to convince individuals so that they would choose to disqualify themselves from Heaven—by rejecting their Creator.

Charles Darwin's father taught him that there was no Creator God; Creation had created itself. His mentor at school was also a militant atheist. Charles worked hard to eliminate any vestige of Christianity from his thinking. In his autobiography, he flatly says that the Christian faith is manifestly false.

While it is impossible to disprove God's existence, Darwin planned to come up with an intellectual explanation of how there *could be* a world without God. So, he came up with a hypothesis to take God out of the picture. His strategy was to render the Creator obsolete in the minds of others.

Darwin mistakenly concluded that monotheism 'evolved' from polytheism. That was the key to his explanation of the existence of religion. According to Darwin, Christianity is nothing more than superstition that humanity ought to leave behind. His belief was that man is alone in the Universe and that we are 'evolving' into a higher creature. His explanation of The Descent of Man is sheer speculation without a shred of historical evidence. But according to textbooks foisted on our schoolchildren, he was an impartial, entirely objective scientist with no agenda, with no ax to grind.

You can make a good case that Charles Darwin is the devil most responsible for the collapse of Western Civilization, or 'Christendom' as it was once called. He was committed to the 'murder of God.' His theory was communicated to him by spirit beings for the express purpose of opposing what he called "the doctrines until held now by Christians."

Darwin admitted that his motivation for writing *The Origin of Species* was "to disprove the belief in the separate creation of species." He would add, "I can entertain no doubt that the view that each species has been independently created is erroneous." He proclaimed, "In a series of forms graduating insensibly from some apelike creature to man as he now exists, it would be impossible to fix on any definite point when the term 'man' ought to be used."

He decided that all life, including man, had evolved from lower life forms. Now Darwin had no evidence that humans had ever evolved; he only surmised his theory based on anatomical similarities. He sought to destroy belief in Adam and Eve.

His theory also rejects any essential distinction between human beings and animals. If Man is nothing more than an accidental animal, what moral basis is there to oppose rape or infanticide? How can humans have any code of morality if we are nothing more than random chemicals that come together for a brief time? We kill chickens and cattle by the billions, why not people? That is what led to the thinking of Lenin, Stalin, Hitler, Mao, and Pol Pot. What are a few million people anyway? Just a bunch of molecules, right? All we are in this view is instinct and animal behavior. Who can say that *anything* is wrong?

Many evolutionary scientists have now given up on the gradual model of evolution proposed by Darwin. Some are so desperate to hold on to a godless Universe that they postulate 'punctuated equilibrium.' This half-baked, poorly supported scientific hypothesis appeals to men who are running from God. The atheistic worldview behind it is imbued into our children with the authority of our government. Why should they not act like animals if that is all they are?

Darwin's ideas had a profound effect on John Dewey, the 'Father of American Education.' Dewey was successful in implementing the indoctrination of Secular Humanism—a godless religion—into American children through government schools with compulsory attendance. What is impressive is, despite cradle-to-grave brainwashing, the vast majority of Americans believe in God anyway. That seems supernatural to me.

The idea of Natural Selection is that the environment changes the form of living creatures. For instance, if, for a few years, all the leaves on the trees are uncommonly high, only the long-necked giraffes will be able to reach them. The shorter-necked giraffes will starve to death, and only the long necks will live to reproduce. So in time, all giraffes will have longer necks than they had before. Such notions came from man's long history of breeding horses and cattle to purposefully achieve particular characteristics, which is not natural but *artificial selection*.

One significant factor was ignored regarding the human race, and that is that a man will get massive biceps from working as a blacksmith, but his baby will not be born with them.

Just because men are physical beings does not mean that it is all we are. And it makes no sense to insist that we are nothing but Matter because *we are alive!* And most Matter isn't. Life remains a mysterious force. When you view a corpse at the funeral home, it still has the molecules. We are still recognizable, but it is decidedly missing the life force.

The earth-shattering thing about Darwin's big idea was that it dispensed with the idea of a Creator altogether. All of life was explained as *eat or be eaten*. Individuals that survived had developed natural capabilities to catch their prey and escape those who hunted them.

The part of Darwin's idea that indeed made no sense was that over enough time brand new kinds of living creatures would appear. There is no proof that this has ever happened. But those who latched onto it as gospel did so *because they wanted the world to be godless* so they would not have to answer for their immorality. And to appear smarter than everybody else—more advanced.

Now what came next was the idea that if all living creatures, including human beings, 'evolved,' *everything else must evolve*, such as religions, political systems, technology, etc. With technology, that is demonstrably true. This does not mean it must be valid for everything. Part of the idea was that anything lost was not worth having, or it would have survived the selection process, and whatever is new must be automatically better. So Man began to crave novelty, loving the new just because it was new.

Darwin missed the boat because 'the survival of the fittest' only explains the elimination of the unfit from the gene pool. It cannot account for the production of new characteristics, or anything new, such as a new species. In other words, long-necked giraffes did not *become* long-necked by natural selection; the short necks just died out. Still, there arose generations of people eager to get rid of any transcendent purpose for our lives.

Right on the heels of Darwin came other thinkers who decided that—because of Darwin's Natural Selection—disease, famine, and war were natural things, neither good nor bad but necessary to check population growth, mainly to weed out the weak ones. Therefore, Christianity was in the crosshairs because it had established a colossal system of charity.

Wherever Christians went in the world, they would feed the hungry, clothe the cold and naked, house those without shelter, set up hospitals for the sick, take care of the mentally ill and physically disabled. All of which was artificially thwarting Darwinism, and therefore artificially propping up the weakest members of the race that ought to be dying off for the betterment of our species. And worse: Allowing those weak ones to breed more of the same. Starvation, pestilence, and bloodshed were nature's way of making the human race stronger.

Evolution became a religion to some. The first definition of 'religion' is "a set of beliefs concerning the cause, nature, and purpose [or lack of purpose] of the Universe." They felt that everything should be subsumed under their new god: Science. They began to declare that the *theory* of man descending from a single-celled ancestor was a *fact*. One that could be easily observed by anyone smart enough to see that rain falls from the sky. There is a problem. To quote Jacques Barzun: "If you make Chance your creator, you are likely to get nothing but monstrosities as your creatures; you cannot make an alarm clock by whirling bits of scrap iron in a closed box."

Promoters of science have convinced many that whatever some scientists say is the end-all-be-all of truth. You can see it in the way they frame statements: "Science now says," or "We now know." But among all scientists, their *presuppositions inform their results*.

The majority of scientists followed Darwin. Not because his ideas were proven, far from it. They assumed them to be true because *they wanted it to be true* that living creatures had not been separately created; that man had descended from an apelike animal; that the supernatural did not exist; that everything is reducible to particles. That is scientific materialism, a philosophy *masquerading as scientific fact*.

Scientific materialism, or scientism, would be used to justify some pretty abhorrent behaviors in subsequent decades. After all, should not the strong put the weak out of their misery and end their bloodlines to make the whole human race more robust and create a new, improved civilization without the defectives? Would this not advance evolution?

The story of insect and animal life is one of chase, capture, and death. Nature is cruel. Darwin had believed that not only were some individuals further evolved than others but also whole races of people were more highly developed or woefully primitive and savage. All kinds of schemes were proposed to remedy that situation, biological segregation, sterilization of inferiors, and mass reproduction by the fittest, selective breeding—and instigating wars. It did not cross their minds that it *is the most robust, not the unfit* that are usually killed off in wars. Our best warriors go into battle; the weak, the feeble-minded, the disabled, and the elderly stay home.

The famous atheist philosopher T. H. Huxley served as the guru to a generation of college students in Europe as the 19th century wound down. He could be counted on to lead the way in bashing the Bible, scorning Christians, preaching that nothing is real except sensations, and worshipping the scientist as the new priest of the enlightened.

In response, American historian Henry Adams predicted wars were coming on an enormous scale because, having declared that God is dead, European intellectuals had embarked on a course of cultural decadence, which would feature corruption, perverse art and literature, widespread mental problems, and homosexual behaviors. Since Darwin had shown 'might is right,' there was nothing wrong with taking what you want, including another man's wife, children, or property. Cheating people, if you can, will prove they are inferior to you. Wiping out your neighbor by violence, brutalizing and degrading others, proves your superiority.

Natural Selection can help us see what life forms survived but not how those life forms came to be. Perhaps the 'Origin of Variations' might be a better term, to borrow from Samuel Butler. He also maintained that human beings do what they do because *they want to*, at least above the involuntary stages such as digestion, etc. In other words, people's physical actions, except for pure reflex, are expressions of mental activities. People make efforts; they endeavor with purposes first formed in their minds.

But Darwin had banished the mind from the Cosmos. Since minds could not be scientifically measured, they must not exist, except as mere Matter moving around at random. However, we all know that life is more than a box of atoms. Darwin said that our thoughts are nothing more than secretions of the brain. But as George Roche points out, "Thinking is something we do, not something that happens to us."

After his death, Charles Darwin's son Major led the movement. Major Darwin declared: "The unfit amongst men are no longer necessarily killed off by hunger and disease, but are cherished with care, thus being able to reproduce their own kind, however bad that kind might be." Major proposed an end to Christian charity because bad breeding would lead to a ruined civilization. Darwin's cousin Francis Galton launched a religious crusade to save the human race through selective breeding. He proposed meticulous physical examinations of all human beings before they were allowed to breed, and forced labor camps for the unfit.

German scientist Ernst Haeckel (1834-1919) took the baton next. He would preach eugenics, as well as abortion, infanticide, euthanasia, and finally, the forced liquidation of weaker races. Haeckel and his acolytes made Darwinism a pantheist neo-pagan nature-worshiping religion. He proclaimed that to believe humans were different from animals, that a Creator exists, that Heaven exists, and that Jesus is more than a myth, is to be duped by "the ideas of uneducated people."

Exterminate the decrepit was his proposal, stating, "What good does it do for humanity to maintain artificially the thousands of cripples, deaf-mutes, idiots, etc., who are born each year?" Darwin and Haeckel both thought it would be best if "the possibility of transmitting their injurious qualities by inheritance would be taken from those degenerate outcasts." That is a long way from the Gospel.

Charles Darwin had famously written: "With savages, the weak in body or mind are soon eliminated. We civilized men, on the other hand, do our utmost to check the process of elimination; we build asylums for the imbecile, the maimed, and the sick; we institute poor-laws, and our medical men exert their utmost skill to save the life of every one to the last moment. Thus the weak members of civilized societies propagate their kind. No one who has attended to the breeding of domestic animals will doubt that this must be highly injurious to the race of man. It is surprising how soon a want of care or care wrongly directed, leads to the degeneration of a domestic race; but excepting in the case of man himself, hardly anyone is so ignorant as to allow his worst animals to breed."

Eugenics is applying science to the breeding of human beings, something that Darwin obviously thought would be a good thing. He preached that the unfit are a burden on society, and Christian compassion only exacerbates the problem. That is just one link between Darwin's theory and the ideology of the Nazis.

In Darwinism, we see that God is excluded, as is the belief that human beings have an immortal soul and an afterlife. Therefore, since nature has created itself somehow, it can be neither good nor evil; all morality is relative, meaning nothing more than a matter of opinion, like your favorite flavor of ice cream.

Darwin observed that human beings selectively breed for various attributes in dogs, horses, and cattle. He figured that such variations are limitless, and thought maybe animals also would vary so much that over time they could become an entirely different kind of beast altogether. He admitted, "We see nothing of these slow changes in progress." That is how Darwin explained that the whole human race had been fooled into thinking dogs have always come from other dogs and horses from other horses and people from other people. To believe his theory takes tremendous faith. It is to trust something is happening right before our very eyes that no one can see or has ever been able to see.

Although his followers today are reluctant to admit it, Charles Darwin is the father of Eugenics and Social Darwinism. His theory was created to refute the beliefs of the Christians that surrounded him in his society. Ernst Haeckel expanded Darwin's theory into 'Moral Darwinism.' Margaret Sanger and Alfred Kinsey would expand it into sexual hedonism.

Darwin was a great admirer of Haeckel. Both agreed that there is no clear distinction between living things and non-living things (if you can imagine that). Haeckel believed that modern Europe, or at least modern Germany, should emulate the ancient Spartans. "They killed any members of their society who were weak, sickly, or disabled, and only the perfectly healthy and strong children were allowed to live. They alone afterward propagated the race."

The books of both Darwin and Haeckel were best-sellers in Germany. Both were enormously influential in forming the ideology of the Nazis, especially Haeckel's recommendation of a state euthanasia program for "hundreds and thousands of incurables, lepers, people with cancer, etc., who are kept alive without the slightest profit to themselves or society." The problem was Christianity, which was behind the charity programs that cared for such folks.

The Nazis would begin by euthanizing a couple hundred thousand mental patients and disabled persons. Next came euthanizing children who were crippled, retarded, orphans, troublemakers, or mixed race. Abortion and infanticide offered society the best chance to get rid of undesirables early before becoming costly to support.

A scientific fact is something that can be observed. Evolutionists love to claim that their explanation of life is 'a fact.' That is not so. Science does not show it to be so. It is a worldview dressed up as science. To Darwinists, *it must be true*. That is why a famous atheist such as Richard Dawkins writes that our ancient ancestors *must have* had a very simple eye. Since there isn't any proof they did, he adds, "We don't need any evidence for this. It has to be true." Nobel Prize-winning geneticist Thomas Hunt Morgan sets the record straight: "Selection has not produced anything new, but only more of certain kinds of individuals. Evolution, however, means producing new things, not more of what already exists."

Science is about what we can see and measure. But Darwinists make up things that they then call facts. For instance, we can all see that human beings, like many other creatures, have two eyes, two ears, and a nose. The Darwinist adds, "Because we all share a common ancestor." But that is something for which there is zero evidence—we do not see it. It is made up and presented as fact.

Jonathan Wells, a doctor of molecular and cellular biology, writes: "Darwin thought the strongest evidence for his theory was that vertebrate embryos are most similar in their earliest stages; the problem is, they're not. Faked embryo drawings are still used in some modern biology textbooks as 'evidence' for Darwin's theory. Although all species are supposedly descended from other species through natural selection and variation, no one has observed the origin of even one species by this process."

The American Association for the Advancement of Science will make statements such as, "100 million fossils have been identified that prove evolution beyond any doubt whatsoever." That is not true. Fossils do not tell us all living creatures evolved from a common ancestor. As a senior editor for *Nature* magazine confesses: "Fossils are mute; their silence gives us the unlimited license to tell their stories for them. It is effectively impossible to link fossils into chains of cause and effect in any valid way. Everything we think we know has been invented by us, after the fact."

You can *claim* vertebrates evolved from invertebrates and mammals evolved from reptiles and humans evolved from non-humans, but your claim cannot be proved. There is no evidence that a reptile ever turned into a mammal or gave birth to a mammal. There is no evidence there ever was a half-reptile half-mammal either. As Donn Rosen of the American Museum of Natural History says, "Darwin said evolution happened too slowly for us to see it. Stephen Jay Gould said it happened too quickly for us to see it. Either way, we don't see it."

Charles Darwin confirmed, "One cannot look at this Universe with all living productions & man without believing that all has been intelligently designed." Richard Dawkins adds, "Biology is the study of complicated things that give the appearance of having been designed for a purpose." But it has become taboo to say life is the result of intelligent design in our universities, even though there is no better explanation for the origin of life.

As Tom Bethell writes in *Darwin's House of Cards*, "Admitting design in biology would immediately overthrow Darwin's theory. Its whole thrust from the beginning was to eliminate the need for a designer—to persuade us that nature could construct organisms without any 'input' from a designer."

Neurosurgeon Michael Egnor provides some insights: "Your computer doesn't know a binary string from a ham sandwich. Your math book doesn't know algebra. Your Rolodex doesn't know your cousin's address. Your watch doesn't know what time it is. Your television doesn't know who won the football game last night. Your cell phone doesn't know what you said to your girlfriend this morning. People know things. Devices don't know anything. They don't have minds."

The study of biology does not need the Theory of Evolution, which has become a quasi-religion based entirely on faith, not facts. Common descent has never been proved; natural selection does not create new species; no organism departs from its original type. As philosopher William Lane Craig says, "A beachcomber who comes upon a sandcastle recognizes that it's not the result of the action of the waves and the wind, but of intelligent design."

Biologist William B. Provine is honest about what the Theory of Evolution teaches: "There are no gods, no purposes, no goal-directed forces of any kind. There is no life after death. There is no ultimate foundation for ethics, no ultimate meaning to life, and no free will for humans."

Darwin's beef was with Jehovah: "Thus disbelief crept over me at a very slow rate, but it was at last complete. I have never since doubted even for a single second that my conclusion was correct. I can indeed hardly see how anyone ought to wish Christianity to be true."

C. S. Lewis expounded: "If my mental processes are determined wholly by the motions of atoms in my brain, I have no reason to suppose that my beliefs are true. And hence I have no reason for supposing my brain to be composed of atoms. A theory that explained everything else in the whole Universe but made it impossible to believe that our thinking was valid would be utterly out of court. For that theory would itself have been reached by thinking, and if thinking is not valid, that theory would, of course, be itself demolished. It would have destroyed its own credentials. It would be an argument which proved that no argument was sound—proof that there are no such things as proofs—which is nonsense." Lewis also clarified, "What Darwin really accounted for was not the origin, but the elimination of species."

Bill Gates says, "DNA is like a computer program, but far more advanced than any software we've ever created." We all know that only programmers create programs. They do not create themselves.

Another famous atheist scientist, Francis Crick, signer of the Humanist Manifesto, called for a new religion of Secular Humanism to replace belief in Christ. Crick supported eugenics and infanticide. He proclaimed that an elite group should decide who is born, suggesting that since human beings are just animals, we should breed them. And yet, Crick acknowledged that DNA is similar to letters in a written language that must be spelled correctly to convey the intended meaning. He admitted how impossible it would be for "this miracle of molecular construction" to happen accidentally. "All the cells need do is string together the amino acids *in the correct order.*" He admitted that the odds against this are a one followed by 260 zeros!

Since a protein 'evolving' all by itself is impossible, Crick and others, to keep God out of the picture, have decided to believe that life on Earth came from extraterrestrials. This theory is called 'directed panspermia.' Bethell defines it as "self-replicating bacteria originated somewhere in the Universe, spread by intelligent life-forms using spaceships to propel the minute critters through interstellar space."

The astronomer Fred Hoyle agreed, because he saw that life evolving from non-life is just impossible: "The notion that the operating program of a living cell could be arrived at by chance in a primordial organic soup here on Earth is nonsense of the highest order." Many atheists believe in extraterrestrials. Carl Sagan said he "believed in superior beings in space, creatures so intelligent, so powerful, as to resemble gods." Richard Dawkins: "It's highly plausible that in the Universe, there are god-like creatures." Sagan: "There are a million technical civilizations in the Milky Way."

What such men share with Darwin the most is hostility towards the Gospel. Darwin called it "a manifestly false history of the world, attributing to God the feelings of a vengeful tyrant. The Bible is no more to be trusted than the beliefs of any barbarian."

The world's foremost expert on bacteria, Richard Lenski, has been observing them since 1988 without stopping. That is equal to a million human years. *Science* magazine calls him "The man who bottled evolution," and "proved how mutation and selection shape living things." *Discover* magazine claimed Lenski's bacteria "have been evolving in all sorts of interesting ways," enabling us "to reconstruct the history of that evolution in great detail." Richard Dawkins even chimed in with "a beautiful demonstration of evolution in action."

I hate to burst anybody's bubble, but the truth is the bacteria are still bacteria, even after trillions of reproductions over 60,000 generations. They have acquired zero new genetic functions. As scientist Alan Linton writes of his field: "Throughout 150 years of bacteriology science, there is no evidence that one species of bacteria has changed into another. Since there is no evidence for species change between the simplest forms of unicellular life, it is not surprising that there is no evidence for evolution throughout the whole array of multicellular organisms."

One of Darwin's key points was that some human beings, the "savages" and "barbarians," as he called them, are mentally closer to apes than they were to sophisticated men such as himself. He thought it was arrogance that made anyone think human beings were exceptional creatures; "our admiration of ourselves." As he admitted, his object was "to show that there are no fundamental differences between man and the higher mammals in their mental faculties." Thomas Huxley agreed that man "stands nearer the ape than the ape does to the dog." Stephen Jay Gould capped it with this: "Educated people now accept the evolutionary continuity between humans and apes."

Scientists speculate philosophically about what might have happened and then present their speculations to the public as if whatever they can imagine happened happened. As paleontologist Colin Patterson offered, "It is easy enough to make up stories of how one form gave rise to another. But such stories are not part of science, for there is no way of putting them to the test."

Huxley, a big promoter of Evolution, admitted that "an act of philosophical faith" is required to believe in it. Evolution is sold as a scientific discovery when it is nothing of the sort. Darwin admitted he had zero empirical evidence that natural selection had ever produced a new species. Nobel prize-winning scientist Ernst Chain pronounced that the Theory of Evolution rests on such flimsy assumptions it can hardly even qualify as a theory nonetheless a fact. "I would rather believe in fairy tales than in such wild speculation."

Famous geneticist Richard Lewontin goes far enough to proclaim that the "vast weight of empirical evidence" weighs in *against* it being authentic. As George Roche points out, "Evolution is virtually immune to scientific testing, so nothing much will ever be known about it." However, the German geneticist and atheist Gunther Theissen asserts that within the scientific community, "It is dangerous to raise attention to the fact that there is no satisfying explanation for macroevolution."

Science philosopher Jerry Fodor, also an atheist, adds: "More than one of our colleagues have told us that even if Darwin was substantially wrong to claim that natural selection is the mechanism for evolution, nonetheless we shouldn't say so. Darwinism goes literally unquestioned. A view that looks to contradict it, either directly or by implication, is *ipso facto* rejected, however plausible it may otherwise seem."

Scientists have failed to show an evolutionary connection from any lower life form to human beings. Genetic studies on modern humans point to the veracity of the biblical account. According to the archaeological record, man does not gradually appear—he explodes on the scene. Humanity spread around the planet from our first two parents from either in or near Israel.

"The general scientific world has been bamboozled into believing that evolution has been proved. Nothing could be further from the truth." - Sir Fred Hoyle, famous atheist scientist

Karl Marx Will Annihilate You

The foundational idea of the ideology that Karl Marx (1818-1883) published thousands of pages about is laughably wrong. It is that the value of any product is the value of the labor of the man who made it. Therefore, if I buy land, build a factory, design a product, set up a sales staff, marketing team, product distribution, an accounting department, customer service, etc., all of that is worthless. If I sell shoes for $20 and do not give my shoemaker the whole $20 I have stolen from him. This idea only served one purpose: To agitate workers who had almost zero understanding of such matters to make a violent revolution.

To show how silly the underlying premise is, a machine can make shoes faster than a man, and now I have no man to pay at all, which hardly renders the footwear worthless. As Jacques Barzun has noted, "Men dive for pearls because they are valuable; pearls are not valuable because men dive for them."

The value of things depends on how many people want them, how badly they want them, and how many are available. Marx was smart enough to know all of this. But his goal was to use propaganda on working people to justify the ruthless political action that would destroy whole nations, and feature the dispossessing of people who had wealth and land, by killing them if necessary.

The man was wrong about nearly everything. He thought workers in America, once unionized, would overthrow the government. They did not. He felt all the wealth in America would wind up in the hands of just a handful of men. It did not. He thought the middle class would disappear. It exploded in size. He did not believe the lives of working people would improve under capitalism. They did beyond anyone's wildest dreams.

Marx loved the Theory of Evolution and believed it justified his Theory of Communism. He liked to call himself the 'Darwin of Sociology,' as if group violence was a scientific concept. His book *Das Kapital* was dedicated to none other than Charles Darwin. He strove to abolish private property so that all property would belong to the state. He wanted to see vengeance visited upon the upper and middle classes, including terror and bloodbaths, followed by a dictatorship. Marxism led to starvation, torture, enslavement, and mass murder on a scale never seen before in human history. At least 100 million innocent people were killed to create what Marx called Scientific Socialism—a "new and better world."

You could hardly find a more ill-mannered, quarrelsome, malicious drunkard than Karl Marx, who was also physically filthy and stunk to high heaven because he rarely washed. A selfish, angry little man with evil eyes, he was insanely vindictive, filled with jealous hatred, coarse, hardhearted, abusive, sarcastic, cruel, ridiculing, nasty, crude, insulting, and treated nearly everyone with disdain and scorn. Other than that, he was a pretty nice guy. He hardly ever washed his clothes, and in his house, everything was broken and squalid, covered with half an inch of dirt. In the last 25 years of his life, he was covered with boils. Marx considered the rest of the human race to be detestable degenerates. His favorite saying? "I will annihilate you."

If anyone thinks Karl Marx promoted equality for women, look at how he treated them—with contempt. He refused to allow his daughters to go to school. He kept a female slave from the age of eight, whom he would later continually rape. Then he denied his child that she bore him and kicked her baby out of his house. The boy bastard was put into a foster home and was never allowed to visit his mother when Marx was home, and could only come to the back door when he wasn't. She was the only working-class person the supposed champion of the workers ever knew. Helen Demuth was her name. She worked for him virtually her entire life, but he never paid her one cent—what a paragon of love for the poor.

Descended from a long line of rabbis, Karl chose to identify with Satan. He once wrote, "Everything that exists deserves to perish." You should not be surprised to learn that only eleven people attended his funeral. He encouraged ruthlessness, lawlessness, riots, and assassination. His heart was devoid of love for anyone, and he hated humanity and God with a furious rage. Although he claimed to have the answer as to how humanity should handle its economy, he was grossly incompetent with financial matters.

The Communist Manifesto must be the most malicious book ever published, as evidenced by the over one hundred million murders committed in its name. Marx stated: "Communism abolishes eternal truths, it abolishes all religion, it abolishes all morality." That fits right in with his declaration, "Communism begins where atheism begins."

The Devil knows that young people fervently want to change the world, especially after receiving the kind of 'social justice' brainwashing that goes on in our government schools. The problem is that the young know nearly nothing about the world yet, and are therefore prone to devote themselves to utopian schemes that are not based on reality but fantasy.

To Karl Marx, human beings are nothing more than animals with material needs. To read his personal testimony is to discover the thoughts of the Devil himself. When he was a young man, he came under the influence of evil spirits, and suddenly words erupted from his pen full of blasphemy. Marx dreamt of destroying the whole world as he mocked God. Why do so many today—especially politicians and educators—adore the philosophy of Karl Marx when he said he cursed Mankind, wanted to bring the world to ruins, and hated God?

His own father said Satan possessed his son. While Marx promoted atheism to his followers, he and his inner circle believed in God enough to denounce, revile, curse, and contemn Him. The most remarkable thing about him was his burning hatred. His ideas appeal to evil people who want more than anything a religion to replace Christianity. He gave them one, with himself as Messiah.

To Marx, private property was the source of unhappiness. Hence, the state should own everything. And everybody. All options were on the table to wage war against the world into which he was born: schools, culture, guns, bombs—the ends justify the means. He wanted nothing less than to rule the world. To him, there was no God, no basis for law, and no meaning or purpose to life except the will to use force to get what you want. He sought to make a new religion in which instead of God, the people worship the state. In which they will only be allowed to worship the state.

Karl Marx argued that the family was an evil influence on Mankind and should be obliterated. "Abolish the family!" he exclaimed. Along with hating all morality, belief in God, and eternal truths, he despised middle-class marriage and middle-class families, or as he called them both 'bourgeois.'

He called for the abolition of marriage, which he wanted to be replaced with free love, as well as the end of parental influence over children, mainly when it came to their education. He did not want children to even live with their parents. That is the real reason why leftists have always wanted to push women into the workforce: To get ahold of their children. They would call it the 'liberation of women.' One emphasis in communist writings was always to use 'liberation' as a means to the ends of communal child rearing. As Marx said, "When the family ceases to be the economic unit of society, the care and education of the children becomes a public affair."

He writes in his *Communist Manifesto* that for communism to work, Holy Matrimony and Christianity must be annihilated. Communist Party intellectuals know well that Christian principles working within marriage, which features loyalty to your mate and to God, are a substantial barrier to persuading a person to become a communist. Marx argued, "The criticism of religion is the prerequisite of all criticism. Religion is the sigh of the oppressed creature. The abolition of religion as the illusory happiness of the people is the demand for their real happiness."

The fact is Karl Marx was a Satanist. From a long line of godly people, at age 18 he came under the sway of Moses Hess, who initiated the young Marx into Satanism. Before long, Marx would use the word 'destroy' so often that it became his nickname. After becoming a Satanist, he wrote the blueprint for a worldwide satanic revolution, the *Communist Manifesto*. The Soviets and Red Chinese would later follow his prescriptions, as they would murder, massacre, imprison, and purposefully starve countless innocent people to "drive the capitalists out of the world and drive God out of the Heaven."

He wished to draw the whole of Humankind into the pit reserved for the Devil and his demons. In his own words: "I wish to avenge myself against the One who rules above." And that's not all. Check out these utterances of his: "The hellish vapors rise and fill the brain, Till I go mad and my heart is utterly changed. See this sword? The prince of darkness sold it to me. While for us both the abyss yawns in darkness. You will sink down, and I shall follow laughing, Whispering in your ears, 'Descend, come with me, friend.' If there is a Something which devours, I'll leap within it, though I bring the world to ruins—the world which bulks between me and the abyss, I will smash to pieces with my enduring curses. Thus heaven I've forfeited, I know it full well. My soul, once true to God, is chosen for hell."

It is essential to understand that he admits his aim was not to improve the world or reform it but merely to demolish it and enjoy its ruination. He proclaimed: "With disdain, I will throw my gauntlet full in the face of the world, And see the collapse of this pygmy giant whose fall will not stifle my ardor. Then I will wander godlike and victorious through the ruins of the world. And, giving my words an active force, I will feel equal to the Creator."

A man without friends, who did not like people, Marx was a brooder with a bad temper, who kept his wife and children in poverty so he could concentrate on killing belief in Christ. Marx starved three of his children to death, and the other two would commit suicide. His favorite daughter married Richard Aveling, a Satanist, socialist, and evolutionist—ever notice how that unholy trinity goes together? Known for his public blasphemies and odes to Lucifer, Aveling's most famous speech was entitled *The Wickedness of God*.

One of Marx's partners in the First International was Mikhail Bakunin, a Russian anarchist, who described his friend Karl Marx: "Here steps in Satan, the eternal rebel, the first freethinker and the emancipator of worlds. Disobey and eat the fruit of knowledge. In this revolution, we will have to awaken the Devil in the people, to stir up the basest passions."

Bakunin also acknowledged that socialism and Satanism were linked: "The Evil One is the Satanic revolt against divine authority. Satan is the eternal rebel, the first freethinker, the emancipator of worlds." Bakunin admitted that the real purpose for socialist revolutions was not to free workers from exploitation—that was just a cover: "Our mission is to destroy, not edify."

The Italian mass murderer Mazzini said of Marx: "His heart bursts with hatred rather than with love toward men." French socialist Pierre Joseph Proudhon was another colleague of Karl Marx. Check out this lovely quote from him: "Come Satan, slandered by the small and by kings. God is stupidity and cowardice; God is hypocrisy and falsehood; God is tyranny and poverty; God is evil."

The tomb of Karl Marx in London has become a shrine of British Satanism. Everything in his behavior had a demonic character. Isn't it amazing that this man's writings are taught to our children in the same schools that ban the Bible?

At the funeral of Karl Marx, his partner Engels said: "Our dialectical philosophy abolishes all the notions of absolute and definitive truth." Engels explained: "For Marxism, religious criticism and revolutionary action must go hand in hand. Communism alone would achieve atheism, but the atheist propaganda must nonetheless accompany and sustain from the beginning of the effort to achieve communism. Atheist ideology is essential to the Party, even if, in individual cases, it admits believers into its midst."

Karl Marx predicted that getting rid of private property would allow humanity to evolve to a higher state. Leon Trotsky fleshed it out: "Man will become immeasurably stronger, wiser, and subtler. His body will become more harmonized, his movements more rhythmic, his voice more musical. The average human type will rise to the heights of an Aristotle, a Goethe, or a Marx."

Nietzsche to Sartre or Nihilism to Existentialism

Friedrich Nietzsche (1844-1900) was the son of a pastor. He launched a hateful assault on the Christian faith, blaming Jesus for Germany's problems. "I call Christianity the one great curse, the enormous and innermost perversion, the moral blemish of mankind, the most seductive lie that has yet existed."

Nietzsche's view of reality denies any such thing as good and evil. The most powerful persons can impose their will on others, as per Darwin. Thus those with power can define or redefine what is approved or disapproved.

He predicted that his ideas would lead to mass murder in the twentieth century. Having done away with God, morals, virtue, and fear of judgment, man would realize nothing matters except the *will to power*, and worldwide insanity would ensue. His main mission was to "strike a destructive blow against Christianity" so that "with the old God abolished I myself will rule the world." Tell me if that doesn't sound Luciferian.

Filled with satanic hatred of God, Nietzsche pronounced himself "the most terrible opponent of Christianity: the Antichrist Himself." Three months after making this declaration, he lost his mind and spent his last eleven years certifiably deranged.

One might think a crazy man who spent his days hating Christ, who would become the most significant influence on Adolf Hitler and the Nazis, might be shunned today. Instead, our college professors tend to admire him and his work, and many consider him the grandfather of modern psychology. Get the irony there? A lunatic as the grandfather of psychology.

Nietzsche openly advocated for a world without any behavioral boundaries. To destroy faith in Christ, he was willing to use "violence, slavery, danger in the street and the heart, secrecy, tempter's art and devilry of every kind; everything wicked, terrible, tyrannical, predatory, and serpentine in man." He wanted to eradicate "mercy, kindness, pity, generosity, patience, industry, humility, and friendliness."

His philosophy could hardly be more opposite to the teachings of our Lord. Self-glorification with suicidal nihilism was Nietzsche's nirvana. He once wrote: "There is no one among the living or the dead with whom I feel the slightest affinity."

What we need to understand about Nietzsche is that he claimed to be possessed when he wrote his masterpiece, *Thus Spake Zarathustra*: "It invaded me. One can hardly reject completely the idea that I am the mere incarnation, the mouthpiece, or medium, of some higher power."

Friedrich Nietzsche saw that a growing movement among the intellectuals of his day was to deny the supernatural aspects of the Christian religion but keep the Christian morality. To make Jesus not the Son of God but a great moral teacher. That meant that Christianity was built on historical lies, or mistakes, illusions, or hallucinations.

Nietzsche asserted: "They are rid of the Christian God and now believe all the more firmly that they must cling to the Christian morality." But, "When one gives up the Christian faith, one pulls the right to Christian morality out from under one's feet. Christianity is a system, a whole view of things thought out together. By breaking one main concept out of it, the faith in God, one breaks the whole. Christian morality is a command; its origin is transcendent; it has truth only if God is the truth—it stands and falls with faith in God."

His central theme was that faith in God would yield to nihilism—belief in nothing. He announced, "We have abolished the world of truth, nothing is true." Knowledge, wisdom, and virtues are nothing but delusions, in his view. Because if there is no God, there are no facts, no absolute values, no objective truths. "How much must collapse now that this faith has been undermined because built on this faith was the totality of our European morality."

The death of God and the coming of nihilism were bound to have lethal consequences. In 1888, Nietzsche predicted that as faith in Christ faded among the most influential men, "Europe will soon be enveloped in darkness. I herald the coming of a tragic era, the rising of a black tide, there will be wars such as the world has never seen. Thanks to me, a catastrophe is at hand, all the earth will writhe in convulsions, and we must prepare for a long succession of demolitions, devastations, and upheavals."

If Man is not the Image of God, there is no reason individual persons should not be used as material, as tools, as Useful Idiots, like mobs, for a group of motivated men to achieve their aims. And no reason they should not be sent to the Gulag or exterminated in Auschwitz.

Nietzsche wrote that he had been guided by an unseen hand to set up a deliberately anti-Christian philosophy. Instead of loving love, he loved hatred and proclaimed himself hostile to morality. Tormented by the temptation to eradicate the Gospel, he admitted he was jealous of Jesus to the point of lunacy. The Spirit of Evil directed his mind. As that spirit took more control of him, he went insane, and his last writings are full of blasphemy and malevolence.

He proclaimed war against the Christian ideal, to rid the world of "trustfulness, patience, love of one's neighbor, and self-sacrifice. This eternal denunciation of Christianity, I will write it on all the walls so long as I find walls to blacken. I call Christianity the great scourge among all, the most shameful stain of humanity." His horrible end could be the same fate that awaits Western Civilization. His embrace of nihilism and paganism combined with anti-Christian invective are running rampant all around us.

Nietzsche wrote about "the Eternal Serpent," also called "Zarathustra," a demon that falls on him, assaults him, torments him, overwhelms him. It is from this demon that his "pen gushes forth" and creates "his testament, a fifth gospel" that is to abolish the four Gospels of the New Testament. "I have challenged all religions and have made a new Holy Book."

Now he has gone past criticizing Jesus to replacing Him. He is the new prophet repudiating Christ and seeking converts to a new religion. Zarathustra despises the Crucified One above all else. A new religion is necessary to fill the void created by killing God, "If we do not wish to fall prey again to the old idea of a Creator." Zarathustra aspires to be that substitute, our new Redeemer. Come with me, he coos, into what he deemed Eternal Nothingness.

Fyodor Dostoyevsky (1821-1881) discernably saw where atheism leads. His fellow Russian intellectuals claimed it would 'liberate' humankind by casting off Christian morality. They had perhaps started what is known as 'protest atheism'—a revolt against God because of the world he made. Dostoyevsky warned that if you think the suffering and pain is bad now wait until you see what kind of world godless men will make after removing divine limitations to human brutality.

Atheism can legitimize nearly anything. As Dostoyevsky informs, "Now assume there is no God, or immortality of the soul. Now tell me, why should I live righteously or do good deeds? Why shouldn't I, as long as I can rely on my cleverness to avoid being caught by the law, cut another man's throat, rob and steal?" To remove divine limits to human activity will lead to unrestrained evil violence and tyranny, he predicted. And it came to pass in the Soviet Union.

Dostoyevsky saw the dangers inherent in socialism, "that unclean and decadent thing" that embraced atheism. "To annihilate God is the first point in their program and the first watchword spread by their tracts. They undertake to build up humanity without God." The socialists sought to empty Heaven, destroy faith in God, and secularize man so thoroughly that there is nothing left about him that is considered sacred or transcendent. Only then can science save humankind and deliver us to Utopia.

Presciently, Dostoyevsky foresaw that the socialists intended for 10 percent of humankind—themselves—to rule the world. And if necessary, they might exterminate many of the rest. Only then would exclusively "educated men, who, organizing themselves according to scientific principles, would live happily ever after", populate the planet. He predicted over forty years before the Russian Revolution, "Social systems that have no Christian basis (the only one capable of transforming man) inevitably become systems of violence and slavery."

He said that the socialists had formed an alliance with Satan, "the terrible and intelligent Spirit, the Spirit of negation and nothingness," the Spirit of the Antichrist. By denying that human beings are living reflections of our Creator, the principle of human dignity is gone. Souls have no infinite, absolute value, and are thus reduced to being *means not ends* in themselves. Thus is sown the seeds of totalitarian ideologies.

As Henri De Lubac declared: "It is then that Christianity, with its conception of man, comes once again to give hope to the world, without presenting to man suspect novelties, but strengthened by its unchanged doctrine, it comes to save all. What it did for the ancient soul recommends it for humanity today. It comes to gather all that is sought by humanity, the best of its effort, and the best of its thought, to give it a foundation from the deepest source, the most certain origin of man. Christian realism is the realism of fullness. Without hiding man's misery from him, it shows him his nobility as well. A future is being prepared in which we are all invited. The Universe has a meaning to which man is the key. The current ills of man cannot be reduced to some poor organization of society. The ills of man are infinitely more profound, more mysterious, his situation infinitely more tragic, and his alienation more rigorous. This horrible invasive leprosy is called SIN."

Mark Twain (1835-1910) disguised his malicious atheism in good humor. During his day, the most famous writer on the planet mocked Christians and saw the Body of Christ as his hated enemy. He called God "repulsive and malignant." Before he died a hopeless nihilist, Twain wrote out a blasphemous message he had received directly from Satan called *Letters from the Earth*.

John Steinbeck (1902-1968) was awarded the Nobel Prize for his book *Of Mice and Men,* which is filled unceasingly with taking God's Name in vain. One could get the impression that cursing in the Name of the Lord is the book's central message. Not one of the characters in the book has any relationship with God. Still, they mention him in every other sentence. The reader can hardly come away from the story without the impression that the writer repeatedly insults God, does not fear God, and hates God. It is, naturally, required reading for high school students.

Jean-Paul Sartre (1905-1980) was an atheist and communist (ever notice how those two go together) and an antinomian. A stalwart apologist for Stalin's Soviet Union, even after he knew about the Gulags; he described Cuba under Castro (who never held elections) as a direct democracy, and the communist tyrant Tito's Yugoslavia as "the realization of my philosophy." Sartre loved the totalitarian Chairman Mao's murderous Red China while despising America, the land of the free. He encouraged political violence and loved Franz Fanon's concept of liberation through murder, terrorism, and Africans killing Europeans at will.

By the late 1950s, his ugly philosophy became apparent in his visage—a flabby body with the head of a toad, a blotched and pitted face, walleyed with yellow teeth, a man who never stopped talking and never listened to others. In the end, he stood for nothing. As he said himself, "Little by little atheism has devoured everything."

Sartre was an apostate, descended from seven generations of Protestant ministers. His life was a fifty-year celebration of debauchery as a drunkard, drug addict, and serial fornicator. His chief enemy was Jesus Christ. He sought to expel every vestige of God from the world, calling himself the *Chronicler of Hell,* and bragging that he "collared the Holy Ghost in the cellar and threw him out."

The man was unspeakably cruel and treacherous to the only woman who ever loved him, Simone de Beauvoir. He led the Western World into sexual license and nihilism. What naturally followed was the disintegration of the family in favor of profligacy, the promotion of sexual perversion, abortion, and euthanasia.

Sartre suffered from the same destructive fantasies and the same pathological malice towards what is normal that characterizes all devotees of Karl Marx: Hatred of reality. And he had the same tendency to divert attention away from the actual horrifying consequences of Marxism.

Sartre launched the idea – common now - that leftist movements must be judged not by their results but by their intentions, which are always worthy, of course. He preached, "Life is absurd." To be free, a man must be alone since "Hell is other people." Note that God said, "It is not good for man to be alone."

At its core, Sartre's philosophy of existentialism is selfishness. In his view, life has no purpose. Man has no nature, and the Cosmos has no meaning. We only exist, and we exist best when we make ourselves god: "Everything is possible if God does not exist. If God does not exist, we find no values or commands to turn to which legitimize our conduct." That is the deification of Self. All that is left is to live for his next fix, hookup, and television show. Existential man is alienated and directionless.

Along with other leftists, Sartre had the same boogieman to hate: the Bourgeois, which essentially means the middle class. *Normal people*, that is, who are heterosexual, married, good husbands and wives, good fathers and mothers, believe in the Lord, go to church, teach their children well, work for a living, try to get ahead, maybe start a little business, obtain some property, try to behave themselves, do not commit crimes, and long to be free from government interference—This is the monster the Left hates. And the Lord loves.

Sartre is cool for people who do not understand what he is talking about. He helped wreck our world. The abortion movement—a sacrament for Secular Humanism—has destroyed the closest of all human relationships. A billion or two babies have been killed in the wombs of their mothers—the very place designed for their protection.

We have seen a sharp rise in virtually all social pathologies. Nine times more people are lonely today than fifty years ago in the West. The loneliest people in the world today live in America, Australia, Sweden, Britain, and Canada. America is running headlong into bankruptcy, morally and financially. And why not? In the long run, we are all dead.

The Polish poet Czeslaw Milosz (1911-2004) perceptively saw that the ultimate source of the despair, tyranny, and mass murders of the twentieth century was the anti-Christian nihilism. He explicates, "A true opium of the people is the belief in nothingness after death—the huge solace of thinking that for our betrayals, greed, cowardice, murders, we are not going to be judged."

The point of nihilism is that there is no such thing as sin and no future judgment for our sins, thereby liberating us to do as we please. As Alister McGrath says, "The greatest intolerance and violence of the twentieth century were practiced by those who believed that religion caused intolerance and violence."

"For men have become lovers of their own selves, covetous, boastful, proud, blasphemers, unthankful, unholy, without natural affection ... despisers of those that are good ... lovers of pleasure more than lovers of God ... never able to come to the knowledge of the truth." (Paul the Apostle)

Satanic States

It makes ironic sense that the people who taught humanity monotheism—the Jews—would also, after they lost the faith of their fathers, instruct humanity in the substitute religion of atheistic Marxism.

The First International was formed in 1864, in London, with the Illuminati supposedly behind the curtain of a group of socialists, communists, atheists, and Satanists. Its members then set out to make war on Western Civilization by spreading propaganda designed to enrage the lower classes and engineer mob actions, terrorizing friends and foes. Lenin and Trotsky would one day take over an enormous country with these methods. Immorality, especially of the sexual and violent kind, was preached as *good*—*if* it furthered the workingman's revolution.

In 1914, European Civilization began to destroy itself. Many of its intellectuals, leaders, and rulers had forgotten God. Thus an essential part of their humanity was lost. This led from a crisis of civilizational morality to a rage of self-mutilation. The deliberate rejection of the God of the Bible would bring on the twin horrors of communism and National Socialism.

Ideas have consequences, and bad ideas can have lethal ramifications. The bad ideas I am speaking of are: Nothing matters but Matter; God is a myth, and the spiritual realm is an illusion. Even the socialist George Bernard Shaw blamed the First World War on "the Religion of Darwinism."

It was the power of the Church that had held back state power in Europe. It was based upon the conviction that Caesar is not God, and therefore not the ultimate authority. Christianity taught that a transcendent order of justice stands in judgment of public authority.

The two world wars just about killed the Church in Europe. Before World War One, the churches were full; they were half empty in the 1920s. The very idea that Christians would slaughter each other on such a massive scale—fifteen million dead—led to many losing their faith. In the aftermath of World War Two, the pews were three-quarters empty. The horrific slaughters spawned an enormous spiritual loss.

Vladimir Lenin thought he could persuade the Russian people to give up God and embrace his atheism. Within five years of his Bolshevik Revolution, he gave up that idea. He embarked on using force to suppress belief in Christ Jesus, as he put it, by the "protracted use of brutality." Christianity was declared the enemy of socialism.

As Russian historian Mikhail Keller explains, "Lenin, and later Stalin, determined, in order to maintain control of the people, it would be necessary to annihilate the family. The communists encouraged sexual immorality, approved abortion, and forced women out of the home into the workforce, accomplishing its purpose of destroying the Russian family."

No clear distinction can be drawn between socialism and communism. Marx often used the terms interchangeably. Sometimes, he would distinguish socialism as a transitional phase, followed by a higher stage of full communism: The abolition of private property.

As Lenin said, "What is usually called socialism was termed by Marx the first, or lower, phase of communist society." The most widely circulated works of Engels was called *Socialism, Utopian, and Scientific*. The British Communist Party used the term socialism as synonymous with communism. The 1929 Election Manifesto of the Communist Party of Great Britain, *Class against Class*, repeatedly uses the term socialism as the equivalent of communism.

The real purpose of that diabolical ideology we call socialism, is to turn envy into righteousness and justify the resentments of weaklings and failures towards the more successful men. The socialist in America today gravitates naturally to bureaucratic or tenured academic positions, where advancement is by seniority, not merit. There he can nurse his brooding grudges.

Socialism/Fascism/Communism/Totalitarianism are all variations of the same thing, and all rest on a foundation of Atheism. Thus having dispensed with any higher authority, the state assumes absolute dominion over all other institutions, including the family and the Church, which in this evil ideology are nothing more than the inventions of old-fashioned men. Individuals do not have any inalienable rights but only rights granted, or taken away, by the Almighty State.

What follows is a single-party government that kills its opposition and silences dissent by whatever means necessary. It takes total control of education and all means by which ideas are communicated. It loves secret meetings and secret police. It owns everything and everybody. The law becomes what it says it is. And it usually involves a cult of personality around a Lenin, Stalin, Hitler, Chairman Mao, Ho Chi Minh, Pol Pot, Castro, or Obama.

In the 1930s, the leftist Walter Lippmann made this observation: "The premises of authoritarian collectivism have become the working beliefs, the self-evident assumptions, the unquestioned axioms, of nearly every effort which lays claim to being enlightened and progressive. In the name of progress, men who call themselves communists, socialists, fascists, progressives, and even liberals, are unanimous in holding that government with its instruments of coercion must, by commanding the people how they should live, direct the course of civilization and fix the shape of things to come."

The Devil's minions try to claim that socialism/communism is part of Jesus' program. Jesus urged his disciples to take care of the poor with their own resources, voluntarily; the socialist/communist *confiscates your money* to give to others. Jesus would never favor such a thing, and He certainly would not agree with Chairman Mao's ideology. Mao said that he wouldn't mind if *half the people on the planet perished* for the cause of worldwide socialism. The Khmer Rouge regime in Cambodia shows us what socialists/communists are capable of. They massacred anybody and everybody who opposed them.

The Catholic Church has long seen communism for what it is. In 1846, Pope Pius IX warned: "Communism is among the darkest designs of men in the clothing of sheep, while inwardly ravening wolves. Their books and pamphlets teach the lessons of sinning and generate a widespread disgusting infection. These works, well-written and filled with deceit and cunning, are for the destruction of the Christian people by the lowering of morals and undermining the faith that produces the morals;" the endgame being "morals deteriorated, Christ's holy religion despised, the majesty of divine worship rejected."

Pope Leo XIII proclaimed in 1878: "Communism is the final plague which insinuates itself into the very marrow of human society only to bring about its ruin. We speak of men who, under various names, are called socialists, communists, or nihilists, bound together by the closest ties in wicked confederation. They leave nothing untouched or whole, which by both human and divine laws has been wisely decreed for the health and beauty of life. They refuse obedience to the higher powers. They foul up marriage and the family. They debase the natural union of man and woman, which is held sacred. They weaken the family, the cornerstone of all society. The foundation of this society rests first of all in the indissoluble union of man and wife. It is completed in the mutual rights and duties of parents and children. The doctrines of socialism strive to dissolve this union, marriage, which God himself instituted at the beginning of the very world. God ordained parental authority over the authority of the state."

In 1937, Pope Pius XI wrote, "Communism is a satanic scourge, godless, by its nature anti-religious, a perversity and poison that is intrinsically wrong and collectivistic terrorism replete with hate." He denounced it as a "false faith rooted in class warfare," which "conceals itself in a false messianic idea" hatched "by the powers of darkness" and "at its origin primarily an evil of the spiritual order. From the polluted source, the monstrous emanations of the communistic system flow with satanic logic. Communism strips Man of his liberty, robs human personality of all its dignity, and removes all the moral restraints that check the eruptions of blind impulse—refusing to human life any sacred or spiritual character. With the rejection of any link that binds a woman to the family and the home, she is withdrawn from the family and the care of her children to be thrust instead into collective production. The care of children then devolves upon the collective. Finally, the right to education is denied to parents, for it is conceived as the exclusive prerogative of the community."

After the 1917 Socialist Revolution in Russia that would found the Soviet Union, one of the first acts of Vladimir Lenin was to forbid anyone under seventeen years old from being taught about God, Jesus, or the Bible. All education was from removed from parents and churches, making the only lawful means of learning the state school, which was militantly atheistic.

Children were encouraged to tattletale on their parents if they told them about God. Marriage ceremonies were taken from the Church and made the purview of the state. Divorce was made easy, and abortion legalized. The first country to legalize abortion was the Soviet Union.

Feminist Aleksandra Kollontai promoted that development, as well as sexual promiscuity, to "free captive housewives from the shackles of the family," because "women can only achieve equality through the overthrow of capitalism" and in the new utopia, the family would cease to exist. In her view, "Mothers do not have children; all are children of the State. Society will take upon itself all the duties involved in the child's education."

All children are wards of the socialist state. Progressives still feel that way. Melissa Harris-Perry said recently on MSNBC, "We have to break through our kind of private idea that kids belong to their parents, or kids belong to their families and recognize that kids belong to the whole community."

Lenin reformulated the theory of Marx, making it simpler, easier to teach and understand. Lenin also loved the Theory of Evolution, commanding, "Only the strong survive. If anyone gets in your way, kill them."

Mussolini would base his Theory of Fascism upon the Theory of Evolution. Atheism was the belief system of both Lenin and Mussolini. Secret police, murder, and terror were weapons they loved to exercise. Lenin declared, "We will destroy everything! We will destroy the entire bourgeoisie [middle class], and grind it to powder."

Individual human beings mean absolutely nothing in this worldview since man has no real purpose or destiny. The State is all. English socialist H.G. Wells loved Lenin, "A refreshing and amazing little man." Wells said of Josef Stalin: "I've never met a man more candid, fair, and honest."

George Bernard Shaw captured the mood of the anti-religious, defiantly atheistic intellectuals of the 1920s, "We were intellectually intoxicated with the idea that the world could make itself without design, purpose, skill, or intelligence: in short, without life. The first effect was exhilarating: we had the runaway child's sense of freedom before it gets hungry and lonely and frightened."

One of the first decrees of the Soviets had been to replace marriage and the family with free love. A law pronounced in 1919 made it illegal for any woman ages 17-32 to be in a monogamous relationship with a man. "All women become the property of the State," declared the decree.

The government issued certificates to 'working-class men' to have sex with the women of their choice. It also abolished rape on the idea that a woman's body did not belong to her anyway but belonged to the socialist state to be used by her comrades as they wished. One month after a baby was born, the government would snatch it from its mother. It would be cared for and educated by the state, to ensure indoctrination from a tender age in anti-Christian ideology.

The Soviets began their socialist experiment by hating on Jesus, killing priests, and desecrating churches. God was immediately kicked out of all schools, and the teaching of Christianity prohibited by law. Five years later, it was forbidden by law *under penalty of death* for parents to teach religion to children in their own homes.

In 1929, the Soviet Union decreed a five-day week, abolishing the seven-day week based on the Bible and the Sabbath. Atheist propaganda filled the streets, and hundreds of official Museums of the Antichrist opened to mock God.

Christian charity was banished because the state demanded a monopoly on social services. In 1938 alone, 165,200 priests and pastors were arrested and sent to the Gulag for practicing their religion, with 106,800 others executed by firing squad.

Like the American Left today, the Soviets set their sights on Christmas, which children everywhere love. It is therefore hated by Satan and his servants here on Earth. Christmas trees were prohibited. Here is the government proclamation of 1929: "Millions of little children are brought up by very religious grandmothers. For such children, the Christmas tree represents a very great danger. The struggle against the Christmas Tree is the struggle against religion and our class enemies."

Abraham Lincoln once wisely observed: "The philosophy in the schoolroom in one generation will become the philosophy of government in the next." People of the Left are always most interested in getting their grubby little hands on your children. Lenin, Stalin, and Hitler all preached that while it may be hard to change adults' minds; it is easy to mold the minds of Children. If private schooling is outlawed.

In Soviet schools, socialism was presented as the savior of mankind. Religion was to be exterminated worldwide, with the wealth of religious people, and their churches, confiscated. Christians were not allowed to teach school unless they first denied Christ in public. Political Correctness was an official policy. Educators were required to insist that God was a fairy tale, equivalent to goblins and unicorns. The schools were specifically designed to root out any religious inkling among children.

Marxism is Satanism in disguise. It officially denies the existence of the Soul, God, Sin, Heaven, and Hell. It is organized hatred of Man and God. Marxism is often called a religion, as its followers are rabidly devout and have great faith in their ideology. Since it is bitterly hostile to the very idea of God, *it is an evil religion.*

As one famous Soviet apparatchik put it: "Communist ethics make it the highest duty to accept the necessity of acting wickedly." If that doesn't sound demonic, I don't know what does. Marxists hate Jesus because their ideology will brook no rival. Besides, since good and evil only live in the imagination, none of the 100 million murders of its innocent citizens by socialist states were immoral acts. Socialist immorality has *no lower limit*.

When the Iron Curtain finally fell in 1989, all could see the facts about the worker's paradise built by socialism. As described by Christopher Hitchens: "The hideous prisoners, faces grotesque from habitual evil, being herded in sordid dungeons; the desolate cityscapes of concrete slabs under poisoned skies; the filthy yellow waste trickling from a crooked pipeline onto a polluted sea; the excrement-smeared, desecrated ruins of what had been churches, the corruption and the unending official lies." When Mr. Hitchens visited the Soviet Union, he observed, "My Russian acquaintances thought my wife and I were ten years younger than we were. We thought they were ten years older than they were."

Nazism was a marriage of socialism, science, and the occult. Adolf Hitler knew that Nazism could not coexist with Christianity. He imprisoned or executed more than a third of the Christian ministers in Germany. A new Paganism took over, and even judges and the law became anti-Christian.

Nazi Germany was the most educated, progressive, scientifically advanced nation in the world. We see many parallels with the American Left today: Both accept socialism, especially socialized medical care; took prayer out of schools; renamed Christmas and Easter in schools; made abortion acceptable; began to raise children in daycare; built gigantic bureaucracies to command every nook and cranny of everyday life; spent money like crazy people; banned private ownership of guns; instituted Political Correctness; oversaw a rise in perversion, immorality, and crime; and remade schools into indoctrination centers.

Hitler was a Satanist in full bloom. Just listen to his voice and tell me it was not demonic. He had many books on the occult, in one of which he highlighted this sentence: "He who does not have the demonic seed within himself will never give birth to a magical world."

But let's go back a few years to Guido von List, the clairvoyant Armanenschaft occultist who wanted to revive ancient German Paganism under the demon god Wotan. In 1908, the List Society was formed in Vienna. List introduced Occult Runes, one of which would become the 'Seig' for Hitler Youth—and the Double Seig for the Mystical Brotherhood of the SS, those jackbooted goose-steppers. His plan included Christian crosses being pulled up from graveyards around Germany to be replaced by the pagan 'Man Rune of Death.'

In World War One, German soldiers sought protection from charms, amulets, and talismans, such as the Swastika. The last Russian Empress, who was German, the one involved with Rasputin, also liked to wear Swastikas. Hitler idolized List and sought to revive Paganism throughout Europe as an occult religion featuring ritual magic and sexual perversion, with the Swastika as its symbol—replacing the Cross.

Another founder of the Nazi Party was dedicated Satanist Dietrich Eckhart. He claimed to be in direct communication with Satan through séances and declared Adolf Hitler the Antichrist. Karl Haushofer became Hitler's spiritual mentor, as well as introducing him to sadomasochism and other perversions. Together they planned the new religion replete with astrology, clairvoyance, telepathy, hypnotism, and Yoga, with Hitler as the new messiah. Wagner's opera *Parsifal* had imagined an Aryan Messiah, and this idea became the center of Hitler's new religion.

Hitler had long before vowed to follow Satan while standing before the Holy Lance (or Spear of Destiny) in Vienna. Part of his occult beliefs included reincarnation. He claimed to be the reincarnation of Roman Emperor Tiberius Caesar, a habitual sodomizer.

Let's take a closer look at the SS, which was obsessed with secrecy. The forerunner of the SS was the Order of the New Templars, a cult that was deeply into reincarnation, among other things. The Swastika was first used in Germany by this satanic cult. It published a magazine called *Ostara*, the name of an old German pagan goddess. Jorg Lanz von Liebenfels, a well-known occultist who later influenced Hitler, founded the cult in 1907. The potent occult symbol of the Swastika—the ancient Druids in Britain had used it—was adopted by the National Socialists (NAZIs) in 1920, its final design created by the artist Adolf Hitler.

Von Liebenfels would combine science, eugenics, socialism, and the occult, along with 'selective breeding,' to create a new occult religion—Theozoology. According to his views, which the Nazis latched onto, no individuals are equal, no families are equal, and no races are equal—in intelligence, productivity, morals, or criminality.

When Germany began its descent into poverty and misery in the 1920s, the Germans began to look for an earthly Savior. One organization to which they turned was the Thule Society, formed in 1918 by Alfred Rosenberg, dedicated to the teachings of Guido von List. Part of its mission was to declare socialism as the political and economic system for Germany, the Swastika as its symbol, and ancient pagan rituals their means of devotion.

Strange ceremonies and beliefs would begin to mesmerize the German people. At one rally, there were 37,000 Swastikas displayed for the new messiah, Adolf Hitler. Such mass rallies were religious and mystical, designed to promote worship in the new faith. All of these pagans lamented that Christianity had forced the occult underground. It had been kept alive by secret organizations such as the Rosicrucian Order. With the consecration of the Blood Flag, there shall be no God but Germany.

The Swastika was to replace the Cross, as the Nazis believed Darwinism would replace Christianity. According to this view, in tune with the 'survival of the fittest,' only the strong would survive. For Hitler, that meant the Aryan Race, the most highly evolved race, which would eventually develop into new men that would forge a new world—by extinguishing or enslaving all others. The 'sacred mystery of the Swastika' was said to be the symbol of Darwinism and Darwinist Genetics. Hitler sought to launch his new religion of secret demonic knowledge to "wash off the Christian" and promote the doctrines of the Devil.

Before the rise of Hitler, the personal guru of Kaiser Wilhelm had been a Satanist named Houston Chamberlain. Chamberlain claimed that demons wrote his writings while he was in a trance. He also said he saw the demons that inspired him. Chamberlain wrote what demons told him to write, in the grip of a horrible fever. Later, he would say he did not recognize any of the ideas of which he had written.

A fan of his was the young Adolf Hitler, who also mentions the Theory of Evolution over and over again in his manifesto *Mein Kampf*. Hitler considered himself the superman that Nietzsche hoped would arise.

Houston Chamberlain was then the 'spiritual founder' of the Third Reich. Disillusioned with Christianity, he felt the German People must return to Paganism and that it was their destiny to conquer the whole planet. Jesus was out because He was a Jew. And Christianity was a Jewish plot.

The Nazis were the most progressive and scientific rulers in history. Just like today's leftists in America, Hitler tried to eradicate any influence of Christianity in public affairs. The Nazis renamed Christmas 'Winter Solstice' and Easter 'Spring Holiday,' as well as creating state child dedications to replace Christian baptism, and state marriages to replace church marriages.

Hitler banned prayer in schools and substituted teaching Nazism for teaching Christianity. Soon enough, nativity scenes and Christmas carols were also banned from schools, and crucifixes were removed from classrooms with Swastikas put in their place. The Nazis made it a violation of the law to give your child a name from the Bible or the name of a Christian Saint. A new calendar came out that deleted all reference to Christian Holy Days.

Late in the 1930s, Hitler prohibited the printing and distribution of the Holy Bible and demanded that Bibles, crosses, and paintings of saints be removed from churches to be replaced with *Mein Kampf* and Swastikas. Public display of Christian art was outlawed, and no newspapers were allowed to print articles from a Christian point of view. For the Hitler Youth, the Gospel was thrown out and replaced by Hitler's *Mein Kampf*.

By 1939, it was against the law for children's books to mention angels, Christ or Christmas. Instead, they were embedded with Paganism. The Summer Solstice was named an official holy day. God had to be banished to make way for National Socialism. A 1941 Nazi statement says: "The State excludes the Church from everything it considers as belonging to the political sphere. At the same time, the Church is expected to shrivel to nothing."

Many other Nazis were devout Satanists, including Hess, Himmler, and Goebbels. Some Americans today embrace New Age Religion, which is similar to Hitler's occultism. Hitler said: "One can is either a Christian or a German. You can't be both."

One of the stupidest memes floating around social media today is the one that says, "Adolf Hitler was a Christian." What did Hitler say about Christianity? Here are a series of quotes from his lips:

"The reason why the ancient world was so pure, light and serene was that it knew nothing of the two great scourges: the pox and Christianity!"

"Christianity is an invention of sick brains: one could imagine nothing more senseless. Hans Kerrl, with the noblest of intentions, wanted to attempt a synthesis between National Socialism and Christianity. I don't believe the thing's possible, and I see the obstacle in Christianity itself."

"Our epoch will certainly see the end of the disease of Christianity. It will last another hundred years, two hundred years, perhaps."

"The heaviest blow that ever struck humanity was the coming of Christianity. Bolshevism is Christianity's illegitimate child. Both are inventions of the Jew. The deliberate lie in the matter of religion was introduced into the world by Christianity."

"So it's not opportune to hurl ourselves now into a struggle with the Churches. A slow death has something comforting about it. The dogma of Christianity gets worn away before the advances of science. Religion will have to make more and more concessions. Gradually the myths crumble. All that's left is to prove that in nature, there is no frontier between the organic and the inorganic. When understanding of the Universe has become widespread when the majority of men know that the stars are not sources of light but worlds, perhaps inhabited worlds like ours, then the Christian doctrine will be convicted of absurdity."

"Our whole deformity and atrophy of spirit and soul would never have come into being except for this oriental mummery, this abominable leveling mania, this cursed universality of Christianity."

Virtually every other Nazi leader – Hess, Goering, Himmler, Goebbels, Rosenberg, von Schirach, Streicher, and Bormann – expressed a profound disdain and hatred for Christianity. Many Christians courageously stood up to the Nazis, against their persecution of Jews, which was gratefully acknowledged by Jewish leaders. In 1938, Rabbi Morris Lazaron attested: "Never in history has organized Protestantism throughout the world bestirred itself in defense of the Jew and to protect the Jew. More Catholic leaders than ever before have lifted their voices in condemnation of the racial fixation that dictators have used to bait the Jew. No more glorious page is being written in Christian history than Christianity is writing in Germany today. Christianity may yet be the rock on which the German dictatorship will destroy itself."

During the war, Albert Einstein testified: "Only the Church stood squarely across the path of Hitler's campaign for suppressing the truth. I never had any special interest in the Church before. But now I feel a great affection and admiration for it because the Church alone has had the courage and persistence to stand for intellectual and moral freedom."

Fritz Lentz came up with the concept of Racial Hygiene from the Eugenics of Darwin. It was his idea to boycott Jewish businesses, exclude Jews from the Civil Service, remove Jews from teaching positions in universities, and expel Jews from economic and cultural life—just like the American Left wants to do to Christians today. The Left despises Christians just as Nazis despised Jews.

The next big idea was euthanasia for handicapped children, followed by the same program for the mentally ill, and those retarded or deformed—those whose cost to society was too high. It was decided that 10 percent of the population was feebleminded or deficient in some way. To create humanity anew, the Nazis figured they must kill the most talented non-Germans and enslave the rest, particularly the Slavs. Inmates of psychiatric hospitals were lined up and shot (the T4 Program). They euthanized the elderly in retirement homes and decided to kill those too sick to work.

Darwinism had undercut over a thousand years of belief in Christ among the German people, including the Christian dogma that men and women are God's children. It was Darwinism that spawned eugenics—the breeding of human beings to produce a better race. For eugenics to accomplish its goal, they had to stop promoting Christian charity for the weak. Darwin had said that no one was stupid enough to allow the worst domesticated animals to breed. Based on these same ideas, Maury Stokes had founded Planned Parenthood of Britain.

Logically then, the human race would be better off without the lower races, and they could be bred out. When breeding them out began to look like it would take too long, the idea of exterminating them came to the fore. At the least, the unfit should be sterilized. The Race and Resettlement Bureau was created to help. Positive eugenics was also implemented, that is, the selection of 'brood mothers.'

Adolf Hitler was an avid collector of *Ostara*, in the pages of which all of these ideas blossomed. Hitler fervently agreed with Charles Darwin's cousin Francis Galton about eugenics, based on the notion that inferior types have more children. So the state must step in to control human breeding, beginning by excluding alcoholics and the insane from having children.

American 'progressives' had led the way in eugenics and forced sterilizations at first. The Germans studied and approved of the progressive's program in America. Many folks seemed to agree that it was a disgrace for the deficient to reproduce. Because the wants of deficient individuals should count for nothing compared to the needs of the human race and the state. Himmler was obsessed with all of this. The Germans forcibly sterilized 400,000 persons, and marriage was forbidden to any who were diseased.

The clairvoyant Karl Maria Wiligut made the Castle of Wewelsburg the spiritual center for the Pagan Cult of the SS. The SS-TVVT and Death's Head units were formed to quarantine Jews, social misfits, dissidents, and perverts in concentration camps, along with priests and ministers targeted for execution. Abortion was strongly encouraged for all non-Aryans but illegal for Aryans. At Lebensborn, they launched the Spring of Life program to breed super-babies. All of these tactics were to speed up natural selection and evolution.

The Soviets openly preached world conquest—and conquered a third of the globe—while the American Left insisted that they didn't really mean it. Today, the American Left claims Islamists don't mean what they say about slaughtering all non-Muslims, raping all their women, and enslaving their children. Nor do they mean their constant chants, "Death to Israel! Death to America!"

Socialists proclaimed that a scientifically planned and organized society would bring humankind a new high standard-of-living and that the USSR would far surpass the USA. Instead, Russians walked for hours in freezing cold to stand in line for stale bread. And most of the youth of the world would swim across the ocean if they could come to America.

The Soviets declared that one single socialist shoe factory could shoe the nation. When that failed, they claimed that going barefoot was best. Socialists contended that killing tens of millions of people, and enslaving the whole human race, would be beneficial in the long haul because they would destroy capitalism. Socialism is a form of hatred—a sadistic, brutal, inhuman social system. Self-made puppets in search of a master, begging and demanding to be taken care of, favor it.

When the godless left attains a particular measure of power, it usually starts its anti-Christian program by demanding that the Free Exercise of Religion be subordinated to the almighty state. That is a stepping-stone to the ultimate aim: the elimination of religion except for a religion of the state, with it as the provider for all our needs, and destroyer of all that oppose its aims. Of course, progressive ideology today is anti-Christian because Christianity shines a harsh, bright light of truth on its falsehoods.

That is why the French Revolution had as its chief aim the destruction of Christianity, as do the Marxists, socialists, fascists, communists, and all other Leftists, today and in the past. That same spirit animated the Cultural Revolution of the 1960s.

For free people—such as Americans in their original constitutional republic—self-government means the moral government of us by us. Evil people cannot be free; they do too much damage to their society. A dreamer becomes dangerous when you take away his belief in God. He has to find a new religion because man is, by nature, religious. He must serve something more substantial than himself.

Scientific socialists such as Hitler, Mao, Stalin, and Pol Pot committed the most hideous crimes in human history. Josef Stalin said he became an atheist after reading Darwin's books. He went on to murder perhaps sixty million innocent citizens of Russia. The daughters of socialism—communism, fascism, and Nazism—all produced the same results: Existence without life from denying man's spiritual dimension, and ultimately death in Auschwitz or the Gulag Archipelago. What they all stood for finally was hatred of Father God and Jesus His Son.

Enter the Mind Benders

Psychology is the only profession that creates the diseases it claims to cure. Before Sigmund Freud came along, no intelligent adult would pronounce that his own actions were not his fault. Psychology created a new man who is blameless for his failures and not responsible for them because they stem from his childhood when he was innocent.

Since psychology originated in Christian society, there is no question but that Christianity is its target, what it seeks to displace. A sinner is told to "Repent!" by Jesus, but the psychologist says there is nothing to repent for, only things for which you need therapy at $250 an hour.

After World War Two, it became unfashionable to think that heredity had anything to do with how one turned out. Instead, it must be social forces, especially bad family environments. It became accepted that it was only bad childhoods that made for delinquents and criminals. And so the Social Worker Revolution was born.

Christian volunteers had done social work for centuries. But the new paradigm was that Freudian psychology would work better—social work would carry on best without Jesus. Soon, this idea was applied to juvenile and adult offenders. It was observed that criminals have other conduct disorders as well as committing crimes, perhaps mental or nervous abnormalities.

The mind doctors generally concluded that rather than beset by spiritual problems, felons are victims of psychic trauma in their past, that they might not even remember. The remedy was to establish a system of psychiatric clinics alongside all courts and prisons and allow mental experts to guide judges and prison officials to treat those who misbehave.

Some experts said prisons should be eliminated and replaced by mental health rehabilitation centers since criminals were not genuinely blameworthy for their foul deeds. Even the famous atheist lawyer Clarence Darrow argued in court: "There is no such thing as crime. Therefore there is no such thing as a moral responsibility."

Later, the thought that came into vogue among behavioralists was that mothers cause virtually every human problem. Your mother "first stirs up bitterness and revenge wishes in the child, and the hate that burns in the child's heart." So the mothers of the human race were the cause of war, crime, mental illness, marital difficulties, sexual problems, alcoholism, psychosis, and neuroses.

Well, back to the criminals. It turns out that boys who have had therapy, and boys who haven't, grow up to commit about the same number of crimes. Criminals who had undergone therapy in prison committed *more* crimes after they got out than those who hadn't. The longer the treatment, the more crimes they perpetrated, and the crimes were more injurious.

So, you mean to tell me that teaching juvenile delinquents and felons that their villainy is not their fault; that they are not responsible to man or God for their behavior; that they are victims themselves, did not make them go on the straight and narrow? Still, any cockamamie idea is worth a try, except for reading the Bible and going to church.

Research shows that boys who receive therapy have *more* problems as adults than those who do not, such as alcoholism, mental problems, disease, and commission of serious crimes. Dr. Tana Dineen, who practiced psychology for 30 years, says in her book *Manufacturing Victims* that scientific studies show therapy to be ineffective, unnecessary, and often harmful.

Listen to psychologist Roger Mills: "I have personally seen therapists convince their clients that all of their problems come from their mothers, the stars, their biochemical makeup, their diet, their lifestyle, and even the 'karma' from their past lives."

Now according to medical authorities, it is true that our children are exhibiting all-time high levels of anti-social behavior, as well as drug and alcohol abuse and suicidal tendencies. Maybe it is because, for a generation, they have been saturated with 'self-esteem' psychological engineering.

Studies show that psychopaths, sociopaths, narcissists, bullies, murderers, thieves, and the habitually hostile, always alienated, mean, and self-destructive persons, *all have very high self-esteem*. In the end, people with the highest esteem in the world are the most attractive females.

Paul the Apostle warns against thinking too highly of yourself—of esteeming ourselves too highly. Obsessing about your 'self' was promoted by Erich Fromm, who said, "Belief in God is a childish illusion." Fromm believed "the lack of self-esteem is central to the personal and social ills plaguing our nation."

A study by Yochelson and Samenow of the most vicious criminals found that *not one* of them had low self-esteem. Sociological research shows that the higher the self-esteem, the more likely to commit crimes and the more likely one will be immoral, violent, and a sociopath.

Forty percent of American women are depressed, according to a government spokeswoman. Every person in America is damaged emotionally, some say. Various studies conclude that adolescent boys are deprived emotionally and live lives of quiet desperation. They are engulfed by isolation and loneliness. Girls crash and burn under great suffering. Men are in agony, and enraged, having lost their sense of self. Seventy-seven percent of all adults suffer from emotional disorders; the whole country is "officially nuts," reported the *Wall Street Journal*.

Now, a reasonable person might notice that ever since psychology burst on the scene in America in the 1960s, we have seen a tenfold increase in sin—which, after all, isn't your fault. But it is precisely sin that separates us from God and requires repentance to reconcile with God, not therapy.

Our society groans under the weight of ten times as much crime, violence, and immorality as we had fifty years ago. After all, what is attractive about psychology is that it absolves us individually of guilt. It provides an excuse for our wrongdoings. We are nothing more than the product of our genes or social environment: We are all victims!

Due to the determination to have psychology and psychiatry established as 'sciences,' for reasons of prestige, most in those fields, since their founding, have claimed that our thoughts, emotions, behavior, and personality are all purely physical phenomena.

These specialists made grand promises to make society and the world better and safer because they would solve our age-old problems. Finally, in 1979 the American Psychological Association admitted that what it represents is not and cannot be a 'science.'

And notice the irony of a field that denies anything exists such as a 'mind' and yet calls the problems it says it will cure 'mental illness.' Shouldn't it be 'brain illness' if we have no minds outside our brains?

The Father of American Psychology, William James, believed that each of us has a soul that exists in a spiritual realm, apart from our bodies in this physical world. In essence, the spiritual self is who we are, a more concrete, permanent, intimate person than whom we appear to be to others. Your spiritual self includes your personality, core values, and conscience.

But James was not a Christian. He believed in Pantheism—that God is not separate from the Universe, but God is, in effect, the Universe. Therefore he fell into the error of thinking "higher powers exist that are at work to save the world," when the only 'higher powers' he was in contact with were through the Occult. They are out to *destroy* the world and everything and everyone in it.

The mental health industry is booming. Mostly because it creates its customers by selling the public on the doctrine of 'therapism.' Anguished Americans must have an army of therapists, self-esteem gurus, grief counselors, sensitivity trainers, and trauma experts to make it through life. As Abraham Maslow said, "Psychologists will save the world, or it won't be saved at all."

Maslow wanted psychology to replace Christianity. Human beings would be peaceful, happy, and fulfilled as soon as people were accepted and esteemed—just as they are—by others and themselves. He did not believe evil existed, but "a sick culture makes sick people."

Although he is revered in the mental health community, his own studies proved his theories to be completely wrong. His idea that unhappiness was caused by "not being yourself" or "not finding yourself" is false. Sin causes human unhappiness, as does making poor decisions, and not practicing delayed gratification.

One of Maslow's disciples was Abbie Hoffman, a famous Sixties revolutionary, hater of America, despiser of free enterprise, clown, psychopath, drug abuser, and drug dealer. But he did not find solace, his life ending in suicide.

Even the humanist psychologist Carl Rogers believed the mind is much more than the brain. While he rejected Jesus Christ and the Holy Bible, he had a change of heart about the non-material world's existence after he and his wife began consulting mediums in the 1970s. Rogers was the grandfather of the self-esteem movement, the defining question of which is, "How do you feel about that?"

Rogers taught parents and teachers to approve of children unconditionally; to praise them no matter what they do. "The spontaneous feelings of a child, his real attitudes, have so often been disapproved of by parents and others that he has come to feel that the self he is constitutes a person no one could love." Schools should not be for learning about subjects but *personal growth centers*, just a big group therapy session all year long, in which no behavior would be judged.

In the late 1970s, Rogers and his wife began to consult spiritualists and have demonic mystical experiences. Rogers professed: "Helen had been a great skeptic about psychic phenomena and immortality. Yet, upon invitation, she and I visited a thoroughly honest medium that would take no money. There, Helen experienced, and I observed, a 'contact' with her deceased sister, involving facts that the medium could not possibly have known. The messages were extraordinarily accurate. It was incredible, and certainly a non-fraudulent experience."

After his wife's death, Rogers went to the spiritualist again and came away convinced about spiritualism, occult phenomena, and reincarnation. "We were very soon in contact with Helen, who answered many questions. I now consider it possible that each of us is a continuing spiritual essence lasting over time, and occasionally incarnated in a human body. I am open to even more mysterious phenomena – human auras, Kirlian photography, even out-of-the-body experiences. Paranormal phenomena such as telepathy, precognition, and clairvoyance have been sufficiently tested that they have received scientific acceptance."

Rogers wanted to create new people who would "Trust in their own experience and a profound distrust of external authority. They make their own moral judgments. They are nonmoralistic and nonjudgmental—never judging the behavior of others as evil or wrong." The foolish implications of this philosophy are that we should not say that Adolf Hitler, Josef Stalin, Chairman Mao, serial child killers, pedophiles, rapists, and so on have done anything wrong.

Rogers' "Persons of Tomorrow," as he called them, are everywhere today. These lawless, immoral, self-righteous do-gooders produce massive social decline and chaos throughout the Western world. He also taught that adultery was an enriching experience to justify his cheating on his wife as she suffered from terminal cancer. According to him, we should not refer to such relationships with the "negative terms like extramarital affairs or adultery or immorality, because such notions are old-fashioned and ridiculous."

Rogers helped popularize adultery and wife swapping. That resulted in multitudes of divorces, hurt spouses, and emotionally scarred children. Rogers here was partly attacking the belief that people should follow the absolute moral standards and ethical teachings of the Bible. In recent decades, many psychologists, psychiatrists, and counselors have spread Rogers' foolish advice.

"But who defines mental health?" asked Carl Rogers. He argued that because the Menninger Clinic, the Center for Studies of the Person, and the Soviet Union each defines mental health differently, there is no such thing as a definition of mental health.

Rogers' approach quickly deteriorates into an entirely relativistic, existentialist, foolish charade in which the counselors continually smile like Cheshire cats and continuously nod while their clients describe all their wrong attitudes, wicked behaviors, and perversions, without the counselors ever once committing the unpardonable sin of telling their clients that some of their actions are wrong and need to change.

Rogers strongly opposed the Christian idea that all people are born with a sinful nature. Rogers taught that anti-social behavior and crime result from people being socialized wrongly by parents, teachers, and others, and is contrary to their inherently good human nature.

In 1966, Carl Rogers said, "I don't have very much standing in psychology itself, and I couldn't care less. But in education and industry and group dynamics and social work and the philosophy of science and pastoral psychology and theology and other fields, my ideas have penetrated and influenced in ways I would never have dreamt."

These ideas are so ingrained in our fellow Americans by the government indoctrination centers (public schools) that a study of values by political science professor Alan Wolfe found that many people refuse to express moral judgments about even outrageous crimes. Instead, they will say, "Everybody makes mistakes." Even serial killer, cannibal, and homosexual rapist Jeffrey Dahmer's deeds elicited sympathy: "I felt sorry for him," said some respondents. We have lost our will to criticize vicious, heinous behavior.

God has told us that we choose our actions, and the choices we make shape our destinies. Therefore, we are right to praise people who do the right thing and blame people who do the wrong thing, especially habitually. The whole mental health field is not comfortable with personal responsibility, believing the things we do are outside of our control due to genetic predispositions and the environment in which we grew up. That is the crux of the case for nonjudgmentalism. The comic strip *Non Sequitur* shows a mental health facility and reads, 1st Floor: Mother's Fault. 2nd Floor: Father's Fault. 3rd Floor: Society's Fault. Nonjudgmentalism is not the essence of kindness; it is the essence of madness.

The great Swiss psychiatrist Carl Jung was intensely into the Occult. He wrote of visitations he had from demons that menaced and frightened him horribly, while also teaching him what became his theories.

Jung wrote about this in his *Red Book*, but his family withheld that work from publication until forty years after his death. Jung said, about what he learned from these demons, "Everything else is to be derived from this. It began at that time, and the later details hardly matter anymore. My entire life consisted in elaborating what had burst forth from the unconscious and flooded me like an enigmatic stream and threatened to break me."

What did Carl Jung learn from the spirit guides of the other world? "Our unconscious existence is the real one and our conscious world a kind of illusion." A proud Buddhist could not have said it better.

Jung said his personal spirit guide was named Philemon, who would appear and disappear quickly and without warning. Over time, Jung began to admire Philemon, and it is from him that he learned the crucial ideas that still affect human beings today a great deal. Late in life, Jung admitted that he didn't know what the 'soul' is—even though the word 'psychology' *means* its study.

Many headshrinkers who started out as deniers of the supernatural changed their tune because of the experiences they had in their work. Psychiatrist Ralph B. Allison averred, "I have come to believe in the possibility of spirit possession by demonic spirits from satanic realms." Psychologist Edith Fiore came to believe in demonic possession as well.

Thomas Szasz, the famous atheist psychiatrist, admits what psychology is: "The clever and cynical destruction of the spirituality of man." The good doctor had a lot more to say, as well, about important things, such as that *mental illness* is just a term to describe unwanted behavior. What is wanted and unwanted behavior is a judgment call, not a scientific fact.

'Mental Disorder' Szasz called a 'weasel term,' and drug addiction not a disease but a *social habit*. A disease is something a person has; behavior is what people do. Szasz taught that diseases are "malfunctions of the human body, of the heart, the liver, the kidney, the brain. No behavior or misbehavior is a disease or can be a disease. That's not what diseases are."

A disease can be seen during an autopsy but not voted into existence by members of the American Psychiatric Association. Calling people diseased denies them responsibility as moral agents with free will. Szasz said, "One of Freud's most powerful motives in life was to inflict vengeance on Christianity." And Szasz calls psychotherapy "a fake religion that seeks to destroy true religion."

Secular psychologists Keen and Rieff described psychotherapy as "a kind of national religion, with a gospel of self-fulfillment and with therapists as the new priests." Note that psychology often promotes itself as the solution to the same problems that the Bible addresses as spiritual issues to be solved by entering into a relationship with Jesus. A person who does not believe in Heaven cannot possibly show you the way. Since Man did not create himself, he cannot comprehend himself unless he consults his owner's manual, the Holy Bible.

Jesus said you must deny yourself to be saved. When I was young, self-centeredness was considered a grave fault. Today, it is at the center of our culture: self-love, self-esteem, self-acceptance, self-forgiveness, self-awareness, self-image, self-confidence, self-worth, self-control, and self-improvement.

It is an odd thing that people in the mental health field seem to suffer from many psychological problems themselves. Every fourth psychologist admits to having considered suicide, and they commit suicide at twice the rate of their patients. Freud killed himself, but before he did, he said, "Patients are nothing. We cannot help them."

And as Professor of Psychiatry Al Parides notes, "If you look at the personal lives of all Freud's initial disciples, they have an unbelievable amount of particular sexual problems. The amount of deviancy as far as their sexual behavior is enormous." And yet these are the same people who decree: "Parents should be licensed to have children only upon demonstrating a sound understanding of truths dispensed by psychologists."

Here are the actual words of the 'psychologist to the stars,' Kathleen FitzGerald: "Sacred Psychology is exploring and understanding the unique nature, color, and feel of our individual souls. It is about Soul Loss, Soul Retrieval, Soul Care, and Soul Celebration. The Inner Child sends her/his soul into exile until it is safe to return. In Native American spirituality, shamans journey to retrieve soul." Gotcha.

One of the most damaging things in the mental health field is 'regressive therapy.' It has torn apart millions of families by supposedly uncovering memories of sexual abuse by fathers that never happened, as well as false memories of satanic ritual abuse.

The therapist leads a child into a highly suggestive state of mind and then encourages the child to 'remember' what the therapist beforehand has decided she wants her to remember. The right answer garners lavish praise. But the wrong answer is reacted to by the therapist with disappointment and, "Let's try again to remember what your Dad did to you. Didn't he do this? And that?" An adult who won't remember what the psychologist wants her to remember is declared to be "in denial" or "repressing the memory."

While Psychology has always disdained Christianity, it has been known to welcome the Occult, and even promote the demonic as liberating. The Association for Humanist Psychology invited an African witch doctor to its convention, who proceeded to put its president into a trance on stage in front of a huge crowd. An advertisement for the event read, "Journey into altered states of consciousness where one can meet one's higher spirit teachers and the 'gods' themselves. We will be walking and talking with Jesus, blissed out on Buddha, wrestling with Satan, and sighting UFOs."

Swiss psychiatrist Elisabeth Kubler-Ross went nuts after becoming deeply involved with the Occult. Her book *On Death and Dying* influenced perhaps billions of people with her 'five stages of grief' concept. She came to believe she had 'spirit guides' who taught her about apparitions, bilocation (that you can be in two places at once!), astral projection, channeling, reincarnation, and naturally that the Creator in the Bible is "baloney." She ended her life as a lonely, bitter, cuckoo bird.

Dr. Raymond Moody is a psychologist who was featured on the Oprah Winfrey Show to talk about his big book *Life After Life*. In the book he announces that there is no personal God and Jesus is no Savior. There is no Judgment Day, because after death *all of us*, even Pol Pot and John Wayne Gacy, meet 'the Central Force,' a 'Being of Light,' who only loves and accepts everybody without question. Moody is also heavily into the Occult, in particular, 'mirror-gazing' to talk with the dead.

Then there is Betty Eadie, and her book that was even sold in Christian bookstores, *Embraced by the Light*. Eadie teaches that *everybody goes to Heaven*. And, of course, that *there are many paths to God*, Jesus being only one of many. And Dannion Brinkley with his bestseller *Saved by the Light*, which is full of Occult anti-Christian themes such as "There is no Heaven or Hell. Faith is not a requirement, there is no judgment."

Psychiatrist Peter Breggin: "The brain is made up of several hundred billion neurons and trillions of synapses. Each human brain is more complex than the entire physical Universe. Unlike the physical world, the biochemical activities that run the brain remain almost wholly shrouded in mystery. We have no idea, for example, how the brain makes a thought or emotion. At the root of psychopharmacology lies a dangerous assumption that it is safe and effective to tamper with the most complex organ in the Universe! Curiously, in light of so much psychiatric concern about the dangers of biochemical imbalance, all known psychiatric drugs produce widespread chemical imbalances in the brain, usually involving multiple systems of nerves. Prozac is no exception."

Scientists at the University of Wisconsin-Milwaukee found that minnows administered Prozac became aggressive, anti-social, and sometimes homicidal. But why put a fish on Prozac? It's not a fix for sad fish - instead, human medications are ending up in waterways. At a particular dose, the males begin to ignore the females. When concentrations increase, they stop reproducing all together and turn violent: The males start killing the females, and the females don't lay any eggs.

Take a look at all the violence, murder, and suicide blamed on either taking psychotropic drugs or from stopping taking them. All psychiatric drugs cause brain dysfunction. That is how they work. To quote Dr. Breggin once more: "If depression has a biological or genetic basis, it has not been demonstrated scientifically. Biopsychiatric theory remains pure speculation and runs counter to a great deal of research, clinical experience, and common sense. The biochemical imbalance theory has replaced Freud's psychological theory as the most widely accepted explanation for emotional pain and suffering. In turn, Freud's theory had replaced religious explanations, such as original sin, the Devil, and moral degeneracy. The biochemical theory is presented to the public as scientific truth."

Though the concept of evil has been present in all cultures around the globe since time began, it is virtually absent from our field of psychology because the very word 'evil' sounds like a value judgment. We can't have that in our value-free sciences. Psychiatry wants to blame abnormal thinking, emotions, and behaviors on chemical imbalances.

We need to shake off scientism's shackles and face the world the way it is. People are afflicted by unclean spirits and oppressed by the Devil. To discern if a spirit animating some person, culture, or country is good or evil, the only sure test is to compare its message with God's Word. If a zeitgeist, ideology, way-of-life or system of values stands in opposition to the Gospel, it is of evil origin.

In 1971, a *Time* magazine cover story was about B.F. Skinner, the "most influential living American psychologist." Skinner said, "We can no longer afford freedom, and so it must be replaced with control over man, his conduct, and his culture." He also taught that belief in God was nothing more than a backward superstition. Consider this quote from him: "All people are is what society has conditioned them to be." His big idea was that man has no soul, so men and women should be 'conditioned' from childhood to serve the interests of the collective. "To Man as Man, we say good riddance." Arthur Koestler went further, stating that we needed to develop "a chemical to rid man of aggression and put it in our drinking water." By now, we can see a significant switch, as Man has gone from observer to the one observed.

The 'bible' of psychiatric analysis, the DSM, keeps adding more and more disorders for which we supposedly need the help of its profession. Big Pharma loves that because it can come up with a pill to help with every garden-variety disquiet you might imagine.

The fact is, it is normal to experience sorrow and stress and to be discouraged or depressed from time to time. The shrinks are busy making every American a mental patient. They give healthy people unhealthy drugs that are quite addictive and extremely costly to you and our society. The idea that to get through a normal life we are so weak as to require happy pills—not to mention a lifetime of needful 'therapy'—is crazy.

A multitude of drugs has been invented to affect our brains. There are drugs prescribed to help you relax, or become more alert, to be less anxious, to sleep, not to feel sad, to improve attention, improve memory, and to make you feel good. But they do not *cure* what ails you. They only work if you keep on taking them—a great benefit to the pharmaceutical industry whose continued profits depend on addicts.

Psychologists and psychiatrists are notoriously left-wing politically and have grown more and more so over the decades. Democrats return the favor by using taxpayer funds to support their work. Recent research shows that psychologists admit they openly discriminate against any conservatives in their field, denying them referrals, teaching positions, tenure, and employment.

The Mind Benders once boasted that therapy and psychotropic drugs would solve the world's problems through federally funded mental health centers. These grandiose expectations have come to naught as mental issues have become more prevalent since the feds started paying to 'cure' them. Even the *Los Angeles Times* quoted the world's foremost psychotherapist as saying, "I can't think of any fundamental insight into human relations that has resulted from a century of psychotherapy."

In *The Psychological Epidemic and Its Cure* John F. MacArthur, Jr. writes: "The behavioral sciences are not, as is commonly believed, scientific. Neither have they proven effective in changing the human heart. 'Christian psychology,' with its claim of secret knowledge about dealing with people, has made deep inroads into the church. So-called Christian psychologists and psychiatrists have testified that the Bible alone is not sufficient to meet people's deepest personal and emotional needs, arguing before a secular court that God's Word is not an adequate resource for counseling people about spiritual problems—what used to be seen as a vital pastoral responsibility. Too many have bought the lie that a crucial realm of wisdom exists outside Scripture and one's relationship to Jesus Christ—the real key to helping people with their deep problems."

MacArthur also asserted, "True psychology (the study of the soul) can be done *only by Christians*. The secular discipline of psychology is based on godless assumptions. The Puritans, long before the arrival of godless psychology, identified their ministry with people as 'soul work.' Scripture is the manual for all 'soul work' and is comprehensive in the diagnosis and treatment of every spiritual matter, energized by the Holy Spirit in the believer. It is foolish to exchange the Wonderful Counselor, the spring of living water, for the sensual wisdom of the earth and the stagnant water of behaviorism. Why should a believer choose to do behavior modification when he has the tools for spiritual transformation?"

MacArthur concludes, "These doctrines are a mass of human ideas that Satan has placed in the church. Most psychologists epitomize neo-Gnosticism, claiming to have secret knowledge for solving people's real problems. Bible reading and prayer are commonly belittled. Psychologists cannot even tell the sane from the insane. It is significant that one of the biblical names of Christ is 'Wonderful Counselor.' Every need of the human soul is ultimately spiritual."

Every fifth American today is on psychotropic drugs to make it through the day. A mountain of money has been made from the loneliness, disappointments, and unhappiness of Americans.

In 1948, the federal government began backing the mental health professionals with taxpayer funds. At that time, only 9,000 persons were employed as a psychiatrist, psychologist, or mental health social worker. Today there are millions of them. But their work, which began as treating severe mental problems such as psychosis, is now mostly about interpersonal relationship problems, low self-esteem, sexual difficulties, and feeling depressed—part of the human condition in never-ending supply. Everyone could be a candidate for such services, especially as the nation loses its way spiritually.

The ideas of Sigmund Freud are now firmly planted in the unexamined beliefs of the average man and woman. Even as they have been wholly discredited in the scientific community. Research shows that the more mothers know about psychology, the more trouble they have parenting their children. Another study shows that people in the mental health field—whose jobs it is to solve our problems—have no fewer problems themselves and no less trouble with their children than the average parent.

But remember the original claims of this profession: If only we had enough professionals and billions of federal dollars, we would see an enormous decrease in depression, suicide, divorce, and crime. Instead, we have gotten a lot more of all social pathologies since we changed from turning our troubles over to the Lord and His Church to the godless mental health industry.

Psychiatrists say that the most common cause of suicide and mental illness is unresolved guilt. But they never recommend the only therapy that truly works: Telling their patients that God loves them and will forgive them of everything they have done if they believe in His Son. God can cleanse your conscience and set you free; free from sin, guilt, shame, and the wages of sin: Eternal Death.

Since man cannot live with guilt, he will justify what he has done and what he plans to do. We sin willfully, which naturally leads to guilt unless you are a sociopath. You can turn that into godly sorrow, which leads to repentance. Confess to the Father that what you have done is wrong. Ask Him to heal you, and He will.

The Frankfort School Cometh

Some people wonder, What ever happened to America?

Western Civilization was founded on Christianity, a faith that is at the core of traditional American culture. That is why Western Civilization is targeted for extinction by Satan's army. Johann Herder described *culture* as "the life-blood of a people; the flow of moral energy that holds society intact."

Hegel saw culture as "the defining essence of a nation and a shared spiritual force which is manifest in all the customs, beliefs, and practices of a people." It is the basis for a country's manners, art, language, and law. Because our foundation is the Christian worldview, it is the main prize Satan seeks to desecrate. To destroy our traditional culture would ruin our shared values and sense of community that made Americans Americans. Notice, if you will, that our education establishment demands respect for every culture in the world, and the sacred rites and stories of even the most remote tribe, but works to see ours torn to bits. Why is that?

The New Left that emerged during the late 1960s was the brainchild of a group of atheist socialists known as the Cultural Marxists of the Frankfort School. Their raison d'etre was to overthrow Western Civilization. They planned to capture control of the institutions that shape and transmit ideas and values in America—newspapers, magazines, television, film, public schools, and universities—to undermine it from within. Their first move would be to saturate the country with hedonism, a message of instant gratification.

Nearly all of the horrible hokum we suffer today can be traced back to this movement. The list includes the sexual revolution, political correctness, multiculturalism, 'tolerance,' 'diversity,' feminism, special rights for sexual perverts, libertinism, rampant divorce, cohabitation, abortion, atheism, occultism, social justice, historical revisionism, and even Ritalin.

Those who hold traditional values that were nearly universal when I grew up are now demonized as bigoted extremists. Whatever was immoral and shameful is now enlightened and praiseworthy. That is what Nietzsche would call the *transvaluation of all values*. Old virtues become sins, and old sins become virtues. The spirit that rules our age is anti-Christ because it celebrates the antithesis of Christian virtue. Anyone who tries to slow down this 'progress' is deemed hateful and divisive.

The Italian communist Antonio Gramsci (1891-1937) would launch the campaign by pronouncing that the Christian faith was the obstacle to a worldwide communist revolution. To capture the West, it first must be de-Christianized.

Prison Notebooks was his blueprint of how to demolish Western Civilization. Gramsci prescribed "a long march through the institutions," meaning that atheist socialists should infiltrate and take over schools, colleges, the arts, cinema, radio, theatre, and the news media. These transgressors would politicize those institutions to subvert the culture.

Georg Lukacs (1885-1971), a Hungarian Comintern agent for the Soviet Union, helped found the Frankfurt School. He defined his own ideas as "demonic." Lukacs saw "the revolutionary destruction of society as the one and only solution ... a worldwide overturning of values, the annihilation of the old values and the creation of new ones." He instituted sex education in Hungary to teach children how to have sex and all about the joys of promiscuity. Lukacs invented the famous term for it: *free love*.

His teachings were that religious virtues were irrelevant, monogamy old-fashioned, parental ideas about sex backward. He hoped to weaken the traditional family and organized religion, which he said conspired to deprive Man of pleasure. He urged students to rebel against *any* sexual constraints. Lukacs idea was to promote licentiousness among women and children to destroy Western Civilization, with totalitarian communism as the ultimate goal.

The Frankfort School was founded in Germany in the 1920s. One goal was to steal the immense wealth of the West. The strategy was to gradually take control of cultural institutions to dismantle European nations from within. Propaganda would undermine personal responsibility, morality, tradition, community, patriotism, unity, language, and the big one: belief in Christ Jesus.

The Frankfort School was a think tank set up to plot the corruption and overthrow of capitalist countries by systematically undermining their cultures, a strategy known as Cultural Marxism. The method is to brainwash people into accepting the essential elements of socialism without realizing it. After a few generations of this social engineering, radical leftism becomes the new system without a violent revolution.

When Hitler came to power in 1933, the Frankfurt School, whose members were predominately Jewish, fled to the United States, where they quickly found employment at Columbia University. In other words, they were invited to subvert America from within New York City. To kill the country that had given them refuge became their purpose.

They would soon develop a new weapon: Critical Theory. It was the instrument to 'deconstruct' America, particularly the patriarchy, free enterprise, and patriotism. The freest and most prosperous human beings in history must be brainwashed to think America—the only country that has made the average person so free, flourishing, and affluent—is evil, oppressive, and unworthy of love.

One of the Frankfort School's big guns was a protégé of Sigmund Freud, Wilhelm Reich (1897-1957), an atheist socialist of Jewish descent. As a little boy, he fantasized about having sex with his mother. He humped the family's maid as if she were a dog when he was four. At eleven, little Wilhelm was having regular intercourse with a servant girl. By the time he became an adult he was a full-blown pervert. Reich was an excessive masturbator, and a regular at the local brothels, who habitually engaged in sadomasochism and bestiality.

In 1922, Reich went to work for Sigmund Freud. He led a life of debauchery and serial adultery, leaving behind a trail of broken homes, abortions, suffering, and suicides. Naturally, he joined the Communist Party and became friends with John Dewey, The Father of Modern American Education.

Reich's big idea was to fuse Marx's ideology with Freud's psychology. That fusion is what became known as Cultural Marxism. To set man free, he must be relieved of morality. For that to happen he must become free of conscience; a man yielded to his primary biological impulses. What was Reich's rationale? "If you get people involved in deviant sexual behavior, the whole idea of God just disappears automatically."

In his view, a man was nothing more than an erotic impulse. Thinking is the problem; thought is a disease that nullifies our primal urges. The ideal man is, therefore, he who has satisfied his strong libidinal needs. The family must be annihilated because think how it restricts freedom!

Reich decided that the Frankfort School should use sexual immorality to bring down Western Civilization, using 'comprehensive sex education' in our public schools for the indoctrination of the young. Reich coined the term *Sexual Revolution*, a revolution that, he predicted, once it started, "no power in the world could stop it."

Thus, Reich laid out long ago what the new culture of the 1960s would do to our nation's youth. Radicalize them. Teach them to reject work, authority, competition, schedules, accepted customs, and conventions. Persuade them to take drugs to 'expand their minds' and to define their very own existence by creating their own belief system, lifestyle, and culture. But the topper was this: Never judge what anyone else does.

Sexual promiscuity, free love, the rejection of morality, and making pleasure the primary pursuit of life, was his philosophy. Reich saw how to eradicate the family by appealing to women with the idea that they had somehow, without realizing it, been enslaved by a mysterious, nefarious thing called the 'Patriarchy.' Men were the enemy!

The family had to go because it was through the family that men dominated women. Fathers were superfluous; children did not need parenting. Reich believed little children should be encouraged to have sex. "A right to natural love," he called it. He wanted to liberate children because fathers and families had suppressed their sexuality.

Reich taught that monogamy was a load of crap because the same partner could satisfy no one for an extended period. He condemned premarital abstinence and created the idea that the New Left radicals would chant in the late 1960s: Smash Monogamy!

Being such an expert on human nature and thus qualified to prescribe such strange medicine, one would hope Mr. Reich had personally found the happiness he promised was awaiting all who would follow his prescriptions. Alas, in his autobiography, Reich opens the curtain to unveil himself as a pathetic person, eternally frustrated and wracked with strange phobias. The ordinary things we all do with ease every day made him sick with worry. He was unable to form bonds with other human beings whatsoever. He acknowledged, "The most constant presence in my life was fear and anxiety."

Kurt Lewin (1890-1947) was one of the Frankfort School Freudian Marxists. A founder of Social Psychology, he invented *sensitivity training* to fight against what he called religious and racial prejudice. That was to become the tool today's Left uses to force students and employees to accept the leftist worldview and deem traditional values and biblical beliefs unacceptable. Lewin was the father of the indoctrination we now see in the government schools.

Two other members, the infamous Horkheimer and dastardly Adorno, had the insight that America could be sent to the dustbin of history through the psychological conditioning of schoolchildren. This conditioning was to overcome parental authority—an authority that predates the state—by teaching kids that their parents' ideas about the world are wrong. Children would be taught that their parents are racist, sexist, and homophobic. Therefore, parents' social and moral beliefs must be rejected in favor of ideas implanted by the public school.

The new leader would become Herbert Marcuse (1898-1979), *the guru* of student leftists during the counterculture revolution. He convinced many of the Sixties Generation, the most privileged people in the world, that they were living in an intolerable hell. He would harness resentment and turn it into a rage. Since the 1960s, the most effective weapon of the Left, itself filled with hatred, has been to brand their opponents *haters*, an idea birthed by Marcuse.

He argued that American society was sick from having too many sexual hang-ups. What we needed to do was revert to what he called infantile sexuality and progress to polymorphous perversity, in which our "very being is essentially the striving for pleasure." He argued that sexual deviants should be the heroes of our new society; they will lead us to utopia.

Marcuse fomented a cultural revolution to kill the Christian faith and its moral codes. He knew that an immoral society, fixated on sex, would be an easy target for totalitarian communists to conquer. His famous book *Eros and Civilization* was called the 'bible' of the 1960s counterculture. In it, he lays out his plan: The body, in its entirety, would become an instrument of pleasure. What we needed was to eliminate the repressive order of procreative sexuality and enjoy "primary narcissism" for the "redemption of pleasure."

What is the purpose of all this? Besides sexual pleasure, we get that part loud and clear. "This change in the value and scope of libidinous relations would lead to a disintegration of the monogamous and patriarchal family."

This man was enormously popular among college radicals of the Sixties. He was their master and told his acolytes to extinguish faith in God. *Eros and Civilization* was all about hatred of America, the middle class, marriage, capitalism, and Christianity.

Marcuse deemed *any* sexual restraint 'sadistic' because nothing should stand in the way of the gratification of lust. The only way to be free was to explore ever stranger sexual adventures, with no limits. That is radical hedonism, trying everything at least once, separating sexuality from any notion of biological reproduction, with the homosexual as the standard-bearer for the new sexual liberation.

The Baby Boomers knew neither hardship nor war when they first arrived on campus in 1964. They were living a life of ease, comfort, and luxury. They were spoiled, affluent, confident, carefree, and bored. The answer? Sex, drugs, and learning to hate your country. Marcuse would provide the hippie movement with a steady stream of propaganda to sanctify their rebellious impulses. He invented the slogan of the young, 'Make love, not war.'

What Marcuse labeled, *liberating tolerance*, he defined as "intolerance against movements from the Right but tolerance of movements from the Left." The new 'tolerance' is only tolerant about sex, pornography, filthy language, bad manners, obscene art, idolatry, sacrilege, and blasphemy.

Movements from the Left included the activism of various groups that Marcuse encouraged to self-identify as oppressed. He called for a coalition of blacks, feminists, immigrants, sodomites, atheists, socialists, criminals, and Third World 'people of color,' to see themselves as victims. Victims of systematic, institutional discrimination, bigotry, and oppression, hell-bent on overthrowing white male power, thereby tearing down capitalism, the country, and the world.

Marcuse made no secret that he was willing to stamp out academic freedom to see "the withdrawal of toleration of speech and assembly from groups and movements" that were conservative. He argued for 'the cancellation of the liberal creed of free and equal discussion.'

The university atmosphere we see today, with its vigilant policing of ideas and politically driven censorship policies, was given its intellectual legitimization by Marcuse. His views have formed the intellectual foundation for the academic Left, and for the machine of political correctness that drives much contemporary media bias.

The Left today trumpets their superiority because they are tolerant, and you are not. Still, theirs is not authentic tolerance because it is not tolerance to tolerate only the ideas with which you agree. The Left does not tolerate opinions with which it disagrees, as we all know. Leftists live by a phony 'tolerance,' which means everyone must tolerate their views, but they must not tolerate conservative views. The Frankfurt thinkers set in motion the trend of silencing opponents rather than to engage in dialogue with them.

"To understand the Student Rebellion of the late 1960s, the Counterculture of the Woodstock Generation, we must see how the Devil manipulated those young people through Herbert Marcuse and the Frankfort School," writes Roger Scruton.

Michael Lerner lived with Herbert Marcuse before becoming the mentor to one Hillary Clinton. Lerner would teach Hillary what he called the 'The Politics of Meaning,' which uses politics to provide meaning in the otherwise meaningless lives of the godless.

Lerner leads the Network of Spiritual Progressives. This organization promotes the idea that if you believe in some kind of higher power, what *it* wants from you is for you to work through a totalitarian government to redistribute wealth.

He also is part of the Beyond Marriage campaign, according to which there is no possible arrangement of people who should not be recognized as a 'family' and therefore entitled to a wide range of legal benefits. Economic benefits for deviant sexual relationships is the main thrust of their group. "Marriage is not the only worthy form of family or relationship. It should not be legally and economically privileged above all others," Lerner declares.

The result of the Long March of Cultural Marxism is a generation of people who have no guardrails, no standards of right and wrong. That leads to moral anarchy. All they have to guide them are their feelings. The media readily manipulates such people. Marketing is the application of the knowledge of human psychology to the task of persuasion. Not to persuade the intellect of people; to sway them emotionally.

The New Left now calls its believers 'progressives.' They long for a world with less and less European people, no traditional families, and no religion. They promote degeneracy, ugliness, and false history. Progressivism is societal rot; it eats away at the foundations of society until it falls in on itself. What are left are the decayed remnants of a once-great civilization, the one time envy of the world.

The Cultural Marxists unleashed a tide of spiritual darkness that has crept over America. They believed in nothing except tearing down what others held as cherished beliefs. These men fled Nazi Germany and were saved from the gas chamber when given sanctuary by America. They repaid our country by making their primary work to defile all that is sacred to us. It was President Franklin Roosevelt and the Rockefeller Foundation that brought them to America.

In their view, Christianity was the towering obstacle to humankind 'evolving' to a higher state, 'progressing' to a marvelous future by annihilating God's moral laws. Part of the plan was to reduce the human race to the level of beasts in our minds. And to blur the lines between masculine and feminine. It was a program to rework the human psyche so that we would be devoid of thought and logic, only operating on feelings and emotions.

All of these men shared a hatred of the middle class and its values, the repudiation and annihilation of which justified every form of rebellion. Our middle class, or 'bourgeoisie' as they called it, was the envy of the world. It was admired for its order, safety, social continuity, goodness, love, faith, hope, discipline, literacy, education, stability, trust, worship, devotion, honor, respect, charity, trade, prosperity, freedom, law, and individual rights— especially the right to private property. All of that is hated by the Devil, and so, hated by his servants.

The Holy and the Sacred enrages those who are infested with demons. The Frankfort School invented 'cultural repudiation' and Political Correctness to ban all that is true, first from the university, then gradually from all of society. They worked for Lucifer, all the while claiming to be liberators empowering the oppressed. Consider this; if their arguments are right, there is such thing as 'right'—but denying the existence of right and wrong is at the heart of their ideology!

The progressives would take Satan's advice and use sex as a weapon to ruin marriage, morality, and faith in the Bible. The godless Left had failed to sell the humanity on economic Marxism, and so sought a new strategy to ruin capitalism and Western Civilization. Mass brainwashing was employed to convince the young they were imprisoned by the Christian moral code and needed liberation—to make sex the center of their being, indeed, their very identity.

So here we are. The Bible is denounced as a fairy tale. All groups except heterosexual white males are victims of oppression. The most magnificent and most beneficent civilization ever stands accused of crimes against humanity to make white men feel guilty and morally disarmed until the wealth of the West is plundered and given to people of color from around the world.

The spirit of our age seeks to crush the idea that traditional American values, Western culture, and the West's institutions are *superior*, or that the Christian faith is the One True Religion. The truth is that all peoples, cultures, and civilizations are not equal—some achieved great things, and some didn't. In the story of slavery, Western Man was among the many villains, but he was also the ONLY hero. The West did not invent slavery, but it alone abolished slavery.

In 1965, 94% of women and 89% of men thought America was the greatest country. Now only 51% of women and 58% of men agree. While 66% of Republicans believe it, among Democrats it is down to 38%.

Spike Lee says, "America was built upon the genocide of Native Americans and the enslavement of African people. To say otherwise is criminal." His accusations are utterly untrue. What is undoubtedly true is that America made Spike Lee fabulously rich and famous.

Who believes all cultures or nations are truly equal? If they are, then why are hundreds of millions of people pining to get into Western Civilization? Have all cultures produced equally great works of art, literature, sculpture, music, architecture, economic systems, universities, hospitals, technology, transportation, communication, healthcare, and political systems? True tolerance does not mean we should tolerate utter lies presented to our children as truth. *Western Civilization is superior.*

Test scores of our high school students are among the lowest among modern nations. The portion of our children living in broken homes is nearing half. Teen suicides have tripled since the 1960s. Fifteen years ago, it was lamented as a national tragedy that we had six million drug addicts—today; we have 22 million. Happiness is sought but not found in recreational sex, pornography, alcohol, and drugs.

Virtually everyone in America considered the Boy Scouts to be morally upright in 1980. The Boy Scouts were one of the most respected and best loved of all American associations. They didn't change a thing, but by 2000 the *New York Times* called them a Hate Group. That is the fate of anyone who doesn't go along with the new 'progressive' vision for America. The Long March of America's Cultural Revolution succeeded beyond the wildest dreams of all but the most starry-eyed utopians.

Polls taken in 1968 show that Americans, by wide margins, strongly opposed Affirmative Action and legalizing abortion. Americans were firmly in favor, by huge margins, of posting the Ten Commandments, reading the Bible, and children praying together in public schools. What Americans wanted was ignored by the powers that be.

Leftists are vicious and hateful. They routinely call splendid Christian leaders "The American Taliban" and slur fine men who happen to be conservative politically Nazis and Fascists. Anyone who disagrees with them they immediately call names (sexist, racist, homophobe, mean, hateful, extremist) instead of arguing against the truth claims anyone might make with a worldview that opposes theirs. As McLuhan said, "Moral indignation is a technique used to endow the idiot with dignity."

Pat Buchanan once observed, "The sexual revolution has begun to devour its children." The statistics on abortion, divorce, collapsing birthrates, broken homes, teen suicide, school violence, drug use, child abuse, spouse abuse, violent crime, incarceration rates, promiscuity, sexually transmitted disease, illegitimate children, and falling test scores, show a decadent society that is decomposing and dying. Empty nurseries and full waiting rooms outside the psychiatrist's office testify that all is not well.

This is a war for the souls of our children. The Antichrist is trying to annihilate America—to obliterate Christianity. A demonic culture is being forced onto our children. The Heartland does not want to tell New York, Los Angeles, and San Francisco how to live, but NY, LA, and SF will not let the Heartland keep the kind of society in which it wants to live. As David Horowitz says, "Inside every liberal is a totalitarian screaming to get out."

At the core of multiculturalism is anti-white-male hatred— unless, of course, the white male practices homosexual behaviors, which is his only way to escape being hated as an 'oppressor' and join the beloved groups entitled to exclusive rights and privileges.

According to the leftist worldview, if one man does better than another, he must have robbed his fellow man. If one family is more prosperous than another, it must have exploited other families. If one town is more successful than another, it must have oppressed the town next door. If one country is wildly successful beyond all human imaginings, and others wallow in a standard-of-living that has not changed since time began, it must be because the greatest country stole the resources of backward nations. If the followers of one religion have tremendously surpassed all others in the human race—indeed lapped them—then they must have held their feet down on the necks of all others whilst they ran.

The reason for this is that the true narrative of humankind shows that the one thing individuals, families, towns, and nations are not is equal in is their abilities, accomplishments, and perceptions of reality. And that, my friends, makes a sham out of the entire Marxist ideology that permeates the Left today in America.

That ideology teaches victimhood from kindergarten onward to everyone except heterosexual males of European descent. To them, it inculcates shame and guilt. You end up with a group that has the most to be proud of feeling ashamed, and groups with very little indeed in which to have pride encouraged to be proud of nothing or some imaginary something. Through his agents, men and women, Satan infects the world with Tall Poppy Syndrome and Crab Mentality.

That is happening in America through deconstruction—the tearing down of meaning, purpose, and faith—and by the falsification of history. All historians have to choose from infinite possibilities what is essential to learn, know, or teach. So if the truth is that the Founding Fathers were the wisest assemblage of men ever to launch a nation, the anti-Christian professor must deconstruct that notion before it might make founders of other countries look not so smart. And more importantly, before faith, liberty, and economic freedom start to be seen (rightfully so) in an attractive light.

Thus, the Founding Fathers become just a bunch of racist 'slave owners' and, therefore, morally illegitimate and not worthy of admiration. As if being slave owners is for what they are famous. There were millions of slave owners when the Founding Fathers lived, nearly all of whose names were quickly forgotten. And there are more slaves on this planet today than at any time in the past. But there are not millions of men who founded a nation as awesome as the United States of America.

History should be a search for truth and a journey to explain reality to others—how the world we are in became the way it is. That is why history has been set aside in public schools in favor of 'social studies,' designed to permeate impressionable young minds with the propaganda of Secular Humanism.

The founders of 'Social Studies' had nary a Christian among them. They were socialists, part of a movement created by anti-Christian men to become sort of a counterfeit Christianity—the ethics without the supernatural, metaphysical heart that produced the ethics. And most of all, a secular religion without virtue and without a God who expects anything from us. Matter is all that matters to these folks. Their heroes are Darwin, Marx, Nietzsche, and Freud—the Four Horsemen of the Apocalypse.

Leftists by the millions make a living today from the very act of tearing down the country they so despise, in education, government bureaucracies, and the 'culture industry.' Their poisonous ideology is driven by the terrible sins of hatred, envy, resentment, grumbling, and covetousness. Its heroes are those who refuse to accept reality, who are mentally defective, emotionally immature cowards.

Christians see America's past as glorious; anti-Christians see it as shameful and wicked. "To destroy a people, you must first sever their roots," stressed Solzhenitsyn. "Who controls the past controls the future. Who controls the present controls the past," declared George Orwell.

So the plan was to make America loathsome and its history despicable to her children. And divide kids in the school into children of villains or children of victims. Do not let them know that Americans invented almost everything worth inventing. Do not let them know that Americans have a glorious history, better than any other nation of all time. America is well worth loving among nations, but the opposite is taught to its young. They are cheated out of their right to know the extraordinary story of America.

Why are the men and women of the Left so hateful towards Jesus? Dr. Samuel Johnson explains: "Such is the state of a man abandoned to the indulgence of vicious inclinations. He justifies one crime by another; invents wicked principles to support wicked practices; endeavors instead to corrupt others, than own himself corrupted, and to avoid that shame which a profession of his crimes would bring upon him, calls evil good, and good evil, puts darkness for light, and light for darkness. Having long neglected to obey God, he rises into rebellion against Him."

The godless leftists who have foisted all this evil on humankind lived private lives of abhorrent immorality themselves. Maybe all they really wanted was approval.

The Religion of Secular Humanism

"The purpose of a man is like the purpose of a pollywog - to wiggle along as far as he can without dying." ~ Clarence Darrow

Secular Humanism is a religion. The American Humanist Association has a religious tax exemption status approved by the federal government. Nine times, the *Humanist Manifesto* calls Humanism a religion. The so-called 'Separation of Church and State' has driven God-based religion from the public schools only to be replaced by the man-based religion of Secular Humanism.

The Humanist magazine featured an article that boasted: "The battle for mankind's future must be waged and won in the public school classroom. The classroom must and will become the arena of conflict between the old and the new, the rotting corpse of Christianity and the new faith of Humanism."

Secular humanist Paul Blanshard writes: "I think that the most important factor moving us toward a secular society has been the educational factor. Our schools may not teach Johnny to read properly, but the fact that Johnny is in school until he is sixteen tends to lead toward the elimination of religious superstition."

Paul Kutz, a signatory of *Humanist Manifesto II*, announced in its preface: "Humanism is a philosophical, religious, and moral point of view." Kutz calls for the establishment of secular humanist churches.

John J. Dunphy, writing in *The Humanist*, declared: "Secular humanist teachers must embody the same selfless dedication as the most rabid fundamentalist preachers, for they will be ministers of another sort, utilizing a classroom instead of a pulpit to convey humanist values in whatever subject they teach, regardless of the educational level—preschool, daycare, or large state university."

The day God was kicked out of our government schools by the Supreme Court is the day the government schools should have been closed down and replaced by private education. *We the People* are supposed to be running this country, not nine unelected men in black robes.

For fifty years, Christians have been forced to fund the destruction of their society due to the indoctrination of our children into the secular humanist religion. Advocates for Secular Humanism have been quite clear and explicit about using government schools to promote their faith and to undermine Christian beliefs and values. Secular humanists should fund their own schools.

Oh, it has been a neat trick, so give the Devil his due. Darwin, Marx, Nietzsche, and Freud are taught to our children unopposed by the teachings of Jesus, Paul, Luke, and John. In other words, the almighty state's authority forbids a worldview with God in it, but a satanic worldview is authorized. If our federal government wants to fund education, it should give parents an annual voucher for $10,000 for each child that the parent can spend on a Christian school or a secular humanist school. School Choice.

From the book *Understanding the Times* by David Noebel, we learn: "Often people get their beliefs like they catch colds—by being around other people! And since ideas are everywhere—on television, in books and magazines, at the movies, and in conversation with friends and family—it's easy to pick them up without considering whether they're worth believing. Regardless of where they come from, the ideas we embrace about the nature of reality lead to a set of core beliefs, which in turn form convictions about how we should live meaningfully. Each religion attempts to explain what it is to be a human being and how we should then live. You'll notice books on 'secularism' and 'atheism' in the religion section. Even atheists have a set of beliefs about the cause, nature, and purpose of the Universe. All worldviews are religious."

The motto of Secular Humanism is *Good without God*. The primary identifying characteristic is its disbelief in God and disdain of any worldview with God in it. Although secular humanists claim their views are the opposite of religion, they are devoutly religious.

Scientific materialism is the cornerstone of Secular Humanism. Calling it 'science' and not the dreaded 'religion,' it has become the religion of our government schools. The so-called 'separation of church and state' has been diabolically used to brainwash our children into the worldview of Secular Humanism by calling it science. It is false science to cloak philosophy or ideology in scientific authority to support the beliefs of individuals or groups by using biased interpretations of evidence that cannot be tested. In other words, in textbooks, classrooms, scientific journals, and television, a godless view of reality *is presented as the scientific view*, which it is not.

Secular Humanism indoctrinates our children into four big lies that undergird the rest of its worldview: 1) The progress of humankind is all because of science and Christianity has worked against it all along. 2) Science has proven religious beliefs are false. 3) Educated people believe in science, not in the Christian faith. 4) Only science presents the whole of reality as it is.

Modern science is, in fact, the child of the Christian religion. The Bible shows us that God created a rational Cosmos organized by natural laws that we can discover with the rational minds He gave us for this purpose. The Universe, designed by God's supreme intelligence, can be investigated by the cognitive abilities of human beings created in His image.

The secular humanists approach the study of the Cosmos in a manner that purposefully and systematically excludes the divine. Not because this approach is natural but because they IMPOSED it on the Cosmos, refusing to consider anything but a godless universe.

That is not as 'new' as its disciples would have you believe. Epicurus promoted the idea that the world's study should have as its aim to 'liberate' the human race from belief in God, immortal souls, and the afterlife—2300 years ago. And a couple of hundred years later, Lucretius promulgated the idea that the Universe was the result of pure chance without guidance or purpose.

The foundation of all worldviews centers on the questions, Who is Man? And who is God? Christianity and Secular Humanism answer these two questions in opposition to each other. This is a cosmic battle between truth and lies.

The existence of God and the Truth of the Bible are what's under attack. Secular Humanism has no answer to the questions, "What is evil? Why is their order instead of chaos? Why is there something instead of nothing? Where did the Cosmos come from? Did it have a beginning? If so, what was there before the beginning?" "Only Christianity provides a unified answer for the whole of life," reasoned Francis Schaeffer.

Every worldview necessarily entails a view of morality. The secular humanist religion makes Adam indistinguishable from an animal, stripped of anything that would make him distinctly human. Therefore it follows that the purpose of a man's life can mean no more than the pursuit of pleasure and avoidance of pain; hedonism undisturbed by any desire or fear beyond self-gratification, with sexual gratification the highest aim. In this view, the fact that children are the result of sexual intercourse is a horrible burden, not a blessing. It requires a denial that our sexual organs are designed for any purpose above making us feel good.

We need to understand then that here we have a clash of moral views that underlie our culture wars. Since, in the secular humanist religion, human beings are nothing more than a random conglomeration of atoms, *there is no basis for any morality*. It follows that no sexual act can be intrinsically wrong—which is a vital attraction of this worldview. Every pleasure can only be good; no one can be wrong about what feels good to them, and no one may make moral judgments about what makes someone else feel good. If it feels good, do it.

'Humanist' has become a word for those who have abandoned belief in God. Some refer to such people as 'secularists.' They tend to gravitate to careers in education, entertainment, media, and government. That is how they have ascended to positions of authority in these fields, by which culture is formed and transmitted. However, having abandoned God, their true spirituality and morality are skewed, making their influence anti-God. We cannot provide a sound foundation for morals and behavior when everyone's guess as to what is right or wrong is as good as anyone else's. People gradually come to believe that they have the freedom to engage in any behavior they choose. In effect, they make themselves gods.

The heartless core of this religion is that nothing but physical forces exist. Therefore, there is no God, especially no God who intervenes in the world, making prayer worthless and our minds and souls nothing but brain activity. But science has no instruments or methods to detect the non-physical world. And to say that human beings have no souls or minds contradicts the way we experience life. To teach the young that our consciousness, beliefs, desires, and intentions are all an illusion is not based on scientific facts but a demonic worldview.

The 'principal architect' of the field known as 'social science,' Emile Durkheim, wrote that scientific thought is the "only a perfect form of religious thought." Therefore, it would eventually entirely take the place of faith in Christ. Many people equate their newfound atheism to a religious conversion, declaring, Science is a religion and its philosophers are the priests of nature. Albert Einstein said: "In this materialistic age of ours the serious scientific workers are the only profoundly religious people." What is the essence of this religion? *Science provides the only real knowledge.*

Christianity, capitalism, and social conservatism are the enemies of progress, according to Secular Humanism. Its central tenets are statism, income redistribution, unionism, government management of the economy, womb-to-tomb provision for its citizens, and libertine social policy. This ideology includes the belief that courts, bureaucracies, and schools should be used to accomplish goals that would never be approved by *We the People.* Utopia can be created here on Earth, but only if all members of society are conditioned in childhood to hold the values that the Left idealizes.

If you take the secular humanist worldview out to its logical conclusion, Matter is all that is real. If it takes the shape of a dog, or cat, or human being, that means nothing. The whole is less than the sum of its parts because only the components, the atoms, are real.

That is opposed to the way humans naturally interpret reality, in which a house is a real thing that existed first in the architect's mind. The builder decided in advance what material was to be used to create it—the material follows form. In the secular humanist view, things *only appear* to be designed.

Secular humanists once taught that atoms were eternal, but now we know that is not true. Therefore, nature cannot be its own cause, since if atoms are not immortal; they could not have always existed. Physical reality exists and must have come into existence— must have been created—at some point in time. In this material world that we temporarily inhabit, nothing cannot cause something. A cause other than nature must have created nature. Isaac Newton grasped that atoms alone could not produce an orderly reality without divine aid from a Grand Designer.

The objective of Secular Humanism is to eliminate the moral boundaries that were created by God. Morality is, in fact, the ultimate conflict between God and Satan. If this plane's sensual pleasures increase, the belief in and worries about the hereafter will decrease. To dissolve the assumption that you have an immortal soul would help remove belief in godly morality. To convince your fellow man that the Universe is nothing but materials would help diminish faith in the Lord. The scheme is to redefine what is real and what is not real. Not based on scientific facts but theories of men—the priests of Secular Humanism.

Naturally, if you buy into the secular humanist worldview— that all is but an illusion (eerily similar to Buddhism in that regard)—politics becomes your means of salvation. Since the Cosmos is purely the result of chance and is entirely amoral, what are fought for are the maximization of your rights to pleasure and the minimization of any barriers to your gratification. Sexual desire is easily aroused and more easily satisfied without the impediments of love, marriage, family, society, or any moral code. With good and evil out of the way, we can dispense with the very concept of vices and virtues.

Secular Humanism requires enormous faith that evolution occurred. No experiment can demonstrate that it is more than a nightmare. Darwin knew that every view of morality entails a picture of the Cosmos to support it. Only a secular humanist worldview can think nothing of the slaughter of hundreds of millions of innocent human beings—we build abattoirs for animals, don't we?

Only this worldview can make a hero out of Alfred Kinsey and his satanic subject, Mr. X. Kinsey believed that adult-child sex was natural—why would it not be if we were nothing but random chemicals? Kinsey also thought it was childlike to oppose bestiality: "To many persons, it will seem axiomatic that two mating animals should be individuals of the same species. Such beliefs are immature."

There are no moral standards in a universe defined by chance. Ethical principles, therefore, are nothing more than individual preferences. As the militant atheist Richard Dawkins said, "We cannot admit that things might be neither good nor evil, neither cruel nor kind, but simply callous—indifferent to all suffering, lacking all purpose." Even though that is precisely what he believes.

The Christian faith teaches us that God outlines right and wrong. We are free moral agents who choose to do one or the other personally. Secular Humanism dominates public discussion and our public school dogmas. Its philosophy is all about societal sin—not personal sin. That enables the most immoral and irresponsible among us to assuage their guilty consciences by supporting the politically correct public stances regarding society's crimes, real and imagined.

Secular humanists infested the Supreme Court. In the 1960s, for the first time in American history, they would cast God, the Bible, and prayer out of our public schools. That was a sharp blow against the traditional values that had formed the bedrock of America.

As our society became more godless, abortion, perversion, pornography, and promiscuity ran amok. The effect of all of this has been the creation of the most troubled, confused, unknowledgeable citizenry America has ever had. We suffer from an epidemic of sexually transmitted diseases, fractured families, and millions of children with no idea who their daddy is.

The people behind the deconstruction of the American Way of Life are known by many names. They may be called atheists, progressives, secular humanists, or social liberals. Regardless, their goal is to replace belief in God with faith in Darwin's Theory of Evolution, with the state as the new god, and people as mere animals, apes with thumbs. These progressives rightly calculated that the easiest way to overcome the will of the people in a democratic republic was through the nine unelected, appointed for life, Supreme Court Justices.

I am amazed at the numbers of politicians who claim to be Catholics but support abortion and homosexual behaviors. They claim to have erected a wall between their private beliefs and their public stances. No other group engaged in public policy does so. Why should only Christians take this position? Secular humanists certainly do not.

Man is a cosmic accident; he has no purpose; his life has no meaning. This is the philosophy of the godless existentialist. It comes from a lethal combination of the four most influential of all atheists: Marx, Freud, Nietzsche, and Darwin. As the French writer Emil Cioran asserted, "Skepticism is the sadism of embittered souls."

Progressives are moral relativists, which means they do not believe that concrete right and wrong exist, or that anything substantive can be said about morality. This leads to apparent problems since Hitler, Stalin, and Mao all thought the murder of tens of millions of people was perfectly righteous—providing it served the interests of the state. They never thought killing tens of millions of people was WRONG.

Relativism forbids distinguishing between moral codes and fosters self-indulgence. Don't be judgmental! Out go civility, manners, and morals—mere shackles on our freedom. Nothing is revered. Permissiveness, pleasure first, no criticism allowed, the praise of the crude, vulgar and sordid. It is not good to eliminate the boundary between what men can do and what they should do.

Secular Humanism is accepting of paganism, occultism, and various other New Age beliefs. It is under the influence of Marxism; its creed is all things anti-American. Secular Humanism is hostile to tradition, custom, orthodox religion, crèches, crosses, bible studies, any mention of the Lord on school property. But witches are OK; they hustle to accommodate Muslims with foot-washing stations; they approve of burkas.

It is secular humanists who have changed the traditional school holidays from Christmas break to winter break; spring holiday in place of Easter; fall break in place of Thanksgiving. They are more agreeable of Labor Day, Memorial Day, and Independence Day—providing the celebrations are not in tune with the original intent of those holidays.

Knowing that God is watching us creates self-control. Wisdom and virtue create human happiness in society. Vice and wickedness are destructive.

Secular Humanism is anthropocentric: Man is the center of the Universe. This religion denies the existence of God and makes Man a god to be worshipped. This view is decidedly opposed to the wisdom of our Founding Fathers. Liberty was not for individuals to pursue every whim or instinct.

Edmund Burke professed, "The only liberty I mean is a liberty connected with order; that not only exists along with order and virtue but which cannot exist without them. The effect of liberty to individuals is that they may do what they please: We ought to see what it will please them to do before we risk congratulations."

Secular Humanism promises individual freedom without limits, most of all, freedom from the Christian faith's moral strictures. We can see the results all around us: moral poverty, moral anarchy. Secular Humanism is a bedfellow with socialism and communism. Karl Marx said, "Communism is naturalized humanism."

A people who no longer have faith in God, but place their hope in social progress achieved through the power of the state; a populace devoid of spirituality, and free from religious responsibility; is ripe for the pickings by those who would impose a communist, atheist, totalitarian state on us.

Progressive atheists suffer under the delusion that social science can perfect human societies, if only they could relieve people of their belief in God. They took control of our school systems and taught generations of children that they were random cosmic accidents raised from primordial goo—rather than the Image of God, as the Bible teaches. Ridding the public schools of God, the Bible, and prayer were the keystones that the progressive atheists needed to push their worldview on our children.

Over the past several decades, progressives would work through the courts to prohibit public expression of our constitutional right to Free Exercise of Religion. Christmas carols and manger scenes began to disappear from the American landscape. Even *Merry Christmas* came under prohibition in many parts of American life. The ACLU has advanced most of all this evil.

Secular Humanism will continue to grow like cancer if we do not cut it out. It is a parasite, so bent on the destruction of faith in Christ that it will destroy itself and its host nation, and bring the whole of humanity down if it must, in the effort. It is insane to give government absolute power when it has no absolute truths by which to govern.

Even John Gray, an atheist philosopher, believes the new militant atheists (Dawkins, Sam Harris, and the like) have gotten louder in recent years because they are worried that religion and belief in the supernatural is flourishing instead of declining. Russia has more occult healers than medical doctors; 38 percent of the French believe in astrology; and over one third of the Swiss agree that "Some fortune-tellers can foresee the future." Nearly everyone in Japan has his or her new car blessed by a Shinto priest. The idea that religion is fading away is demonstrably false.

Similarly, sociologist Rodney Stark says: "It is a very religious world, far more religious than it was 50 years ago." Of the world's population, 81% belong to an organized religious faith; 74% say religion is an integral part of their daily lives, and 50% have attended a place of worship in the past seven days.

The secular humanists call for the government to solve all our problems. But they deny the only real solutions: individual responsibility, right conduct, renunciation of sin, and relationship with God. As the darkness creeps over our land, haters of wisdom take command. They spread false values, filth, and decadence. At the same time, they assault the moral and religious foundations of America, to destroy it from within, in what is truly a rebellion against God, led by the Evil One and those who serve him. You can tell this by the focus of the rebellion's fury: The Light of the World.

Hollywood

In Aldous Huxley's vision of a *Brave New World*, no Big Brother is required to deprive people of their history, maturity, and autonomy. He foresaw the day when people will come to love their oppression and adore the technologies that undo their capacity to think. As Huxley remarked in *Brave New World Revisited*, those who are ever on the alert to oppose tyranny "failed to take into account man's almost infinite appetite for distractions."

Martin Luther said we all have gods; it is just a question of which ones. Graceland still receives 750,000 visitors a year, as pilgrims travel to their shrine. Celebrity relics are coveted, bringing hundreds of thousands of dollars at auction. Hard Rock Café ships mementos of stars around the world, just as the Church of the Middle Ages used to ship its relics to cathedrals.

The rise of the anti-hero to replace the genuine hero has been a salient feature of Hollywood since the late 1960s. A hero demonstrates extraordinary courage through deeds, self-sacrifice, devotion to duty, and prowess in the conquest of evil, thus providing a role model for those who become aware of his exploits.

The anti-hero is a character that is a bad guy—the sort for which one does not cheer in real life. But Hollywood can present the bad guy in such a way that filmgoers do root for him, even if what he is up to is evil. The anti-hero is often a sociopath, notably absent of what are the traditional heroic qualities.

Hollywood is on a mission to destroy patriotism, the family, the Church, and every last vestige of morality in America. It glamorizes sexual immorality and deviancy through the screen images of the most beautiful people in the world engaged in such. It promotes the ideals of socialism, Secular Humanism, and of the criminal as victim of a corrupt society. Religious people are not portrayed except as hypocrites and bigots. But it is brilliantly produced, which makes it difficult for most people to turn away.

What kind of spirit do we discern behind Hollywood films since 1970, focusing on wanton sex, violence, gore, the objectification of women, and the contemptible ridicule of people who believe in God as superstitious rubes?

By 1992, an Associated Press poll would show that 81% of Americans believed motion pictures contain too much violence and vulgar language; 72% said too much sex. A mere 3% responded that television promotes positive values, while well over half found television programs offensive in general. Two-thirds believed TV should stop ridiculing traditional values; even more objected to the way it mocks Christians.

What group ever advocated for *more obscene language* in movies? Just take a poll and ask, "Do you wish movies featured *more* profanity?" and see if you get even *one* "yes." Hollywood holds you in contempt. Nobody ever walked out of a movie thinking it would have been great if only the characters had cussed more.

By now, our minds have been trained not to notice obscenity in movies. In the critically acclaimed and quite popular film *GoodFellas*, there is an obscene word uttered every 32 seconds for well over two hours, including 246 'fucks.' Hollywood claims dirty words are essential to depict Americans realistically, but great movies were once made *without any* obscenities uttered. Even PG films today use mountains of profanity. Hollywood is not portraying real people. It is leading people to talk that way.

According to philosopher Roger Scruton, "Obscenity is a direct assault on the social order, which has personal love as its goal and fulfillment. There is no doubt the normal conscience cannot remain neutral towards obscenity, any more than it can remain neutral towards pedophilia and rape."

As film critic Michael Medved has written, "Hollywood assaults our most cherished values and corrupts our children. The dream factory has become a poison factory." But the critics, who are very influential over what we watch, love nasty movies with malignant messages. For instance, critics raved about one film that featured brutal criminals smearing a man's body with feces, which they then rubbed in his eyes and shoved down his throat, before they peed on him. Meanwhile, we see someone French kissing a corpse, a boy's belly button carved out, a man's face scalded, people copulating in garbage full of maggots, and finally, the celebration of cannibalism.

Medved found the critics' glowing reviews more disturbing than the sickening movie. They used words such as "excellent, profound, powerful, intelligent, exciting, and splendid." When, according to Medved, it was, in fact, a "putrid, pointless, pretentious piece of filth; brutal, nightmarish, and sadistic."

When Medved upbraided his fellow critics about just this one single film, he was savagely attacked as "an old-fashioned, right-wing bigot" who is "narrow-minded" and on a "moralistic high horse." You see, a film critic is not allowed to critique the presented *message,* and indeed not *the morals* of what is shown. That will get you branded with a Scarlet J for Judgmental.

Even the ancient pagan Greeks would keep suffering and humiliation off the stage as unfit for public consumption. Moviegoers today are trained to enjoy desecration. Propriety is long gone, and utter shamelessness reigns. The exhibition of the most graphic violence, and the anguish of those on the receiving end, has become a staple of 'entertainment.' Displays of corpses, many mutilated, including those of children, scarcely raise an eyebrow among the jaded. Every obscenity must be portrayed, supposedly in the name of freedom. All sense of decorum must yield to titillation.

Hollywood's glamorization of smoking in the 1930s and 1940s was mostly responsible for the millions of young people who then began to smoke. Hollywood also glamorized the use and abuse of illegal drugs in the 1960s and 1970s, and young people by the millions became both drug users and abusers. Now Hollywood glamorizes sodomy.

The fact is that Hollywood discriminates against conservatives—and especially against Christians. If a Hollywood person converts to Christianity, he or she can expect to lose friends, contacts, and employment immediately. If you disagree with the Democratic Party, you can kiss your career goodbye as a mainstream actor or filmmaker.

No one in Hollywood disputes that the sort of blatant discrimination suffered by Christians in the entertainment business would not be tolerated against blacks or atheists or communists or perverts or any other group of Americans. When asked about it, the responses are "I'm happy about it," and "I hope so," and the more thoughtful, "Anyone who denies it, is not telling the truth. It is unquestionably a barrier to working in Tinseltown. If you favor any *slightly* conservative position *on any subject* in a meeting, you will be stabbed in the back, discredited, smeared, and blacklisted. On the other hand, the most wildly radical position is applauded as open-minded."

But what kind of people are they to tell us how to think? Their own lives reek of open drug use, out-of-wedlock children abandoned after birth to babysitters, and serial relationships in a group seemingly unable to be faithful to anyone.

Their films portray belief in God or love of America with ridicule and contempt. Republican politicians are shown as villainous creeps. While genuinely oppressed people from around the globe literally risk life and limb to come here to America, Hollywood says our country is the great oppressor of the world.

Listen to the words used by Hollywood types to describe conservative people, the very people who pay perhaps half their salaries by purchasing their products: "Republicans are repugnant reptiles" (Julia Roberts); "Republicans are horrible people" (Moby); "Republicans are fucking idiots" (Jennifer Aniston); "I hate George Bush. I despise him. He makes me feel ashamed and humiliated to be an American" (Jessica Lange); "The American Flag is an embarrassing joke" (Robert Altman); "Bush and Cheney are fucking crypto-fascists" (John Cusack); "The election of George Bush did as much damage as the 9/11 terrorists" (Alec Baldwin).

Here is a couple more: "Naked men marching for gay pride and burning the flag makes my heart swell with pride. I get choked up over it. Except for burning it, whenever I see the American flag, I am insulted because this country was founded on a sham by white men who were rich slave-owners" (Janine Garofalo); "Charlton Heston should have been shot" (Spike Lee). It would take a whole chapter to list the horrible things said by Hollywood types about President Trump.

You will hardly ever hear an actor—even after they have become filthy rich off the backs of regular Americans via capitalism—*say anything good about America*. As a group, they seethe with hatred of America. They send that message around the globe unmistakably, as entertainment starring these anti-Americans is our country's second-largest export. No wonder the world hates us. They are encouraged to hate us by our most famous people!

When Mel Gibson wanted to make *Passion of the Christ*, all the big wigs in the business said *nobody* would want to see it. Even after it grossed over $600 million in movie theatres—one of the all-time most successful films ever made—critics hated it, calling it a lurid, pornographic, repulsive, extremely sadistic, sadomasochistic, snuff film.

Leftists predicted that the movie would result in massive violence against Jews, but nothing happened at all. The only consequence was the one the godless probably feared the most—millions of new converts to Christianity.

Now don't be fooled by cries of censorship from the people who produce our entertainment. They will try to tell you that *they must* shove every degradation and transgression down your throat every day *because not to do so would be censorship.*

Here is why that is poppycock. Every year Hollywood gets thousands and thousands of proposals for movies and TV shows, out of which only a fraction are ever made. In other words, they choose what they portray out of almost unlimited options. Are all the ideas they reject being censored? Does every script ever dreamt up have a right to be filmed?

Everything that is made requires an investment of time and money. It is chosen because it conveys messages and value judgments that the makers of it want to express. The existence of some horrible behavior does not mean *it must be shown on the screen.*

Hollywood will stop a project or alter a script if any loony leftwing outfit objects, or might object, such as groups representing women, blacks, Hispanics, Indians, animal rights, the environment, or people who practice sodomy. But Hollywood is eager to ridicule Christians, and blaspheme God. There is no doubt that the single issue where Hollywood and Americans differ most dramatically is the faith and mores of Christianity.

The elite in America is proud to hate on Christians, exhibiting strident bigotry in the name of tolerance. To mock and ridicule Christians has become stock in trade for beloved entertainers such as Garrison Keillor, who goes way out of his way to insult Believers. Keillor preaches that we should have our voting rights taken away for believing in Jesus—to thunderous applause from his live audience.

It has not always been this way. There was a time when Hollywood respected its audience; when it portrayed the good that God's People do in the world. But no more.

Even a minister is likely to be shown—if he is shown at all—as a Bible-toting, pompous, self-righteous hypocrite who is a pervert, sadist, lunatic, or vicious murdering psychopath that slaughters while quoting Scripture. And here's the critical thing: These disgusting movies usually fail at the box office, costing the film industry billions of dollars. They don't care.

That is how a discerning eye can see they have a demonic hatred of Christ, and no matter how much it costs; they will assault Him and His followers at every turn. But the critics are particularly enthusiastic about blasphemous films. Any insult to Christians is defended as *art* by Hollywood, no matter how gross and offensive it is.

Now, you may ask *why* Hollywood is so anti-Christian? One famous producer responded to that question by saying that he has never been inside a church. In his industry, he is not aware of *one person* who goes to church regularly, as perhaps half of his potential patrons do. Why should we expect entertainment that is virtuous, decent, clean, and wholesome from such people? But think of this: If movies and television suddenly produced righteous, proper, clean, and wholesome products, would that not influence society in that direction?

Make no mistake about it: Hollywood is resoundingly anti-American. In its eyes, "America is no damn good." Sean Penn speaks for many in his business: "I was brought up in a country that relished fear-based religion, corrupt government, and an entire white population living on stolen property that they murdered for."

Not surprisingly, Hollywood is chockfull of people with severe mental problems. One study showed that over half of all producers, directors, and writers are in psychotherapy. In Beverly Hills, there is one psychiatrist for every 130 residents—by far the highest concentration in the world.

Actors are often strange. Peter Sellers once said, "If you asked me to play myself, I wouldn't know what to do. I do not know who or what I am. There used to be a me, but I had it surgically removed."

I would expect that people who spend their whole lives pretending to be someone else might have personality problems. And Hollywood is legendary for drug addiction, drunken debauchery, and complete lack of sexual morality. It is famed for erratic behavior, disorientation, dementia, and sheer insanity. For this reason, motion pictures specialize in making the crazy person the hero of the movie, the enlightened rebel. And whereas, in the old days, Hollywood hid the loony antics of its stars, today it promotes them as a way of keeping them in the spotlight.

Actors are crazy about causes. They are obsessed with appearing to be secular saints *who care more* than any of us possibly could (because we are backward types who love Jesus). They are often rewarded with Oscars for playing the deranged, the disadvantaged, the mistreated, or the hooker with a heart of gold. Phony Hollywood actors specialize in *acting* like they care for the afflicted or oppressed.

Hollywood gave an Oscar to *Hearts and Minds*—a propaganda film for the Vietcong communists, an outfit that murdered about a million people—for which it was given a standing ovation at the Academy Awards.

Imagine the hypocrisy of Hollywood, where the elite use the best tax accountants in the world to avoid contributing their fair share to fund the big government programs they always favor for those less fortunate; have illegal aliens do their grunt work for five dollars an hour around the estates on which their mansions sit while complaining about the minimum wage; drive huge SUVs and fly private jets leaving behind an enormous carbon footprint, while complaining about global warming; protest school choice for their fans while their kids to go $30,000 a year private schools; have armed bodyguards while preaching that everybody else should have their guns confiscated; live in extremely segregated neighborhoods while preaching integration; rail against capitalism while it feathers their nests; and bash America, the only country where they would enjoy the freedom they do.

These phonies live in $14 million Malibu mansions but preach to the masses how great socialist countries are like Cuba and Venezuela; loving up Hugo Chavez, Fidel Castro, and his old buddy Che Guevara. I guess they are just acting.

Cuba hasn't had a free election in over fifty years; HIV positive people are locked up in concentration camps; artistic freedom is nonexistent; any Cuban who disagrees with Fidel was imprisoned or murdered. But countless celebrities with the last names of Spielberg, Stone, Costner, DiCaprio, Glover, Coppola, Depp, Harrelson, Walken, DeNiro, and Redford glorify Cuba as a worker's paradise. A far better country than nasty old hated America. Others named Robbins, Sarandon, Belafonte, Streisand, and Whoopi regularly hate on America and ordinary Americans.

These evil ingrates mainly seem to love to agitate to free murderers from prison, in particular, killers of police officers. And then there is Oprah Winfrey, a black woman who became one of the world's wealthiest individuals by preaching to women and blacks that they are the perpetual victims of the world. In fact, 'Woe is Women' is a considerable business catering to the oppressed and depressed American females.

The consequence of continually viewing an alternative reality in total moral anarchy is that those who grow up seeing it become confused about how they should then live. If the traditional family is destroyed, we will no longer be as healthy as we once were, spiritually, emotionally, mentally, or physically. TV and movies are in the business of shattering taboos. Even incest, bestiality, and cannibalism are not off-limits.

Beauty was the purpose of art before the 20th century. In the past 100 years or so, art has undergone a profound change. Its new mission is to create the unbeautiful—to shock, subvert, and transgress in increasingly novel ways.

Scenes of beauty give way to scenes of destruction and sacrilege. The beautiful art that has been created, such as that by Thomas Kinkaid and Norman Rockwell, is laughed at by art critics as pure kitsch. I believe there remains a great hunger in the human soul for beauty in art.

The purpose of art that is critically praised today is to desecrate and despoil what it means to be a living, loving human being. Art critics are not interested in work that is not disturbing, perverse, and unsettling. Work that meets their approval, as sufficiently decadent, is not reviewed as much as praised and promoted. All of the sacred things we hold dear are to be destroyed through the spirit of modern art, in particular, anything held Holy—set apart for God.

I read an explanation for this lack of beauty in modern art: When the twentieth century began, *everything* had been done that was possible to do in art, as relates to beauty. All was left was to reject everything that had been done by making 'art' that ridiculed the idea of art itself—through primitivism and decadence.

Filippo Marinetti launched this movement in 1909 when he published the *Futurist Manifesto*. It declared: "Art can be nothing but violence, cruelty, and injustice." Marinetti proposed that we "destroy the museums, the libraries, every type of academy, and create the maximum of disorder." The ideas of surrealism followed, which, simply put, are to unleash the horrors of the subconscious and make what this world has deemed obscene and sick to be taken for granted as normal.

The goal is to destroy the culture. Anything established must be denigrated, authority must be denied, clear meaning must be muddied, life must be disintegrated (decomposed, dissolved, demolished); the most base and primitive sensations must be glorified. Duchamp and Picasso got the ball rolling. Andy Warhol tried to finish the job.

Today, by use of spectacular digital effects, Hollywood makes the Occult seem glamorous and exciting as it glorifies satanic rituals in ways that are genuinely stunning visually. But God is banished because He is patriarchal. Hollywood seduces our impressionable youth, providing Lucifer with a powerful weapon by which he opens the door to demonic oppression and possession.

Just look at Harry Potter, how he attends the 'Hogwarts School of Witchcraft and Wizardry.' Harmless fun? There he learns spells, magic, and diabolical rituals from the witches and warlocks on staff, as well as how to communicate with spirits.

Harry has a mark on his forehead, a lightning bolt, which many of his young fans mimic on their noggins. Known as the *Satanic S*, it symbolizes Lucifer being cast out of heaven, becoming Satan. Hitler used the *Double Satanic S* for his prized SS.

Harry Potter creator J.K. Rowling admits she received inspiration for her characters through communication with the spirit world. Rowling represents the Black Arts as an alternative religion for the young, complete with levitation, animal sacrifice, astral projection, contact with the dead, crystal gazing, and demons.

Now, celebrities love esoteric religions. For instance, Madonna is a huge fan of Kabbalah's occult practice, along with many others, including Courtney Love, Roseanne Barr, Goldie Hawn, Naomi Campbell, Diane Keaton, and Laura Dern.

This is not altogether a new thing. Back in the 1920s, Greta Garbo and Charlie Chaplin were followers of the Hindu occultist Krishnamurti. Zen was a big deal for the Hollywood set in the 1960s, followed by all the variations of New Age Religion. Even Charlie Manson had his fans in Tinseltown. But he didn't have as many as Satanist Anton LeVay, adored by stars from Sammy Davis Jr. to Marilyn Manson.

Deepak Chopra took center stage in the 1990s, thanks to a big boost from Oprah Winfrey. His disciples included Cindy Crawford, Demi Moore, Michael Jackson, and George Harrison. Meanwhile, Carole King gave a swami 700 acres of prime real estate in Virginia to build Yogaville. Roma Downey, Rikki Lake, Anne Rice, and others preferred to contact the dead through medium John Edward.

Some fellow named Jack Pursel once announced that a demon named Lazaris inhabited his body. He gained 25,000 followers in Los Angeles, including Shirley MacLaine. Also beloved by MacLaine and by Yanni and Linda Evans was Judy Zebra Knight, who channels a 35,000-year-old evil spirit named Ramtha.

Ramtha is described as "once the ruler of Atlantis but now part of a brotherhood of superbeings who love us and hear our prayers." If you think that story is unbelievable, consider that the Federal Aviation Administration gave $1.4 million of taxpayer money to Ramtha to train its employees on how to manage stress. What does Ramtha recommend? "We must stop worrying about right and wrong."

Now, Ramtha's message is eerily similar to what became the most popular book in La La Land, *A Course in Miracles*: There is no sin, there is no truth, and Christianity is false. "God is neither good nor bad. He is entirely without morals and non-judgmental. There are no divine decrees. Hell and Satan are vile deceptions of Christianity, a product of your insidious Bible, which you are advised not to read. There is no such thing as evil. Nothing you can do, not even murder, is wrong. Every vile and wretched thing you do broadens your understanding."

In Hollywood, the most intense hatred is directed towards anyone who speaks of love for Jesus. Even a cross necklace is taboo unless, like Madonna, you are using it to commit sacrilege. But this only applies to Christianity. You can tell everybody in Tinseltown that you have become a Buddhist, Hindu, Muslim, Satanist, or best of all, a New Ager that is *a spiritual person who hates organized religion*. Everybody will think it's cool.

The elites of our culture, the celebrities, are the most morally perverse among us. With the family, the schools, and even some churches abdicating their responsibility to teach virtue to our youth, the young look to the celebrity culture for role models. Without a stable family, and with no extended family of positive role models, with society telling them everything is permissible except having sound judgment about what is right and what is wrong, our new generations have no one to imitate except the famous. And imitation of adults by children is what children do naturally.

The problem is that while celebrities can be drug addicts, stay drunk half of each day; have rampant sex with hundreds of partners, experiment with various perversions; live a life of serial marriages, illegitimate children, no family life, and single parenthood: These behaviors are a recipe for disaster for regular folks. The typical person is not rich and famous and in-demand, regardless of their behavior because of their 'talent.' As was pointed out succinctly in a 1993 editorial in the *Wall Street Journal* by Daniel Henninger: Everyday people need society to erect guardrails, to keep them from running off a cliff.

Progressives embrace the idea that the elimination of taboos is the path to happiness. In Hollywood, this is hailed as pushing the envelope—when old taboos like selfishness, profanity, promiscuity, bastardy, adultery, sexual perversion, violence, blasphemy, and sacrilege are celebrated. Ted Dalrymple observes: "The prestige intellectuals confer upon antinomianism soon communicates itself to non-intellectuals. What is good for the bohemian sooner or later becomes good for the unskilled worker, the unemployed, the welfare recipient—the very people most in need of boundaries to make their lives tolerable or allow them to hope of improvement."

The Idiot Box

"Being unable to cure death, wretchedness, and ignorance, men have decided, in order to be happy, not to think about such things. The only thing that consoles us for our miseries is diversion, and yet this is the greatest of our miseries. For it is this which principally hinders us from reflecting upon ourselves, and which makes us insensibly ruin ourselves. But diversion amuses us, and leads us, gradually and without ever adverting to it, to death." ~ Blaise Pascal

If an alien were learning about America from watching our television news and entertainment, he would never guess that Christianity plays a role in American life that is greater than anything else except family and work. What Hollywood does best is produce political statements ridiculing traditional family values, while cramming decadence down the throat of America. The most critically praised films and programs are most often those that normalize the abnormal and wicked, or show contempt for the souls who inhabit Flyover Country. We have become a nation fascinated with deviancy. The programs on TV are called that for a reason: they program young minds.

Television advertising works by ingraining specific images and messages in our minds to change the way we think and act. Laughably, some TV producers try to claim that their regularly scheduled programming does not do the same. What Hollywood does is lead us to imitate what it decides is the way we ought to behave by repeatedly showing us specific behaviors and attitudes. All this is candy-coated with extraordinarily exquisite images and excellent actors of great beauty and fame.

Think about the fact that companies will spend billions of dollars to persuade you to buy their products based on thirty seconds of words and images. Think about the fact that many in Hollywood, when speaking on the record, make the ludicrous claim that what we see in tens of thousands of hours of watching television programs persuades us of nothing.

If celebrities do not influence people, why are they immensely well paid to endorse products, services, politicians, charities, and activist groups? Movies and television programs not only entertain us; they teach us what the people who produce them believe about conduct, mindsets, and socio-political issues. If you do not also read, the messages received can confuse you about what is fact and fiction, virtue and vice, truth and falsehood.

There is no doubt Americans are obsessed with celebrities. And there is no question that the entertainment industry has redefined what is normal decorum. It is the most dominant influence on Americans, deciding what is cool and uncool. Do you think that watching TV for 1,400 hours a year does *not affect* how you feel, think, and act? An American child will spend fewer hours *in its lifetime* talking with his or her father than they will spend watching television *by the time they are five years old*.

Gorgeous actors portray loveable characters that mouth liberal positions in a way that suggests the truth is being spoken—and everybody on TV agrees who is acceptable and who isn't. Leftists love to shock Middle America to normalize ever more sinful behavior. Which should make you ask: Who is behind the curtain?

Whoever it is, has already warped the minds of tens of millions of souls. A lot of it is done with laughter. Every comedy presents an anti-Christian worldview. People identify with TV characters. They wish they had friends like them. You are watching the slickest propaganda ever produced.

Bathing yourself in one hour of television should be enough to convince you that the Devil wants you to imitate what you see on the idiot box he rules. And then consider how many people emulate the look and behavior of those they only see on the screen. They want to be like them if they can because celebrities are the heroes they admire the most.

Lifelong immersion into an artificial reality cannot help but influence what we become in our daily lives. The silliest sitcom is expressing someone's values and telling us how someone wishes us to behave. As Ben Stein observed, "It propounds a particular view *of* the world *to* the world continually."

Television is an agent for social change that is decidedly against God's moral laws. Intellectuals from Los Angeles and New York use it to make Middle America change its ways. Producers admit they "want to guide" and "educate" Americans. And this is a small group of people. It is estimated that only 150 people in the television industry can produce or not produce any particular point of view.

Hollywood's creative community sees itself as a group of educators, with television as a vast classroom. They are serving up sugary entertainment laced with medicinal messages. As Garry Marshall said, "It's cleverly disguised to look like something else. The people who produce programs believe that the alternative reality they create can change the real world." Leonard Goldberg confessed: "I think it is the responsibility of television not only to entertain but to offer guidance." Earl Hamner added, "What you see on any television show reflects the morals and the conscience of the people on those shows."

Fathers are superfluous; friends are better than family, out-of-wedlock births should make you proud. That is the world according to the left-wing propaganda that is well written, professionally acted, and pulchitrudinously filmed. Are there any shows on TV that promote traditional family values besides *Duck Dynasty* and the *Duggars*? Do not presume the power of television can be taken lightly. Scientific studies show it is a very relaxing narcotic that is highly addictive.

Primetime television has been pushing feminism for decades. TV has long valued its female customers more than men. One reason is channel surfing—women don't do it; they will sit through the commercials more often than males. Female television writers and producers are influential in the business, and every one of them is a feminist. One study found that among them is *not a single pro-life person*. Not one, even though the country is about half pro-life.

The people producing television almost all vote Democrat; support the homosexual movement; love abortion; scoff at Jesus; mistrust business people outside of their own business; want your guns taken away; think labor unions are fantastic; and are disgusted by conservative people, whom they sneer at as racist, sexist homophobes. Their message is socialism, yet the power players are all fabulously wealthy because of capitalism. *Because of the very people they despise that watch their entertainment.*

It hasn't always been this way. Television completely changed in the 1970s, from a pro-America message—even pro-traditional values and morals—to a theme of subversive transgression. Rebels became the new heroes. Crime was no longer due to character flaws but the fault of our society. Violence was now rarely condemned as immoral. But over the decades since, it has been the most transgressive series that flop, which shows Hollywood was not merely giving the customer what he wants.

It was only after *All in the Family* became the biggest show on television that Hollywood was taken over by militants who were atheists, feminists, and anti-Christian. The industry gradually became uniformly leftist from top to bottom, with executives such as Ted Turner becoming wealthy beyond imagining from viewers whom he later called "bozos" and "losers" because they believed in Jesus.

At least one scientist's studies show that thousands of murders per year in America are the direct result of being desensitized by violent television programs and that our crime rate would be half what it is if TV did not exist. While it has not been proven that watching violent shows can make an adult commit violence, research clearly shows that it does have that effect on some individuals who have grown up watching violence from a young age.

TV skews our perception of race, too. Martians watching television commercials would assume there has never been a backyard barbecue without a black man present. In the artificial reality that is television, there are twice as many blacks as there are in the real world. Maybe this is because blacks watch 50 percent more TV than the rest of us.

African-Americans are one-third of the teachers and professors shown on television—a far higher percentage than in real life—as well as every fourth police officer, every fifth entrepreneur, every eighth lawyer, and every tenth doctor. Black culture is presented as urbane, vibrant, and exciting while white men are hopelessly square.

The favorite image of blacks in film and television is as the victim of bigotry, including by our criminal justice system. But they are shown as being far less criminal than they are in the real world. In real life, blacks commit a third of all violent crimes and half of all murders. You wouldn't believe that from watching television, where blacks commit only eight percent of murders and other crimes. In real life, a white person is ten times more likely to be assaulted or murdered by a black person than the other way around. But TV shows blacks as victims of white criminals twice as often. I only mention this because it is yet another severe skewing of reality. It is a deception. And Satan is the master of all deceivers.

Hollywood also hates businessmen—somewhat strange since Hollywood is a huge business. Capitalists and executives are routinely portrayed as greedy, unscrupulous, dastardly villains. Three out of four business deals shown are immoral or illegal. One out of seven businessmen is a criminal in this alternative reality.

Hollywood is so far to the left that denigrating conservative people is always included at dinner parties but never the other way around. Actress Patricia Heaton tells of when she dared at a soiree with television people to say, "I love President Bush. My husband and I voted for him." Audible gasps were the only sound. Heaton said, "Literally, you would have thought I crapped on the table."

Depending on television and motion pictures to explain existence only shows we have retreated from reality into a world of magic. Even reality shows are not real. If the most prized value is to entertain us, the world will become a place where lies are right, as long as those who make a living pretending to be someone else present them.

Many people do not know this, but militant atheists produced *Star Trek*. One of them, Brannon Braga, said, "Religion sucks! How can we get the other 95 percent of the population to come to their senses about that?" Notice there is no God in *Star Trek*. There is no religion. It has been long left behind by men in the future.

Series creator Gene Roddenberry was virulently anti-Christian and longed for a cosmos where everyone is an atheist. At the same time, it is curious that Roddenberry said he received messages and scripts from a group of spirit beings posing as extraterrestrials known as the Council of Nine. They told Roddenberry they were from "Deep Space."

So I tune in to the Smithsonian Channel to see what kind of programming is being paid for with our tax dollars. The first show I see teaches us, "Islam ruled in Europe for 800 years, which was the golden age of peace and tolerance, where Muslim culture was head and shoulders above any other civilization on Earth, but graciously it shared its miraculous inventions with the West, until Christian Europe waged war on the Islamic Empire in the name of Christ for no reason, and Christian Europeans created damaging consequences that will last for thousands of years." Oh, and "the word *Jihad* only means *western fear*."

NONE OF WHICH IS TRUE! It is shocking how full of false statements and poisonous propaganda the program is.

I turn to the History Channel, whose programs are used quite often in our government schools. I hear the narrator say this little tidbit: "A lot of things in the Bible don't hold up in view of modern science." He did not mention a single specific thing. Just said, "a lot of things." I can't think of anything for which that is true. I smell the Devil.

The History of the World in Two Hours is a documentary that millions of children have watched, produced by the History Channel. It matter-of-factly states that the first humans were black, and they evolved from an animal in Africa. Europeans and Asians evolved from them. The Europeans got lucky because of the type of plants and animals they had where they accidentally went to live. Later, man learned to talk, which gave him an advantage over animals to exploit. There is no God in the picture at all.

But the science shows are the worst, especially *Cosmos*, the widely and wildly praised television series for children that has become a staple in schools as well. The most militant atheist in Hollywood produces the show. It stars one of the most militantly atheist scientists in the country. Both of them freely admit they presented lies as truth in the series, laughingly calling the lies "taradiddles." They assert that lies are acceptable as long as they disabuse children of the idea that the real Cosmos has a Creator.

The series begins with President Obama endorsing it on behalf of the United States Government. The second he is done, the narrator says, "The Cosmos is all that is, or ever was, or ever will be." That is not science. That is atheism masquerading as science. Next, the kids are dazzled by visually stunning state-of-the-art CGI and then taught by the smooth-talking Neil DeGrasse Tyson, the Obama of science.

Tyson's task in the first episode is to teach children that religion stands in the way of intelligent people, the progress of science, and the betterment of humankind. He goes on and on, implying that Christians are suppressing the freedom of thought and the free speech of scientists. On the contrary, the freedom of thought and free expression of anyone who disagrees with atheism is suppressed in the scientific community.

The second episode assures kids that Tyson understands their need to 'feel special,' a need Christianity supposedly satisfies by telling them that they are more than just another animal. He then teaches them the theory that they are descended from lower life forms, i.e., from an apelike ancestor. Tyson tells children this as if it is a proven scientific fact, which it is undoubtedly not. By the third episode, he teaches our children it is a mistake to believe that anything is sacred or that life has any meaning.

The truth is that every one of the scientists who created modern science, in what we call the Scientific Revolution, was a devout Christian. For but one prominent example, Isaac Newton became a scientist because of—not despite—his Christian faith. They believed in a personal God who created an orderly, logical, mathematical Creation that He wanted us to investigate. They saw science as a religious duty and thought Nature had laws because above Nature was a Legislator.

Tyson never mentions any of this. Tyson does rightfully admit that "science depends on the fearless questioning of authority," but are scientists free to question the descent of man from simpler life forms without professional repercussions? Can a scientist doubt Darwin in public and get away with it? No and no.

Later in the series, Tyson says, nobody knows where life came from, although he is willing to entertain any idea except God the Creator. He confesses that all living creatures contain a language written in an alphabet with letters. His only conclusion is that it arrived on Earth from space. From God? NO! From extraterrestrials.

Tyson does not tell the kids that God is even a possibility. Nor does he admit that his view is one with which very few scientists agree. One who does is Francis Crick, who wrote about it: "An honest man, armed with all the knowledge available to us now, could only state that in some sense, the origin of life appears at the moment to be almost a miracle."

Tyson teaches kids to get rid of "the delusion that we have some privileged position in the universe." Well, who says we do? God our Father, that's who, as Tyson well knows. That is whom he despises.

He makes sure children see him as the ultimate authority on these matters, and that they should join him in ridiculing the idea that "our ancestors believed that the universe was made for them"—which was the view of all the men who launched the Scientific Revolution. (As a side note, Tyson also tells your children that anybody who denies man-made climate change is a Nazi.)

In an interview on PBS, Tyson admitted he went way beyond science because he believes that faith is not reconcilable with reason. "God is an ever-receding pocket of scientific ignorance," he ignorantly claims. His producer added, "There have to be people who are vocal about the advancement of knowledge over faith."

The message of *Cosmos*: Christianity is for the ignorant; Atheism is for the enlightened. Did you get that, children?

One famous historian of science says that his community of scientists "has reacted with consternation to the historical components of *Cosmos* because it is troubling that the forums in which the public gets the most exposure to the history of science also tend to be those which it is the least responsibly represented." But a well-known biology professor countered: "It's all right to teach false claims to students so they'll accept evolution."

The media loves to promote the demonic idea that human beings 'evolved' from lower life forms. The worst offender is the Discovery Channel, which tells us there is no doubt about it. The folks at PBS are the next worst. They use taxpayer money to lie to our children about their origins. The media vastly overstates the evidence for the supposed 'descent of man.' They mislead us about the facts and omit facts that prove them wrong. They portray anyone opposed to this diabolical theory as backward and ignorant—people who think the Earth is flat.

Intelligent Design has been so well shown to be true that the godless, including Discovery, now promote a new idea that we are intelligently designed but by space aliens. Any idea is plausible to them as long as God is not in it.

The government-controlled PBS shows children a series by Bill Moyers and Joseph Campbell that proclaims Jesus is a myth— not a historical person. Campbell blasphemously says in the program, "the impulses of nature are what give authenticity to life, not the rules coming from supernatural authority."

As Dave Hunt rebuts: "On the contrary, the 'impulses of nature' give us the tooth and claw law of the jungle. The personal Creator commands us to love one another. If evolution were true, then whatever man did, from muggings to murder to war, would be a natural act against which no complaint could be raised. Police, courts, prisons, and criminal accusations would have to be eliminated. There is no right or wrong in Nature. Whatever Nature and her offspring do is simply 'natural.' If Man is a product of Nature through evolution, then whatever he does must likewise be natural. "

Hunt continues, "For the entire furor that is raised over the possible extinction of a species, such as the Spotted Owl, hasn't evolution been doing away with species for millions of years? Nor has any species ever tried to rescue another species from extinction. Then why should Man be the first to do so? By destroying creatures standing in his way, man, as the ultimate predator, would only fulfill his evolutionary purpose as the 'fittest' species that can survive at the expense of all others."

As presented on television and in newspapers, the news does not report the facts of events so much as present how the Main Stream Media wants you to perceive events. A poll of those in television and print media found that they vote for Democrats over Republicans by a 12 to 1 ratio. But they claim to report the news without bias. If you believe that, I have some prime Florida swampland to sell you.

Consider the coverage television gave to Martin Luther King Jr. during his civil rights campaign. Dr. King reported that whenever he would talk about the Christian basis for his work, either the cameras would get turned off or it would be edited out. He said: "They aren't interested in the *why* of what we are doing, only in the *what* of what we're doing, and because they don't understand the *why* they cannot *really* understand the *what*."

Television news anchors and reporters regurgitate propaganda from pressure groups they favor, at the expense of honest reporting. That is especially prevalent in the department that decides which stories to air, and which they do not air. They judge stories that disprove their pet theories about life not worthy of reportage, but even the most minor story that justifies their worldview (atheistic progressivism) quite worthy of your time indeed. The same is true of newspapers.

There is no need to take my word for it. Here are some quotes from those involved in the MSM, when asked about bias in favor of progressive social liberalism in the newsroom:

"Too often, we wear liberalism on our sleeve and are intolerant of other lifestyles and opinions. We're not very subtle about it at this paper: If you work here, you must be one of us. You must be liberal, progressive, a Democrat. I've been in communal gatherings in the *Post*, watching election returns, and have been flabbergasted to see my colleagues cheer unabashedly for the Democrats." - *Washington Post* editor Marie Arana

"I worked for the *New York Times* for 25 years. I could probably count on one hand, in the Washington bureau of the *New York Times*, people who would describe themselves as people of faith." - Former *New York Times* reporter Steve Roberts

"Of course it is biased. These are the social issues: gay rights, gun control, abortion, and environmental regulation, among others. And if you think the *Times* plays it down the middle on any of them, you've been reading the paper with your eyes closed." - *New York Times* Public Editor Daniel Okrent

"Where I work at ABC, people say 'conservative' the way people say 'child molester.'" - ABC 20/20 co-anchor John Stossel

"There is a liberal bias. It's demonstrable. You look at some statistics. About 85 percent of the reporters who cover the White House vote Democratic, they have for a long time. There is, particularly at the networks, at the lower levels, among the editors and the so-called infrastructure, a liberal bias. There is a liberal bias at *Newsweek*, the magazine I work for." - *Newsweek* Washington Bureau Chief Evan Thomas

"There is no such thing as objective reporting. I've become even craftier about finding the voices to say the things I think are true. That's my subversive mission." - *Boston Globe* environmental reporter Dianne Dumanoski

Brainwashing

Secular Humanism is the official name for Atheistic Socialism, the predominant philosophy of America's education establishment. Every day we send to public schools our most precious gift, our children, to be 'educated.' Joe Larson wrote in the *Eagle Forum*, "Test scores have been declining for decades, as the numbers of children who cannot read continue to increase. Although earth worship, paganism, and the occult flourish in public schools, the Greatest Story Ever Told, based on the greatest book ever written," which tells of the greatest teacher who ever lived, is not used or even allowed.

Socialism was invented by Satan and propagated by his mouthpieces. It has always targeted education as a means to its ends. One of his first worker bees was Robert Owen (1771-1858) of Britain, who proclaimed that all of man's problems stemmed from Christianity. Owen thought up the idea of brainwashing the minds of children with socialism and anti-Christianity through a national system of secular schools. He and his followers, secretly at first and always hiding their true motives, went to work to persuade public opinion that the state should educate children at taxpayer expense.

The state would take over many functions of the Church in Europe and America in the 20th century. In social services, and most notably in education, which had long been a religious endeavor, governments would first restrict and then eliminate the Christian point of view.

Horace Mann (1796-1859) was the 'Father of Public Education' in America. He worked tirelessly to convince legislators and the public of the need for universal public schools. But, as historian George Marsden notes, "Mann emphasized the religious and moral dimensions of the common schools. He insisted on the importance of daily reading of the Bible, devotional exercises, and the constant inculcation of the precepts of Christian morality in all schools." Mann declared, "to civilize the nation," what should be taught to public school pupils was the "ultimate triumph of all-glorious Christianity."

McGuffey's Readers textbooks were the backbone of American schools between 1836 and 1960. One hundred twenty million were sold during that period, ranking third in sales among all books, trailing only the Bible and the dictionary. Thirty thousand copies are still bought each year for private schools and homeschooling. Education included as its most crucial component the teaching of moral and spiritual values. William Holmes McGuffey's twin loves were education and the Gospel. He stressed, "The Ten Commandments and the teachings of Jesus Christ are not only basic but absolute."

McGuffey Readers taught children about the Creator, Divine Providence, the sinfulness of man, and salvation as available only through Christ. The public schools replaced the *McGuffey Readers* in the 1960s with secular humanist textbooks. At that time, American schools were acknowledged worldwide as the best in the world. Now we rank near the bottom of developed nations.

The government schools successfully expunged God. They now do the Devil's work by blowing out the light of belief in God among the young. That is why they should not have a financial monopoly over the educational dollars of parents.

'The Father of Modern Education' is John Dewey (1859-1952). Dewey was the leader of the teacher's union, an atheist, socialist, and co-author of the *Humanist Manifesto*, which calls for Secular Humanism to become the new religion of America.

The *Humanist Manifesto* was designed to replace "the fables of Christianity," which Dewey called "powerless, insignificant, and backward." It specifically states that there is no God; rejects the supernatural; deifies science; and declares that religious worship and churches should be eliminated. Dewey also belonged to 15 communist front organizations.

John Dewey was unquestionably the single person in United States history who most determined the direction of our public education system. He set the curriculum of government schools for generations. It was Dewey, profoundly influenced as he was by Darwinism, who put godless humanism at the center of American education. John Dewey may have shaped more American minds than any other individual.

Because of his 'work,' by the 1970s, virtually every textbook in America was scrubbed clean of any positive mention of Jesus, God, the Church, the Holy Bible, or God's moral laws. It is because of him that our schools went downhill, not based on the needs, talents, abilities, and gifts of our children, and not to promote academic excellence or build character, but as laboratories of social engineering; to create an unwise, unintelligent, ungodly social consciousness, thereby to mold future society according to Satan's vision.

We can see the results: children who grow up to glorify sexual perversions, support socialism, and disdain God. Johnny may not be able to read, but he can use a condom.

Dewey's mentor was G. Stanley Hall, a Darwinist and atheist. Hall believed in selective breeding, forced sterilization, and prohibiting charity for the poor, the sick, or the disabled, so they would die off sooner and not produce offspring. He had the same view of those with emotional problems, mental illness, or mental retardation. Hall was a doctor of psychology who invented our very idea of 'adolescence.' To him, Jesus was a fraud, and God is not there.

After visiting the Soviet Union, Dewey wrote six articles on the wonders of Soviet education. He admired the Soviet Union, which instituted his teaching plans before America did.

The John Dewey Project on Progressive Education at the University of Vermont explains that the overarching goal was to destroy the entire American culture by undermining its belief in individualism, capitalism, and traditional values, in particular, Christian morals. The progressive educational philosophy consists of these fundamental beliefs: An absolute faith in science and the Theory of Evolution; an idea that children can be taught very much like animals utilizing behavioral psychology; a conviction that there is no place for Christianity in education; and traditional values are an obstacle to social progress that had to be removed.

Dewey sought to spread his 'progressive' ideas through the American Public School System. The idea was for the schoolhouse to replace the family and the church at the center of a child's life during his or her formative years. He explained that his plan must be put into action in small steps as not to raise alarms. Parents and taxpayers must be tricked, or they would put a stop to it. But in the long run, schools would reject biblical morality, shun Jehovah and Jesus, abhor the Founding Fathers, and paint an awful, dishonest picture of America to schoolchildren.

Modern science had destroyed the ancient view that the Universe has a purpose, Dewey alleged. Science is the only means to truth, and its truths are subject to change, so, therefore, there is no such thing as objective truth—all truth is relative and changeable, in his view. According to him, "The Universe is self-existing and not created. The nature of the Universe depicted by modern science makes unacceptable any supernatural. Man is at last aware that he is alone."

The fact that worship is a worldwide phenomenon makes it a vital part of humankind. But Dewey sneered at religious people as misguided simpletons. He believed that with his guidance, the little people could be trained to let go of their beliefs, habits, thoughts, desires, customs, and social institutions. His goal was to use the schools to undermine faith in God, and diminish confidence in the American Way.

His strategy involved first indoctrinating America's schoolteachers. For that purpose, Dewey founded the Columbia University Teachers College, right next door to his partners at the Frankfort School. It became the model for teachers colleges across America. The Frankfort School also provided the philosophy for the National Education Association (teachers union), spearheaded by Dewey.

Through Dewey's Teachers College, he taught the professors who would train America's teachers. Thus the goals of public education have been radically transformed—intentionally perverted—by progressives over the past fifty years. Every public school teacher in America must be trained and certified by a teachers' college. Therefore, the way to brainwash millions of Americans is to proselytize those who will teach children.

John Dewey also founded the American Association of University Professors. Today it has 47,000 members. The AAUP was explicitly formed as a progressive movement that had a goal of defeating Christianity in the name of a new god named Science. The AAUP wanted the Creator eliminated from universities, as well as American culture and the public square. In 1988, the AAUP declared that *Christian schools and colleges* forfeit the right to represent themselves as authentic seats of higher learning.

It was not until 1918 that the government made going to school mandatory in America. Not long after that, we see godless progressives infiltrate the education establishment to brainwash our children. Today, the schools have lost their primary mission: to transmit knowledge, wisdom, morality, and civic virtue. That mission was drowned in a morass of social engineering designed to level everyone down.

By the 1920s, a movement had begun to cleanse the public schools of Christ. The people in this movement claimed that education should be neutral about God. But the same group demanded the teaching of Evolution, inherent in which is an atheist worldview.

The public schools had been founded on the idea that virtually all Americans believed in the same truths. These truths rested on a Christian foundation. Progressive voices were clamoring for that to be set aside, and teaching to be based solely on science. The schools had already taken over what had been the function of parents and churches in educating the young. Now progressives wanted schools to become America's new church of science.

The Supreme Court ruled in 1923 that one of the freedoms guaranteed in the Constitution is "the power of parents to control the education of their children." That was reiterated in 1972, and again in 2000: "It cannot now be doubted that the Fourteenth Amendment protects the fundamental right of parents to make decisions concerning the care, custody, and control of their children."

However, other court rulings have since undercut this fundamental right. The 2006 *Fields v. Palmdale School District* decision proclaimed that regardless of what you want as a parent, government schools can teach your child "whatever information it wishes to provide, sexual or otherwise."

Another federal judge ruled that a school can *force* your child to watch a one-hour video that falsely presents as an indisputable fact that people who practice homosexual behaviors cannot help it because "they were born that way," and "there is nothing wrong with" sodomy.

A federal court would later decide that a father couldn't prevent his child from being taught the glories of the homosexual lifestyle *in kindergarten*. Another federal judge ruled that children could be *forced* by a school to attend a program *advocating* homosexual behaviors. That means that parents are losing the fight to be the moral educators of their children.

Before the 1960s, our courts had rarely considered cases about the First Amendment guarantee that *We the People* would always remain *free to exercise* our religious beliefs *everywhere*. The only restriction on religion was that the federal government was not allowed to establish a national church. There seemed to be no problems between Church and State. Lawsuits in the Sixties launched *a new prohibition movement* by atheists to kick God out of education. The Supreme Court would declare God persona non grata in public schools.

Ever since God was booted out of our classrooms, fewer Christians have chosen to go into the teaching profession. That was not the only reason. At the same time, the far left-wing extremist teachers' unions took control of the schools, thanks to new legislation by Democrats. They controlled the federal government entirely in the 1960s. Those twin terrors, combined with the federalization of education, have caused the quality of education to plummet.

Many conservative people do not believe in unions and do not wish to join one. As a result, more and more anti-Christian teachers, hard-core leftists, have moved into the field. Why did leftists want to gain control of schools? To make them better? No. They were already peerless on the planet. What was the problem with our schools then?

The problem was that Americans were a conservative people, who were proud of their country and their faith in God and of the free enterprise system that they rightly understood had made them the most privileged people who had ever lived. Still today, a significant majority of U.S. adults think Christmas should be celebrated in public schools. Seventy percent also believe religious symbols like crosses and Christmas nativity scenes should be allowed on public land. That is what leftists hate and want to kill.

The most malicious ploy of the Devil was to take control of our system of education. Every leftist propagandist knows the best way to take over a country is to brainwash the children. The idea is to make children accept atheism, socialism, and immorality. Karl Marx said, "We make war against all prevailing ideas of religion." As Vladimir Lenin made clear, "Atheism is an integral part of socialism."

The godless have permeated our society with the myth that when you step on public property, you lose your constitutional right to your Free Exercise of Religion. That is the opposite of the truth. But under this myth, our government schools generally forbid the mere mention of Jesus' Name as if it is obscene—while encouraging and celebrating *real obscenity*, such as sexual deviancy.

The ACLU intimidates school administrators and municipalities by writing threatening letters that falsely announce a fictitious law demanding 'separation of church and state' has been broken. A suit is pending that will cost massive amounts of money to defend, money that is not in the budget. A decision is made that the best thing to do is just cry uncle.

To remake government schools into indoctrination centers for Secular Humanism, the Left had to get God out. It could only implement its plan using federal power because all the local school districts across our land would never agree. Every part of its program was opposed by 90 percent of American parents. *We the People* had to be disempowered for the sake of a leftist Utopia.

Today, American schoolchildren are in sensitivity training and indoctrinated into the Devil's Matrix of Darwinism, multiculturalism, political correctness, self-esteem, identity politics, white privilege, moral relativism, tolerance, social justice, and anti-Americanism. It is now impossible to find a textbook that gives an accurate account of Christianity's formative role in American history.

One key to ruining our children was 'self-esteem.' God said we must not esteem ourselves higher than we ought. We should be humble, not proud. The self-esteem movement taught our kids to applaud themselves because it's "all about you, what you like and want." Congratulate yourself, feel good about yourself, but for no good reason.

The claim was that this nonsense would "inoculate us against the lures of crime, violence, substance abuse, teen pregnancy, child abuse, chronic welfare dependency, and educational failure." Instead, all of those pathologies increased dramatically, and the children think far more highly of themselves than they should. For instance, before international math competitions, the Americans predicted they would finish first, but came in dead last. Our students lead humanity in only one category: Thinking they are awesome geniuses.

It comes naturally to a child, and to most adults, to be selfish, envious, and vicious. To curb our natural inclination towards evil, it is a beneficial restraint to have disapproval in our society. Many people would do many things if they didn't worry about what others thought, such as their friends, parents, pastor, teachers, society, and government. And, most of all, what God would think of them. So that is what an evil culture strives to eliminate—any sanction, shame, or 'judgment' of behavior, especially any restraint on sinful deeds.

The perception of reality requires distinguishing the truth from falsehood. It is an individual act of a single mind. The goal of modern education is to produce people incapable of discerning the true from the false and the good from the evil among people, and among states. After all, no one's views have any more validity than anyone else's, even the dullest student.

When an ignorant adolescent is asked to air his views, his ignorance is flattered at school. An ignoramus is treated as an authority. All opinions are significant just because somebody holds them. Incoherent youth don't know anything, so they posture and parrot platitudes and recite bromides they learn from teachers.

Christianity was kicked out of schools over a simple one-sentence prayer that merely acknowledged God and asked His blessing on children, teachers, parents, and country. God, the Bible, prayer, the Ten Commandments, the virtuous, and the biblical were taken out of classrooms to be replaced by the bad, immoral, sinful, and evil.

George Roche says that the kind of people "who argue voluntary prayer in schools is 'establishing' a state church have no such qualms about funding Darwinist enterprises with tax dollars extracted from people with different religious views." Such people lie when they claim that it is a 'scientific fact' birds evolved from reptiles. But such claims are the bedrock of the Theory of Evolution. If it didn't happen, and there is no proof that it did, then evolution didn't happen.

Children should study the Bible in school because you are not well educated if you haven't. The Bible is the foundation of America; of our founding documents, system of government, laws, people, customs, conventions, manners, morality, and traditions, not to mention our religion, as well as the cornerstone of Western Civilization. It is full of psychological insights and history. The atheistic government schools will not allow the Bible. The spirit that animates such an anti-Bible atmosphere wants to create adults who do not believe in God, or any supernatural dimension, or a transcendent moral code.

The government schools have been taken over by people with an evil political agenda. At the founding of America, education had been a private matter, in the hands of parents and churches. Its reason for being was to pass on to the young the knowledge, wisdom, and morals of previous generations, as a means to create self-sufficient adults, virtuous citizens. The aim of the diabolical plan now in motion is to produce adults who will accept Secular Humanism, with its attendant atheism, socialism, and nihilism.

Everybody has a worldview. The term worldview refers to the framework of ideas and beliefs through which an individual interprets reality and interacts with it. Whether they know it or not, every person has one, whether they can define it or not. Therefore, nobody has a neutral worldview. Not even a professor or schoolteacher or writer of school curriculums. Some claim they compartmentalize or privatize their beliefs into public and private spheres. Politicians will sometimes claim that, as an individual, they are opposed to this or that, but as a public official, they have the opposite view. That is merely mendacious.

A person's worldview colors all of their attitudes and reactions to events in all aspects of their life. Someone's values are always being advocated, even in so-called neutral settings. People who think administer public schools and that thinking reflects their worldview.

Psychological experts play a significant role in our children's lives through government schools. They greatly exaggerate the claims of science, and since they are seldom believers in Jesus; they work to prevent faith from developing in their charges. What secular humanists do is see to it that only their worldview is taught to children.

No nation in the history of this planet has done more good for the human race than the United States. But our children are taught that America is a racist, hostile, imperialistic force. They are imbued with the diabolical notion that capitalism and free enterprise are malevolent. The name for this is social engineering. It denies reality. It is censorship of the truth, and it is dishonest. God never smiles upon wholesale false witnessing. It is the Adversary, who is the Deceiver of Man, behind it.

The secular humanists are quite proud of kicking God out of our government schools. By labeling the views and values of Christians as 'religion,' and therefore excluded from the classroom, primarily where the young are taught about their world, those who reject Father God have given themselves a monopoly over young minds, legitimized their worldview, and delegitimized the worldview of traditional America. That is dangerous because history shows us clearly that a society which is atheist by force is a home for Satan, e.g., The USSR and Red China.

There is nothing whatsoever in the Gospel about indoctrination. Telling people the Good News is not indoctrination. All individuals have free will. People should think for themselves. But children should be shown the truth, which is this:

Most people living now, and most people who have ever lived, believe God the Creator made this world and all that is in it, especially all living things, in particular, Humankind as the Crown of His Creation. God made you. He sees everything you do. He loves you. He has a purpose for your life. However, some people believe the Cosmos came into being all by itself, that non-life became life through some cosmic accident, and human beings are nothing more than animals evolved from lower life forms randomly. In their worldview, there are no moral laws except those in fashion at the moment—constructs of Man subject to change at any time, and only relatively valid. Under this system, known as scientific materialism, only Matter matters. Your life means nothing and is without purpose except perhaps in your head. You are free to believe what you will, children, the Almighty State will not choose for you by excluding either of these worldviews from our schools.

Textbooks such as *Across the Centuries* blatantly lie about the world we are in by making the absurd claim that Islam "liberated women" while never mentioning Muslim terrorism. It also says, "Jerusalem is where Jesus was crucified and buried" without mentioning the Resurrection, which is the foundational aspect of the Christian faith. But it claims Jerusalem is "where Mohammed rose to Heaven," which is not even in the Koran, and for which there is no evidence.

Other textbooks treat the claims of Islam as historical facts, while the truths of Christianity are "what Christians believe." Stories about Mohammed or Buddha are presented as factual events, but whatever is said about Christ is qualified by "what Christians believe." They all neglect to mention that Mohammed was a warlord who persecuted people of other beliefs. Not only did he own slaves, but he was also a slave trader.

Islam is tolerant and peaceful; our textbooks propagandize, when, in fact, Islamic nations are politically oppressed, socially repressed, and women are subjugated. Research, science, and technology are stagnant, and literacy runs about 50 percent in Islamic countries. Arab slave trading of blacks is described as an opportunity for social advancement for blacks.

Secular Humanism is a New Age Religion that shuns moral absolutes and teaches situational ethics. It demands the presentation of the Theory of Evolution as the only possible explanation for humankind's biological origins. It belittles free enterprise and promotes One World Government. Thanks to its efforts, the Supreme Court decided that, on the one hand, mere exposure to ideas that contradict Christianity is no problem, but mere exposure to Christianity is a no-no. It is OK to promote New Age Paganism, the Occult, and Witchcraft.

For the most part, textbooks represent the worldview of atheism and socialism. Publishers consider it a badge of honor to have offended Christians but are quite sensitive about offending the Left. Internal memos from textbook publishers show they believe Christians who complain are "totalitarian censors," but when progressives complain, they are termed "positive pressure groups."

Dr. Paul Vitz has studied our government school curriculum. He notes that in sixty Social Studies textbooks from ten publishers, all of them intending to introduce the child to contemporary American society, there is not one reference in word or image to Protestantism. There is nothing in either word or picture that suggests the existence of that aspect of our society. But Native American religion receives sympathetic treatment, with discussions of an Indian rain dance and prayer to Mother Earth.

In our textbooks, there is the almost complete eradication of the idea of a traditional family (husband, wife, children) as desirable or even ordinary. Thus, a family is usually defined vaguely as a group of people or the people you live with. Zero of the textbooks mention marriage as the foundation of the family; zero even mentioned the words *marriage, husband, wife, homemaker, or housewife*. Marriage has no relevance to the definition of family. By contrast, there are countless references to women working outside the home in various occupations.

Zero of 670 stories and articles studied have the content or central motivation derived from the Christianity. Zero mentions even once the name Jesus. By contrast, non-Christian religious ideas are frequent: six stories have Greek or Roman pagan religions as an essential part of the story; six feature ancient Egyptian, Polynesian, or other pagan religions; 13 feature magic. Many of the stories have magic as central to the plot and the story resolution.

Dr. Wayne Grudem observes, "What is taught in school has a strong formative influence on children's values and goals. Particularly in the elementary years, the textbook a child uses is his primary source of information about the entire world outside his own circle of family and community experience. An entire generation of American children is growing up with an idea of American culture and society in which religious convictions of Christians, traditional family values, traditional male/female roles, and conservative political and economic positions play no significant part."

Grudem notes, "Of course, the child may still see these values represented in his or her own home life and community, and that is good. But it still would be hard for the child to escape the conclusion that his or her own experience is abnormal or unusual - for it is clearly not representative of what is approved by those intelligent people who write textbooks and who certainly know what the whole world is all about. What then will happen? At best, the child will feel embarrassed and defensive about his own unusual religious beliefs and traditional family structure. At worst, children will grow up with a very positive disposition toward accepting the liberal political perspective and the anti-Christian religious and moral perspectives portrayed in these textbooks."

As Dr. Grudem asks and answers, "Why are social studies important? Because it is here that the child learns what society is all about, and particularly, the child learns what America is all about. Zero out of sixty textbooks (approximately 15,000 pages) have even one word referring to any religious activity in contemporary American life. None of these texts have even one mention of people who go to church, who worship or pray, or have any religious influence on their lives or society. It is common to treat Thanksgiving without explaining to whom the Pilgrims gave thanks."

Children are taught to see themselves as no more important than animals. The horrible consequences of this are all around us. For one obvious example, 'childhood depression' was non-existent before the schools became hostile to God. Think about that, with creature comforts abounding that were unheard of in the past, our children are growing more and more depressed. If they are loved by their parents, have toys and gadgets up the wazoo, plenty to eat, a temperature-controlled environment year-round, beautiful clothes, plenty of friends, fantastic opportunities, and an unprecedented level of personal freedom, how can they be depressed? God is missing from their lives. Their school treats Him as a fairy tale or, worse and subtly, ingraining in kids that life has no meaning beyond physical pleasure. Maybe they are even worse than animals, causing global warming, extinction of other species, ruining the environment—part of a plague that the world would be better off without. What are they to do with that God-shaped hole in the hearts?

At the heart of Western Civilization has always been the concept that human beings are primarily spiritual beings, meaning that the search for transcendent truth, for metaphysical meaning and purpose, is the fundamental fact of the human person. John Taylor Gatto writes: "Western spirituality granted every single individual a purpose for being alive. It conferred significance on every aspect of relationship and community. In Western spirituality, everyone counts. It offers a set of practical guidelines. Nobody has to wander aimlessly. What counts as a meaningful life is clearly spelled out."

Every single study shows that people who believe in God are healthier psychologically and in every other way. They are better able to cope with life's vicissitudes and adversities. The best way to produce healthy adults is to get rid of atheist education and replace it with godly education.

But the one thing that would do the most good is the one thing banned from the atheist schools because it undermines the secular humanist worldview, especially the Theory of Evolution. The Bible teaches us that life after death and preparing for it is more important than living for the moment.

There is a relationship between your belief about humanity's origin and your moral views. For but one example, the more a person believes in Creation, the less he or she is willing to accept sexual intercourse between two unmarried consenting people. "Wrong thinking always begets wrong behavior," contends Ken Ham. "There is a connection between origins and issues affecting society, such as marriage, clothing, abortion, sexual deviancy, parental authority, etc." Researchers Morris and Morris state, "A person's philosophy of origins will inevitably determine sooner or later what he believes concerning his destiny, and even what he believes about the meaning and purpose of his life and actions right now in the present world."

Years ago, many people correctly forecast that the teaching of concepts that rely on a purely naturalistic explanation of the world, such as the Theory of Evolution, would eventually lead to a decay of American society. Atheist schools lead to self-destructiveness and suicide. Nobody ever heard of children killing themselves before God was kicked out of our schools, but today it is the 6th leading cause of death for children under fourteen. And what do teachers say about their students? Ninety percent of them claim disruptive behavior is a severe problem in their classrooms; 70% say their schools are plagued by stealing and vandalism; half say drugs and alcohol are used during school hours; 44% say there is violence against students, and 24% say there is violence against teachers.

Now we have 'values clarification,' which means children are taught radical nonjudgmentalism. There is no right or wrong; nothing is moral or immoral; there is only what is acceptable *to you* and what is not. Virtue is optional, as is vice. Masturbation, wife swapping, and cannibalism are morally neutral.

Fourth graders must decide themselves what is good or bad because no civilization or religion has ever reached any conclusions worthy of being passed on to our young. But this approach is not totally 'values-free.' It judges as dangerous any values parents might impart into their children, such as honesty, responsibility, loyalty, self-control, or duty. The main idea is that children by ages eight or nine ought to have the ability to form their own wisdom. And that morality is a personal thing you can choose to meet your inclinations and urges.

Common Core will dissolve whatever sovereignty states, local school boards, and parents have left. On top of that, tests will be rewritten to make the right answers the ones that fit progressive ideology in regards to global warming, sexual deviancies, the descent of man from ape-like ancestors, abortion, promiscuity, open borders, etc. etc. etc. AND taxpayers will have to fork over an extra twenty billion dollars to have their heritage and nation destroyed by Common Core.

The data-mining element of Common Core is most troubling. It violates students' privacy and their families through the gathering and sharing of personal information with the federal government. Schools are to record every child's hobbies, psychological evaluations, medical history, religious affiliation, political affiliation, family income, behavioral problems, disciplinary history, and dreams.

At the very least, a free people would expect their schools would not work fulltime to undermine the faith and morals of the parents who send their children there. It is plain silly to act like the schools are 'neutral' when they teach kids that Heaven is empty, and the Universe was not created.

If Man is his own god, he can write his own rules. Government schools teach our children that all life descended from a single-celled ancestor 'naturally,' which implies that any 'supernatural' explanation is false. Incredibly, a federal judge ruled that it is unconstitutional for a public school to tell its students that the Theory of Evolution is a theory!

The theory is based on the notion that life forms progressed from simple to complex as time went on. But astrophysicists calculate the odds are nearly infinite against bacterial life ever evolving into the human race—no matter how slowly. Darwin's idea that more robust, healthier animals are more likely to survive the savage struggle for survival in the wild certainly makes sense. But how did we get here in the first place? Where did life come from?

There are two main views. One view is that God, who existed before the Universe was born, created all that exists except Himself. That is, by far, the belief of the vast majority of all human beings alive today, and of all who have ever lived. But it is a view *forbidden in government schools.*

The view of a small minority of people is that the Universe was created without God because there is no God. To them, God is something human beings imagine to be real but isn't; the Cosmos is nothing but physical stuff; science is the only guide to any knowledge. This view *is allowed in our government schools.*

Richard Dawkins says, "A tiny bacterium who lived in the sea was the ancestor of us all." Children are taught that human beings evolved from a common ancestor, along with all other living creatures, from way back in some primordial soup. And that this happened because random variations of life forms eventually evolved into human beings. Which, of course, means we are not done. Human beings must also evolve into something higher yet because evolution has not ended and will never end until all life ends. So the only difference between man and animals is one of degree—not one of kind. In other words, animals are just like us, except we are further on up the road.

To say that man has evolved is a cruel joke. The latest study shows that the average human being is dumber today than in ancient Greece 2500 years ago. Another bit of recent research shows that the average person in Britain is not as smart as they were in the Nineteenth Century. Man sometimes *devolves*—we see civilizations go backward into Dark Ages. We may be headed for one now.

Man was never without the same emotions and intellect that you have now. When you read Shakespeare, or even the Old Testament, you know instinctively in your heart that the people you are reading about are people just like you and me—even way back then.

In that meaningless materialist universe in which children are taught to put their faith, there is not even free will. Any notion that you 'decided' to do something is an illusion. As Steven Pinker said, "We dispense with all morality as unscientific superstition." Of course, he does. *That is what his worldview is for.* That is the only benefit of his religious views: to eliminate morality.

Mathematicians say that our Universe coming into being from nothing all by itself is statistically impossible. The field of paleoanthropology is full of embarrassing frauds, fictions, and hoaxes. Our students are told that fish somehow 'evolved' into amphibians, which evolved into reptiles, which evolved into mammals, which evolved into human beings. There is no proof that any of these steps ever happened. And yet it is presented as indisputable fact to minds that are not old enough to know better.

The British Museum of Natural History has the world's most extensive collection of fossils, including some sixty million. And yet they do not have one that shows any kind of animal becoming a different kind of animal. However, a children's educational book shows a dinosaur hatching the world's first bird from its eggs. *The Wonderful Egg* is loaded with plenty of other scientific errors. Still, it is highly recommended by the American Association for the Advancement of Science, the American Council on Education, and the Association for Childhood Education International.

An article in the *Wall Street Journal* laments that some Americans still believe in God. It prescribes a remedy: "The secret may be to reach children with the right theory before *the wrong one* is too firmly in place. We should teach children the theory of natural selection while still in kindergarten instead of waiting, as we do now until they are teenagers."

The "wrong one" mentioned is, of course, belief in the Creator. The article admits, "If you wanted to explain most of the complicated objects in my living room, you would say that somebody intentionally designed them—and you'd be right. Even babies understand that human actions are designed to accomplish particular goals. Preschoolers begin to apply this kind of design thinking more generally. By elementary-school age, children start to invoke an ultimate God-like designer to explain the complexity of the world around them—even children brought up as atheists. They explain biological facts in terms of intention and design."

So you see, children have intuition. When they look at life around them, they intuitively believe that living things are designed with a purpose. It's only after indoctrination at their government school that they can be dissuaded from thinking that the world is designed. According to a *Psychological Science* report, research shows "children in preschool and early elementary school show biases that the world was designed to explain the origins of natural objects' properties by reference to functions."

Young children can grasp all on their own that mechanical devices do not make themselves. So the schools must use Orwellian mental manipulation, *designed* by psychological professionals trained to understand how young minds operate, to brainwash children into Darwinism.

The trust of a little child is supremely precious, according to Jesus. If someone were to ill-treat that tender faith, the Lord said, "It would be better for him if a millstone were hung around his neck, and he were thrown into the sea, than that he should offend one of these little ones."

So, you intuitively know that bricks, shoes, smartphones, satellites, and robots do not appear all by themselves. Someone smart thought them up, designed them, and made them. Kids are told that far more incredible things, such as dragonflies, hummingbirds, dolphins, and horses, did appear by accident, and no one thought them up, designed them, and made them.

To tell children in a government school that it is at least *possible* the Universe is created, will get you written up in the newspaper: "The Taliban has invaded Ohio . . .. Know nothing fanatics intent on twisting science to accommodate their pet biblical phrases . . . Knuckle-Dragging creationists are waging a state-by-state jihad against real science . . . the ignoramuses."

Many a child has had their belief in Christian mores demolished by government schools. The result is an immoral and antisocial teenager, whose school has taught that sex is great without love or marriage, which leads to the epidemic we see around us of promiscuity, perversion, pornography, teen pregnancy, abortion, unwed mothers, fatherless children, welfare dependency, emotional problems, mental problems, spiritual problems, prostitution, and sexually transmitted diseases that might be incurable, cause sterility and lead to an early grave.

Look at a list of the top 100 books assigned to children in our government schools. Authors who are militantly anti-Christian wrote over half of them. I challenge you to name more than one writer on such a list who is a known Christian; more than one book that extols Christian values. How can this not harden children's hearts against faith?

The homeschooling movement was sparked by the anti-Christian agenda of the government schools. Even the extreme far left-wing progressive liberal Mario Cuomo sent his children to a Christian school, explaining, "The public schools inculcate disbelief in God."

Now that Christians are leaving the public schools, the secularists are aiming at homeschooling. Homeschooling parents do a better job for vastly less money than government schools. Homeschoolers score 71 points higher on the SAT than the national average—for one-tenth of the money. They do better on the ACT, have higher GPAs in college, and have higher graduation rates. They also dominate academic competitions, such as the National Spelling Bee. Furthermore, private schools do a better job for half the cost because they do not have to do what the federal bureaucrats command in regards to curriculum and teaching methods.

As Ann Coulter has written, "Has anyone else noticed that even though liberals are constantly lecturing us that the key to education in American is small class size and more money for teachers that what they are really saying 'less work for more money.' Liberals hate homeschoolers, who have the smallest class sizes around (and they loathe Christian private schools with smaller class sizes than public schools). Liberals have turned public school teaching into a babysitting service with the goal to indoctrinate our children in godless lifestyles and godless worldviews."

Militant atheists admit that they favor censorship against freedom of expression when it comes to one area—parents teaching their children about Jesus: "Children have a right not to have their minds addled by nonsense. And we as a society have a duty to protect them from it. So we should no more allow parents to teach their children to believe in the literal truth of the Bible than we should allow parents to knock their children's teeth out or lock them in a dungeon." That is Lucifer speaking through the mouth of one Nicholas Humphrey, atheist professor of psychology.

The child has been taught to invent his own reality through child-centered education. He now tries to rescue himself from being cut adrift by adults who were supposed to nurture and guide him. Without navigational aid, he seeks experiences but not responsibilities. Defiance, rebellion, and transgression are the order of the day, an outlet for the rage at having being *de facto* orphaned by the Cosmos in which he finds himself. Drugs numb the pain. And sex. Being taught that he is nothing but an animal, he lives for the moment, seeking to satisfy his every urge. There is no need for courtesy or manners. He knows not what they are for. He is alienated.

You don't have to take my word for any of this. One of the people in charge of deciding what kind of education our kids should get drops the façade and tells us how he feels. "Every child in America entering school at the age of 5 is mentally ill because he comes to school with certain allegiances to our founding fathers, toward our elected officials, toward his parents, toward a belief in a supernatural being, and toward the sovereignty of this nation as a separate entity. It's up to you as teachers to make all these sick children well — by creating the international child of the future." (Chester M. Field, Professor of Education and Psychiatry at Harvard University)

Led by a local teachers' union, a protest arose against school board members who wanted to emphasize America's unique merits, with the intolerable *old-paradigm* notion that America is the best country. Such ethnocentric teaching, the protestors argued, emphasizes one culture over another. Therefore it breaks a state law in California that requires multicultural education, which, as Berit Kjos notes, "trains students to view the world and its people from a *global* and *pantheistic* perspective rather than from a *national* and *Judeo-Christian* perspective."

Comprehensive Multicultural Education is a popular textbook. Its goal is not to teach factual history but a new commitment to universal oneness that must supersede loyalty to God and country. Children must reject their *old* home-taught faith or stretch it far beyond biblical boundaries to include the world's pantheistic, polytheistic belief systems.

In 1985, the ASCD (Association for Supervision and Curriculum Development), the influential curriculum arm of the powerful National Education Association, "urged representatives of Western nations to press for the development of a *world-core curriculum* based on the knowledge that will ensure peaceful and cooperative existence among the human species on this planet."

'Knowledge' that would ensure peace and cooperation? What kind of knowledge would that be? *Education Week* explained: "The world-core curriculum would be based on proposals put forth by Robert Muller, assistant secretary-general of the United Nations, in his book *New Genesis: Shaping a Global Spirituality*." This 'global spirituality' would include Buddha, the Occult, Yoga, Theosophy, the New Age teaching of Alice Bailey—and 'The Great Invocation,' which is an occult prayer to be used around the globe to invoke a global outpouring of spiritual light and power.

In his well-endorsed book on holistic learning, Andy LePage promoted Muller's vision of a World Core Curriculum on holistic learning, *Transforming Education*. In the nineties, it spread into local school districts. Berit Kjos says, "The new path to peace mapped out by leading educators looks more like the mystical steps to Occult Oneness described in James Redfield's top-selling *Celestine Prophecy*."

Teaching occult formulas for empowerment to help students *feel* good about themselves, and using cooperative learning so that all will progress to the same mediocre level. This kind of 'education' leads to global socialism, not to the type of freedom the American Republic has offered people from around the world. It follows the blueprint of Soviet indoctrination. It aims to destroy everything that Americans once called good.

C. S. Lewis argued that liberal ideology seeks to use government schools to create "men without chests"—men who will accept a totalitarian state dictating their lives as long as their bellies and groins are satisfied. The higher self of man is eliminated, leaving behind only the lower, base, animalistic man. Leftists focus on class, racism, sexism, homophobia, and inequality because these things help them forget man's real problem: Sin. Wickedness. The depravity that we can see all around us.

Our public school system miseducates children by repressing the truth about human existence. American culture is producing fewer and fewer sane people. The Antichrist indoctrinates the young through our education system. Self-esteem therapy is extraordinarily dangerous as it riles up people to hate because of real or imagined injustices. It creates narcissism and sometimes violence.

There was a time in our past in which schools needed the permission of parents for their children attend. Decades later, that was reversed, and a law enacted that made it mandatory for all children to go. Laws were eventually passed that granted educators more authority than parents over their children's education. If we are nothing but beasts, as the secular humanists believe, then what are schools for? Beasts cannot be educated; they can only be trained.

Lucifer's Headquarters

The university is a Christian invention. And yet the Devil speaks through men to claim that Christians oppose education. It is no secret that our universities have, for well nigh 50 years now, been at work trying to despoil America by undermining our nation's inherent Christian worldview. Humble fathers and mothers rear their children in good Christian homes; they scrimp and save to send their kids off to college, only to see them return as atheists/socialists/nihilists.

The universities swim in what philosopher Roger Scruton calls "a culture of repudiation "that renounces Western Civilization—the greatest of all man's inventions—and our values and identity as Americans. Every positive aspect of our heritage that most all Americans were once proud, and traditional patriots are still proud of today; our colleges obliterate.

According to the National Health Interview Survey, only 1.6 percent of Americans identify as homosexual. But a survey of Millennials shows that THEY THINK 20 percent of Americans are homosexuals. This is the result of massive propaganda. Now I'll tell a fascinating tidbit that explains a lot about the atmosphere on our college campuses. Ten percent of college professors say they are homosexual—six times the percentage in our general population.

Universities offer twice as many courses on multiculturalism and gender studies as they do American literature. The purpose of gender studies is to affirm homosexual behavior and silence those who disagree—especially those with biblical objections. Christians founded the vast majority of these institutions of higher learning. However, today students with religious beliefs are ridiculed, vilified, and discriminated against due to the work of homosexual activists. 'Tolerance' really means intolerance for any viewpoint that does not affirm homosexual behavior. Religious freedom is suppressed on almost every college campus.

At Temple University, the freedom of speech argument was used to stifle protests about a school play, which portrayed Jesus Christ and Judas as homosexual lovers. And yet a Christian was denied the right to put on a play *about the real life* of Jesus, after objections by homosexual activists.

Thomas Jefferson proclaimed, "To compel a man to furnish contributions of money for the propagation of opinions which he disbelieves and abhors, is sinful and tyrannical." Yet this goes on every day at college campuses where mandatory student fees fund radical organizations that openly promote perversion. Resident advisers at some major universities are forced to watch X-rated homosexual films as part of their mandatory sensitivity training.

The atheist philosopher Richard Rorty expressed the opinion of many college professors, which is that their job first and foremost is "to arrange things so that students who enter as bigoted, homophobic, religious fundamentalists will leave college with views more like our own, and escape the grip of their frightening, vicious, dangerous parents."

Conservatism is a philosophy of love, loving the virtuous and the valuable, protecting the wisdom that our ancestors bequeathed to us. The Left is about desecrating what men and women cherish, and defiling innocence.

It is no longer surprising when our children go off to college and learn to vilify traditional moral values. The colleges will say that all they want is for kids always to *question* time-honored codes of behavior. But the single answer the professors proclaim and reward is, No.

Political Correctness is a tool used by the Devil's minions to vandalize Western Civilization. It is a vicious instrument used to enslave the mind and deny all that is true. PC is used to cancel free speech, and end free thought by way of 'speech codes' and 'thought crimes.'

Its manipulators are ever busy, coming up with new things that cannot be said or thought. The origin of this evil weapon of mass destruction is the Soviet Union, a place built on an odious ideology that no sane person who ever lived under it could admire.

Students at American universities are routinely fed a series of whopping lies that create a false narrative of how our current world came to be. It goes like this: 'Western Civilization went through 'dark ages' because the Church forbade people to learn anything except the Bible. Crusaders attacked peace-loving, far-advanced Muslims for no reason. The Crusaders were just ruthless marauders looking for someone to slaughter. Millions of witches were burned at the stake. Courageous people finally challenged the Church, launching a Renaissance, which led to the birth of modern science.'

There is only one thing wrong with this narrative: it is a lie from beginning to end, created by the Father of Lies, and spread by his servants. The Scientific Revolution only happened once and in one place in world history: Christendom (the former name for Europe). Not in Arabia, India, China, Africa, or even among the Native American tribes.

The denunciation of Western Civilization as 'oppression' overwhelms the atmosphere at American universities. If it is studied at all, it is to denigrate it. The primary reason for this is that our civilization represents Christendom, which is what the demonic genuinely hate.

The anti-Christian ideology is imposed upon students to sever them from their moral and religious roots. Nonjudgmentalism is preached for every culture on Earth, no matter how barbaric—except the traditional culture of our Christian heritage. To value Western Civilization is despised as 'racist.' The truth is that not all cultures are equally admirable, and ours was the best, so the students are brainwashed by the worst lie imaginable.

The 'New Left' spawned by the campus radicals of the 1960s promised utopia. Its progenitors had plenty of theories but no real knowledge—and no wisdom—of how the world works. They demanded reality be something other than what it is. Having shucked off the yoke of their forefathers' worldview, the New Left sought to give their lives meaning through the causes of social liberalism. They have taken over American universities.

One of the most massive donations ever given to a university was the $20M gift to Yale from its alumnus Lee Bass in 1991. The problem was that the money was designated for the study of Western Civilization—once the core of college learning, but in the previous decades deeply deprecated. Eighty percent of donations to universities are earmarked toward specific studies, so that was not an issue. The issue was Western Civilization itself.

In 1995, Yale returned the money to Mr. Bass under fierce pressure from Anti-American multiculturalists. Sara Suleri Goodyear, a professor of English, had this to say about the $20M gift: "Western Civilization? Why not a chair for colonialism, slavery, empire, and poverty?" Geoffrey Parker, a history professor, was quoted as saying, "The major export of Western Civilization is violence."

The New Left has spent decades on a mission to change the worldview of Americans. Central to this plan is to detach people from their loyalties to America, Western Civilization, and Christianity. A large part of the propaganda is employed to convince students that people lived peacefully and in harmony with nature in that once great and noble place known as the Third World. Before the white man exploited and destroyed it.

Fervent anti-Americanism is more prevalent on college campuses than anywhere else in society. American history, free enterprise, and white men are denigrated mercilessly. With twisted logic, the Left asserts that white men were in no way superior in any way to other peoples, and in fact, formed a vastly inferior culture to the Third World. Still, they somehow oppressed everybody else on the planet for centuries—their equals in every way.

The American university is saturated with Christianophobia—an irrational fear or animosity of Christians. An overwhelming number of academics admit they discriminate against Believers. The only group of people that it is approved to express hatred of openly on our college campuses is Christians. There are blatant patterns of prejudice, bigotry, stereotyping, and the dehumanization of persons who follow Christ.

As historian William Ringenberg says, "Explicitly Christian higher education was virtually the only form of American collegiate instruction until the years following the Civil War, while high morals were even more highly prized than academic excellence."

Harvard University was founded in 1636 for this express purpose: "Let every student be plainly instructed, and earnestly pressed to consider well, the main end of his life and studies is, to know God and Jesus Christ which is eternal life."

Columbia University, named of course for Christopher Columbus, was established in 1754 "to inculcate upon tender minds the great principles and Christianity and Morality."

Yale University was born in 1701, "To plant and under ye Divine blessing to propagate in this Wilderness, the blessed Reformed, Protestant Religion, in ye purity of its Order and Worship."

Until a little over 100 years ago, every president of Yale was a minister of the Gospel. At Yale daily life was to be like this: "All scholars shall live religious, godly, blameless lives according to the rules of God's Word, diligently reading the Holy Scriptures, the fountain of life and truth; and constantly attend upon all the duties of religion, both in public and in secret. Seeing God is the giver of all wisdom, every scholar, besides private or secret prayer, where all are bound to ask wisdom, shall be present morning and evening at public prayer."

Yale University now honors Larry Kramer by naming courses after him in 'Gay Studies.' What kind of man is this they revere so? Here are his own words about the dead from the AIDS epidemic: "I listed all the ones I'd slept with. There were a couple hundred. Was it my sperm that killed them, that did the trick? It is no longer possible for me to avoid this question of myself. Have you ever wondered how many men you killed? I know I murdered some of them. The sweet young boy who didn't know anything and was in awe of me. I was the first man who fucked him. I think I murdered him."

And that's not all. Mr. Kramer also wrote these choice words: "In those cases where children do have sex with their homosexual elders, I submit that that often, very often, the child desires the activity, even solicits it, either because of natural curiosity or because he or she is homosexual and innately knows it. Most gay men have warm memories of their earliest sexual encounters; when we share these stories with each other, they are invariably positive ones."

Two ministers founded Oberlin College in 1833. College President Charles Grandison Finney, also a famous evangelist, reported: "A goodly number of our students learn to work themselves in promoting revivals and are very efficient in laboring for the conversion of their fellow students."

Finney gave a speech to his students in 1862 on Moral Depravity. "You can see from this subject why men need regeneration, and also what regeneration is. It is the giving up of the carnal mind, a ceasing to mind the flesh, and giving up the whole mind to obey God. It is a change from being committed to self-gratification to the committal of the whole soul to obey God." Things have changed at Oberlin. Nowadays, about a thousand students attend an annual orgy held on campus with the full approval of the administration.

Some universities *require* students to affirm the goodness of homosexual behavior and will suspend them if they say something as obvious as, "homosexuals could stop doing it." College counselors will not be hired unless they agree with the normality of sexually deviant behaviors. But college faculties can openly mock and ridicule Christian beliefs with impunity. Students have been forced to perform homosexual acts in public against their will or flunk a class. Students have been required to participate in protests for adoption rights for sodomites.

American universities have departments for the study of religion. However, they are, to quote B. Alan Wallace, "the only academic field in which it is commonly assumed that those who neither believe nor practice their subject matter are better able to understand it and teach it than those who do. Indeed, some religious studies departments refuse to hire anyone who has deeply held religious beliefs."

The first universities of America were founded upon a religious vision of Evangelical Protestantism. As of 1900, chapel attendance was mandatory in almost all schools of higher learning. The supreme goal of education was to produce virtuous citizens. But as we know, today religious instruction is nearly nonexistent. In the name of 'inclusiveness,' Christianity has been excluded—forbidden any role in the shaping of beliefs in college. There is no valid reason why God and the Bible should be discriminated against in academics.

The Puritans were the world's biggest believers in higher education, establishing a college a mere six years after landing on Plymouth Rock. New England would soon have the best-educated men on the planet and keep that distinction for some decades. For 200 years, English colleges had a universal creed devised by Dr. Samuel Johnson: "As to religion, there is no intention to impose on the scholars the peculiar tenets of any particular denomination of Christians; but to inculcate upon their tender minds, the great principles of Christianity and morality in which true Christians of each denomination are generally agreed."

College was to promote good habits, proper behavior, and correct morals, to infuse society with Christian virtues, while not at all neglecting a zeal for learning and science. As far as how then we should live, Yahweh's revealed moral law is to what we must conform in our conduct. The judgment, taste, and understanding of ungodly men and women are darkened by sin.

Our most prestigious universities were founded for a far different mission than the pernicious purposes they are used for today. Christians founded all but two of the first 108 colleges created in America. The purpose of them was to provide for a Christian education. To learn what these institutions of higher learning were created for it is instructive to read a few of their mottos:

AMERICAN UNIVERSITY—For God and Country; BROWN UNIVERSITY—In God, we hope; COLUMBIA UNIVERSITY— Psalm 36:10 In thy light shall we see the light; DARTMOUTH— Luke 3:4 The voice of one crying in the wilderness; HARVARD— Truth for Christ and the Church; JOHNS HOPKINS UNIVERSITY— John 8:32 The truth will set you free; PRINCETON—Under God's power she flourishes.

Vigorous evangelicals that declared, "This institution will be Christian in its influence, discipline, and course of instruction," founded Wellesley College. Extensive Bible study was a requirement. The faculty had to be members of an evangelical church. Vassar and Smith were also established as Christian schools.

The University of Georgia, founded in 1785, was dedicated "to a system of public education in the spirit of Christianity with the Bible as the source and fountain of all true wisdom and government."

The University of North Carolina was created in 1789. It required students to attend morning and evening prayers, 'divine services' on Sunday, and every Sunday evening examinations on the general principles of morality and religion with the Holy Bible as the textbook.

By around 1800, Presbyterians were the leading educators in America. Our nation would not have an established denomination. Still, it would have a citizenry trained up with a standard set of beliefs and values. Before the Civil War, American colleges were religious institutions, and 80 percent of college presidents were pastors. Teachers and tutors kept a close eye on students and enforced a strict code of Christian conduct, acting as in *loco parentis*.

Along with morality and spiritual awakenings, America exploded with tremendous progress during this era in technology, law, medicine, industry, and science. As George Marsden writes, "Science was taught doxologically—emphasizing the design in nature for which one should praise the Creator."

It was strongly felt that the increase in knowledge must be accompanied by virtue. Otherwise, as President of Brown University, Francis Wayland warned, "Intellectual cultivation will only stimulate desire, and this unrestrained by the love of right, must eventually overturn the social fabric which it at first erected."

The University of California at Berkeley was founded in 1868 to provide "a Christian education with the American harmony of Christianity and learning under the pervading influence and spirit of the Christian religion." It specified, "A majority of the trustees shall always be members of evangelical Christian churches." The school bears the name of Bishop George Berkeley.

In 1869, the President of Yale, Noah Porter, wrote that American colleges had a moral responsibility to inculcate in students the self-discipline to fulfill their duties to family, friends, community, country, and God. "American colleges should have a positively religious and Christian character," proclaimed Porter. "Religious influences and religious teachings should be employed in colleges, in order to exclude and counteract the atheistic tendencies of much of modern science."

The views of atheists could be presented, but not without the beliefs of Christianity also introduced that refute a godless world. Because to give to students the former without the latter would be to *foster* a godless vision of the Cosmos.

But men were rising infatuated with Darwin, and with Comte's Positivism. They wanted universities to be scientific institutions only—with God banished to the church. Their overarching idea was that belief in Jesus was an outmoded step along the evolutionary path that would before long be as extinct as the Dodo Bird. Science was the only road to knowledge. But in reality, any subject, including science can be taught just as well within a Christian framework—better, in fact.

One of these reprobate men took over the presidency of Harvard for forty years, beginning in 1869, Charles Eliot. His big idea was to replace Christianity with what he named the Religion of the Future, which looks remarkably like the Secular Humanism of today.

Charles Hodge of Princeton told it how it was when he said, "Darwinism is atheism." He saw that Eliot, and others, were conniving to stamp out the authority of the Bible. Eliminating the foundation of everything Christianity stood for, the Miracles of Jesus, His Resurrection, and our chance at Salvation.

In 1872, Ezra Cornell would insist, "It shall be our aim, and our constant effort to make true Christian men. Cornell University is governed by a body of Christian Trustees, conducted by Christian Professors, and is a Christian Institution, as the Public School System of the State is Christian. At Cornell, the teacher shall instruct students in mental philosophy and ethics from a Christian standpoint."

The first President of Cornell, Andrew Dickson White, would have other ideas, which popped into his head after becoming a missionary for Darwinism. His goal was to evict Christianity from the university. In 1896, he wrote *A History of the Warfare of Science with Theology in Christendom*, a vicious vilification of all Christian beliefs, beginning with, "The old theory of direct creation is gone forever. Given all the evidence of human progress, it is incredible that any religion still taught the fall of humanity." And ending with how foolish it would be for any modern man to believe Jesus performed miracles. The Bible had no credibility anymore, he argued, and psychology would banish the supernatural. Instead of Scripture judging scientific theories, science should judge Scripture.

From this man and his book, the idea persists among the public today that the study of the material world and the Christian faith have always been enemies. Or in particular that faith has 'held back' scientific progress, with which no honest historian agrees. This is one of the many ideas that came from academia, was later discredited by academia, but the discrediting part never trickled down to the general public. That is because it is like the media today, which will publish a sensational story on one page of a new happening or novel idea, however dubious, but when the retraction comes, it gets a single paragraph hidden on page 34 that few will notice.

G. Stanley Hall began his career at Johns Hopkins University in 1881. At the time, psychology was part of philosophy. Hall, along with William James, established it as its own field of study. Hall's main thrust was to eliminate Christianity from having any influence in psychology; having decided that belief in Jesus was *unscientific*. He got some pushback from Professor Mark Hopkins, who maintained, "There is an abyss of skepticism and materialism into which, as the greatest of all intellectual disasters, those who cease to believe in the Scriptures are sure to be plunged."

Hall was on a mission to undermine the faith of his students. Psychology should replace Scripture as the foundation of a new world, he believed. And it should deconstruct Christianity by studying it through the lens of "the anthropology of myth, custom, religious belief, symbols, etc., among savages and ethnic stocks."

John D. Rockefeller provided the funding to establish a Christian university in Chicago "for the benefit of his fellow man and the glory of God." Named the University of Chicago, it was founded in 1890 by the American Baptist Education Association. The Baptists knew that it was Protestantism that had made America so great—sparking its love for individualism, democracy, freedom, and free enterprise, arousing a zeal for business, technology, and science, as well as unmatched competitiveness.

The man chosen to lead the new school was William Rainey Harper, who said: "Understand that my special business in the world is stirring up people on the English Bible." Harper had been working diligently to spread the Gospel across America. He directed the American Institute of Sacred Literature, promoting Sunday School and Bible study in public schools and colleges. He also founded the Religious Education Association and led a movement known as 'the Bible Renaissance,' which sought to uphold the Bible as the heart of American life and culture.

The thing that mattered most to Rockefeller was that the University of Chicago would *always* remain a clearly Christian academy. Harper agreed, writing, "Every possible effort has been made to emphasize the fact that the institution is a Christian institution. The first service was a chapel service. The first general university lecture was a Bible lecture. The first faculty meeting opened with prayer."

Harper saw education as part of the Christian mission to the world: "Education will be the watchword of the new Christianity. The Gospel will free men from vice and impurity." Before he died, he wrote, "the University of Chicago has been definitely and professedly Christian. We are citizens in a Christian country, so the University of Chicago is a Christian institution."

The University of Michigan became the leading research university by around 1900. It was an openly Christian institution under the guidance of a marvelous leader named James Angell, who served as president from 1871 to 1909. For Angell, there was no religion worthy of the name besides Christianity. He told his faculty and students: "The Christian spirit, which pervades the law, the customs, and the life of the state shall shape and color the life of the university." Angell also demanded that his faculty possess the "mental and moral qualities that will fit them to prepare their pupils for manly and womanly work in promoting our Christian civilization."

But other voices wanted the universities stripped of any Christian character, or superstition as they called it. Christian theology should be confined to church and the minds of individual believers, they demanded. These men used arguments such as that it was somehow unseemly to portray Christianity as better or above other religions from around the world. More and more academics had begun to doubt the Bible, as many of them announced, due to "the onward march of scientific discovery."

Such men declared that the Bible was just another book, a book of a primitive people at that, an embarrassment to modern intellectual men like themselves. Now that they had Darwinism, for the first time, they had what was at least a somewhat plausible alternative to the Genesis narrative. One of these men was John Dewey, who said in 1892 that if there were a God, He would not have revealed Himself to men.

The future President of the United States, Woodrow Wilson, served as President of Princeton University from 1902 to 1910. The son of a Presbyterian minister, Woodrow was an orthodox Christian who loved the Bible, believed in Jesus as his savior, thought God transformed individuals spiritually, and that God had revealed to us His moral law. Also, he thought that a nation would be blessed or cursed by God in accordance with its actions.

Wilson firmly held that academics were too much in thrall to science, giving it too much prestige, tending to make Man forget what a flawed creature he is. While transmitting knowledge was one purpose of a university, the highest calling was to transform the young into people of good character.

In a speech, Wilson said, "The scientific spirit of the age is doing us a great disservice, working in us a certain great degeneracy. It has given us agnosticism in the realm of philosophy. Experience is discredited. Science has not freed us from ourselves. It has not purged us of passion or disposed us to virtue. It has not made us less covetous or less self-indulgent." But despite his personal beliefs, Wilson bowed to pressure to drop Bible Study as a required course for incoming freshmen.

In 1909, *Cosmopolitan* magazine produced a shocking three-part series, *Blasting at the Rock of Ages*, which showed how disbelief was taught to pupils at American universities. The article, written by Harold Bolce, asserted: "Those who are not in close touch with the great colleges of the country will be astounded to learn the creeds being foisted by our great universities' faculties. In hundreds of classrooms it is being taught daily that the Decalogue is no more sacred than a syllabus; that the home as an institution is doomed; that there are no absolute evils; that immorality is simply an act in contravention of society's accepted standards; that democracy is a failure; and the Declaration of Independence only spectacular rhetoric; that the change from one religion to another is like getting a new hat; that moral precepts are passing shibboleths; that conceptions of right and wrong are as unstable a styles of dress."

Bolce was showing America that our universities were suddenly preaching a new gospel that was opposed to the Gospel of Christ preached in our churches. He had traveled around visiting our highest institutions of learning. At the (Methodist) University of Syracuse, he heard a lecture where the professor said, "It is unscientific and absurd to imagine that God ever turned stonemason and chiseled commandments on a rock."

Bolce also visited many ministers. He concluded: "No greater calamity could befall civilization than the academic destruction of the Gospel that there is but one Name among men whereby humanity can be saved. The unequivocal teaching of orthodox Christianity is that Man is ransomed by the Blood of Christ, which is being repudiated by college professors, who are declaring that the Fall of Man is a myth; that it was a Judean peasant, not a God, who was crucified on Calvary; and that shameful tragedy had absolutely nothing to do with the remission of sins."

William Jennings Bryan, the youngest man ever nominated to be President of the United States, who would run three times for that high office, emerged as a champion for the Bible. Since taxpayers supported most universities, he suggested the immediate termination of any leader of a college working to undermine the Gospel.

Some professors were actively trying to destroy faith in Jesus at many universities. Openly telling young men and women that they should throw their religion away because the Bible is not true. Bryan specifically called out the teaching of the Theory of Evolution, in particular the part being indoctrinated into the young that their ancestors were monkeys, because while "It is true that some believers in Darwinism retain their belief in Christianity; some also survive smallpox."

After the First World War, the slaughters of which cast serious doubts about the virtue of Christian Civilization, a wave of progressive professors became more militant about expelling God from college.

Professor of Psychology at Bryn Mawr, James Leuba, wrote a book detailing his, and his colleagues', disbelief in the Christian faith, asserting that they were superior to it in every way. Included was the idea that as people get better-educated, religious belief will disappear.

Leuba's evidence for this was a study he conducted showing that while 60% of scientists were members of a church, only 53% believed in Heaven. A mere 46% believed in a personal God who might answer their prayers. His main point was that among the most famous, prestigious, influential scientists, all these numbers were lower, with 35% believing in Heaven and 28% in having a personal relationship with God. His conclusion, therefore, was that the more intelligent one got, the less one would believe. (By the way, psychologists and sociologists were and are the least likely to be Believers.)

Leuba would later end up twisting it in the opposite direction, declaring that disbelief in the Lord must *make one a better scientist*. "A decrease of belief corresponds with an increase of general mental ability." He also found that the universities were persuading students to abandon their faith. Leuba claimed that at what he decided were the best colleges, four out of ten students no longer believed in Jesus by the time they graduated, this among young people who were Believers as freshmen. He attributed that to them growing more mature and intelligent due to the influence of their professors.

One thing that had changed was the immigration of tens of millions of Catholics and millions of Jews into America. These new arrivals did not want a Protestant education in public schools or at college. By 1919, Jews in America had risen to 3.5 percent of the population—seven times their percentage forty years earlier. And in America's universities, 10 percent of the students were Jews.

Duke University, founded in 1924, states in its bylaws: "Duke University aims to assert a faith in the eternal union of knowledge and religion set forth in the teachings and character of Jesus Christ the Son of God." Teachings contrary to Christianity would not be taught, said James B. Duke. At the same time, Cornell University was telling its kids that God was "created by the 'folk mind' as the projection of their longing and desires."

The Roaring Twenties had a remarkable effect on college life. The youth culture of the day was one of binge drinking, heavy petting, and fast cars. Young Americans were having too much fun to let God spoil the party. One commentator famously said that their grandfathers believed in Jesus, their fathers weren't too sure, and this generation just ignored Him. They did not understand the Bible—they hadn't read it.

Religious instruction began to disappear, while some departments, notably sociology and psychology, were openly hostile to the supernatural. God was confined to the Theology Department, as far as curriculum goes.

We can also follow the Young Men's Christian Association's (YMCA) demise on college campuses. In 1920, three-quarters of all American colleges had a chapter of the YMCA, and every seventh student belonged to it (90,000 souls). By 1940, less than half those chapters remained, and only one in thirty students took part (50,000). To stay relevant, the YMCA dropped Bible Study and Evangelism, in favor of 'doing good deeds.'

In 1931, historian Carl Becker would write, "It is quite impossible for us to regard Man as the child of God for whom the Earth was created as a temporary habitation. Rather we must regard him as little more than a chance deposit on the surface of the world, carelessly thrown up between two ice ages by the same forces that rust iron and ripen corn. What is a man that the electron should be mindful of him?"

Becker was the President of the American Historical Association, to whom he gave a speech about how history does not exist. Because facts do not exist. Only interpretations exist. For the new atheist, Marxism was attractive, because gave them *something* to believe in.

As late as 1937, the President of Yale spoke these words to his school: "I call on all faculty members, as members of the thinking body, freely to recognize the tremendous validity and power of the teachings of Christ. The maintenance and building up of the Christian religion is a vital part of university life." And in 1940, half of American universities still had compulsory chapel services.

In 1947, Robert Maynard Hutchins admonished: "Civilization is doomed unless the hearts and minds of men can be changed and unless we can bring about a moral, intellectual and spiritual reformation." The problem, he declared, was that education in America "centers upon those aspects of human life least likely to elevate and ennoble the human spirit."

By 1950, an enormous change had taken place. As William F. Buckley Jr. noted, the History Department had become "vigorously atheistic with little mercy on either God or on those who believe in Him." Debunking the faith was a pastime of professors. The Social Science Department treated priests and ministers as "the modern counterpart of the witch doctor."

Either indifference or hatred of religious faith was the spirit of the age. Christianity had been dismissed as a part of the life of an educated person. In the social sciences, faith was ignored as irrelevant to the lives and societies of the human race—an odd position, if one thinks about it. Reinhold Niebuhr put it in perspective: "The religious problem is the ultimate issue in education. Religion deals with the meaning of the whole so that attempting to find meaning in life in anything less than the divine amounts to idolatry."

However! A revival broke out in America's colleges in the 1950s. It featured growing religious interest among students, and serious concerns among faculty and the public about the anti-Christian atmosphere on campuses, which was falsely represented by the godless as 'neutrality.' Campus Crusade for Christ and the InterVarsity Christian Fellowship flourished.

In 1953, a devout Christian took over leadership at Harvard. Nathan M. Pusey rebuked the idea prevalent among liberal 'Christians' that good deeds were what it was all about. We needed to remember: "Faith is the consciousness that moral values and spiritual experiences have a sacred character."

Like other schools, Harvard had become not neutral but anti-religious. It had replaced the True Faith not with nothing but with Secular Humanism. What was at stake was what generations of children would learn about the Cosmos' most fundamental nature. The powers that be had efficiently banished Christ from the very universities that had been created in His Name.

But alas, in the 1960s, what we witness in universities is what George Marsden called a dramatic shift toward dropping distinctive Christian identity. The Christian faith was deemed irrelevant and divisive.

In the best-selling book *Secular City* (1965), Harvey Cox applauded the complete secularization of the university: "The whole idea of a 'Christian' college has little meaning. The term Christian is not one that can be used to refer to universities any more than to observatories or laboratories." Any Christian presence there he called a catastrophe. Man must shift his focus from religion to politics. That was the answer. The religious stage of history was over now, and "man must assume responsibility for his world. He can no longer shove it off on some divine power." So that is what 2,000 years of prayer, worship, and devotion had been all about: shirking responsibility!

It is a diabolical reading of the First Amendment that concludes the government cannot help fund education that includes a religious perspective. That false interpretation without question prohibits the Free Exercise of Religion. By excluding the Christian perspective, our schools implicitly promote anti-Christian viewpoints because that point of view is not banned from schools.

The so-called Blaine Amendments of 38 states prohibit financial assistance to schools whose central character is Christian, or to any colleges that teach from a perspective that there is a God. Schools may and do instill the standpoint that there is not a God and receive government funding galore.

Since the federal government began giving billions of dollars to universities in the 1960s, Christian colleges, especially Catholic colleges, have bent over backward to prove they are secular and not religious—otherwise, no largess for you. Or, as Marsden puts it, they "typically did all they could to demonstrate that their religious commitments made no real difference in how they taught their subjects." Religiously committed scholars and schools face discrimination as a matter of routine.

Satan spread the lie through college textbooks that the original followers of Christ were the very poorest and most miserable and bitter people in the world. These textbooks called it *deprivation theory*, which teaches that people adopt supernatural solutions to their material misery if it is impossible for them to escape it; that such a movement is only found among foolish men without power or position, unlettered men. That comes directly from the sinister atheist Karl Marx, who claimed, "Religion is the sigh of the oppressed creature."

But Paul did not say that *none* of the first Christians were powerful or of noble birth. He said that not many of them were, which means *some of them were*. Well, only some people of any group are powerful or of noble birth. It is known that Christianity spread more rapidly at first among the educated, and women of the upper classes. Pliny said in AD 112 that the Christians were individuals of every age and class. A number of the famous ancient Christian martyrs were, in fact, quite wealthy.

So-called scholars even taught college students that Jesus was illiterate. That is blatantly false. He read from the Torah in synagogues. Throughout His life, we see how immensely familiar He is with the Hebrew Scriptures.

Our universities teach the same thing as stated by both the *Encyclopedia Britannica* and British Museum of Natural History: "Darwin did two things: he showed that evolution was a fact contradicting scriptural legends of creation and that its cause, natural selection, was automatic, with no room for divine guidance or design."

They disregard the fact that our most complex supercomputers are far simpler in design than a living single-celled creature. To say that such an organism arose by random chance out of inorganic material is sillier than to claim computers arose spontaneously one day in an electronics store.

A recent survey shows how well our education system is achieving its satanic aims. Only one in two hundred 18-25-year-olds today holds a Christian worldview—down from one in seven just one generation ago. When people lose their faith, they lose their sense of meaning and purpose, and lose their will to perpetuate their civilization. They stop having children.

Since the 1970s, our universities have been marinated in the idea that the Bible is not historic—which is the primary claim of the Word of God. The Bible is instead presented as nothing but a collection of folklore and myth. The existence of the supernatural is flat out denied.

Students report that they are personally and viciously attacked for expressing a Christian point of view—even in religion or philosophy classes. Saying out loud that you believe in the Bible is sure to result in reduced grades. The Bible is universally rejected on most college campuses today.

Along with the supposed 'evolution of man' from apes is the false implication that being truthful has 'evolved' enormously among men. Postmodern 'scholars' routinely dismiss people who wrote long ago as liars and idiots, especially Christians. The idea is widespread in our universities that all Christian writers in the past were liars—despite that being a grave sin *to them*. But modern scholars who are atheists, now they always tell the truth because they have no bias—*as if* not believing in God makes one objective and honest.

Communists far outnumber Republicans in social science fields. As Bradley C.S. Watson reports in the *Claremont Review of Books*, "Sociologists report they would rather hire a communist than a Republican. Evangelicals and members of the National Rifle Association fare even worse."

Conservative professors are scarce, and in some of the most politicized and fashionable fields—such as gender and cultural studies—none can be found. Our universities expose precious few students to anything like social or cultural conservatism. Because academic liberals rarely ever even meet a conservative on campus, leftists have no reality check.

Conservatives labor under what liberals might call 'systemic discrimination' and 'glass ceilings.' In many fields, conservatives must remain in the closet to keep their employment. But cultural conservatives are the defenders of an intellectual tradition with roots in essential thinkers from the ancient world (Aristotle) to the Enlightenment (Burke). Watson writes, "These people seem to have no natural home in the progressive academy. Jobs for them either don't exist or, if they do, they end up at less prestigious colleges than their scholarly records would predict."

Conservatives of any sort are exceptionally rare at liberal arts colleges, where the transmission of an intellectual tradition might be particularly important. The absence of conservative professors means that most students miss out on potentially necessary correctives to popular culture. "Academic progressivism is a religion of many taboos. For example, most students are unlikely to be exposed to certain research concerning the socio-economic importance of family structure or sexual difference," Watson says.

Conservative professors exist, but research conducted by Shields and Dunn came up with only 153 conservatives out of more than a million professors in the United States, many of whom wished to remain anonymous. The purported tolerance of the academy seldom extends to a faculty meeting where someone proposes a challenge to progressive orthodoxy, especially anything that smacks of cultural conservatism.

There was also survey done that asked college professors to list the two hundred leading intellectuals in America. There was not a single Christian named. Those intellectuals were asked to identify which previous thinkers had most influenced them the most, and twenty-one names were mentioned above all others—not one Christian was among them. What is an intellectual? A person who loves ideas more than people?

George Marsden writes, "One of the strongest current motives for discriminating in academia even against traditional religious viewpoints is that many advocates of such viewpoints are prone to be politically conservative and to hold views regarding lifestyle, the family, or sexuality that may be offensive to powerful groups on campuses. Hence, in the name of tolerance and diversity, academic expressions of such religious perspectives may be discriminated against. Tolerance, one might think, ought to include tolerance of religious viewpoints, including religious viewpoints in academic life. Since religion is integral to most cultures, one might expect that a commitment to diversity would entail the encouragement of intellectual expressions of a variety of religious perspectives, not intolerance toward and exclusion of a whole class of viewpoints."

Feminists have exerted enormous control over education in the United States. They have revised textbooks from elementary school to the highest institutions of learning. Their speech codes and sensitivity training have permeated life at university.

Feminists demanded and won a drastic lowering of hiring standards so that women, minorities, and lesbians could receive preferential treatment at universities. A white man seeking a professorship has no chance against a black lesbian despite a gigantic disparity in qualifications that can be measured. Unqualified professors lead to a lousy quality of education for students. But the agenda of Feminism has nothing to do with education—such as science and mathematics—and everything to do with brainwashing young women into a worldview that is as phony as a three-dollar bill.

Daphne Patai and Noretta Koertge elucidated in *Professing Feminism*: "Our culture, including all that we are taught in schools and universities, is so infused with patriarchal thinking that it must be torn up root and branch if genuine change is to occur. Everything must go—even the allegedly universal disciplines of logic, mathematics, and science, and the intellectual values of objectivity, clarity, and precision on which the former depends. Feminism is not merely about equal rights for women. Feminism aspires to be much more than this. Feminist theory provides a doctrine of original sin: The world's evils originate in male supremacy."

Feminists have implemented 'women's studies' programs at more than 600 colleges. What these programs offer students is not the study of serious knowledge but political correctness to the point of downright silliness. They must adhere to moral relativism because much of what they teach is palpably preposterous.

Students in these classes are commanded to stand up and testify as to their suffering at the hands of men, which is designed to make them both miserable and wrathful. Feminists declare that the oppression of women is worldwide and never-ending. Still, they save their vitriol for America, the supposed oppressor of not only women but of every living creature except white men.

Professor Christina Hoff Sommers believes women's studies programs should issue warning labels to parents: "We will help your daughter discover the extent to which she has been in complicity with the patriarchy. We will encourage her to reconstruct herself through dialogue with us. She may become enraged and chronically offended. She will very likely reject the religious and moral codes you raised her with. She may well distance herself from family and friends. She may change her appearance and even her sexual orientation. She may end up hating you (her father) and pitying you (her mother). After she has completed her re-education with us, you will certainly be out tens of thousands of dollars and very possibly be out one daughter as well."

Christians are systematically silenced in our colleges. Ask yourself, what would happen if other groups, such as homosexual activists, race grievance groups, or vegetarians, were not allowed to share their views on campus?

Christians rightly believe that Christ can and will improve the lives of individuals and our society in general. And yet their message is the only one denounced as delusional, ignorant, and dangerous. The feminists and the Marxists are allowed to shout their destructive doctrines from college rooftops.

Separating Christians out by calling them and their message 'religious' is a devilish trick that has been quite successful. The fact is that the Christians are the only one of these various proselytizing groups that possesses proof their program actually works! Christians ARE less violent; have more stable marriages and families; produce better future citizens; are happier, healthier, live longer, and are far more generous with their time and money to the needy. For any honest person, there is no question that the Christian faith has made the world a far better place, having originated charity, hospitals, nursing homes, colleges, schools, social work, and orphanages, et al.

The kids are suffering from committing so much sin, with the encouragement of the culture and the university. College counseling offices are swamped with students who are spiritually sick. An astonishing 44 percent of college students are reported to have severe psychological problems—nearly triple the percentage reported just ten years earlier. They commonly suffer from depression, anxiety, eating disorders, self-abuse, alcohol and drug abuse, and suicidal orientation. Forty-six percent of college students said they feel hopeless, and 31 percent say they have been so depressed that they could not function. No amount of hedonism can assuage a human heart suffering under the weight of a guilty conscience produced by a mountain of sin. Douglas Axe laments, "Contemplate for just a moment the dystopian vision of a generation of human beings believing in their hearts that they are nothing more than bestial accidents fending for themselves in a world where morality is a fiction."

Leftists control the commanding heights of college, partly by controlling who gets accredited to be a college. As always, sex, or more precisely sexual perversion, trumps all other considerations. At least one Christian college (Gordon) was threatened with losing its accreditation and shunned by its surrounding community because it will not affirm aberrant behaviors—even though its mission was serving the destitute, and it was good at it. Its students worked as free tutors for the neediest children. They mentored teenagers from terrible neighborhoods where they also cared for orphans. On top of that, they volunteered for leper colonies and helped people build homes.

The university is used as a weapon by Satan's servants to push scientism. The funding for research is only available for scientists who will promote a godless universe and the idea that the brain produces consciousness. "Scientists are extremely good at explaining the material aspects of reality. So it came to pass that they came to believe they should be good at explaining all aspects of reality," explains one famous professor at UCLA. But science cannot explain human behavior, or what it means to be a person, a human being in the real world.

The fact is that scientism is like the *Emperor's New Clothes*. It absurdly tells us we are nothing more than a random combination of atoms living a meaningless life, merely smart monkeys clinging to a routine rock hurtling through space on a journey to nowhere. Our own experience shows us how absurd that story is. But in our universities, the myth must be propped up, as the Emperor stands up there, bare-assed naked, thinking he is wearing a marvelous and powerful suit.

On our university campuses, it has been pronounced "immoral for academics or academic institutions to proclaim moral views," says eminent scholar Stanley Fish. But political activism is essential to the academic mission, so says history textbook writer Eric Foner (another atheist socialist). According to him, college professors should encourage left-wing activism to change the world. You see, when they speak sneeringly at 'morals,' they only mean traditional American Christian righteousness. Teaching or advancing left-wing atheist communist immorality is 'political activism.'

Textbooks no longer teach the truth. Instead, they are designed to further the political agenda of the Left. As Robert Bork has reported, there are plenty of "teachers who see themselves as political activists whose campaign headquarters just happen to be the classroom. Professors openly describe themselves as advocates for radical change in society. They teach courses to make converts to an ideology, always a liberal to left ideology."

These actions by American college professors are entirely based on known falsifications. They act like their 'scholarly' research is objective when, in fact, it is designed *a priori*. These professors present their 'research' as expert analysis when, in fact, it is nothing more than propaganda—and they know it. But the public is deceived by this manipulation of reality because the supposed 'expert' appears to be one of the foremost in their field. They are falsifying information to further the political agenda of the progressive Intelligentsia.

Beginning in the 1970s, leftists gradually gained control of the universities by taking over the hiring, promotion, and tenure committees, which they have used to exclude conservatives from colleges in the name of inclusiveness. They learned this trick from the Frankfort School. Gramsci and Marcuse preached that the focus of the godless must be to take over universities because that is where the citizens of tomorrow are taught what is real. The idea was revolutionary tolerance, which meant that to ban conservative ideas and blacklist conservative thinkers was "liberation from oppression."

The student campus radicals from the Sixties have so taken over our universities, that all of the past is now interpreted through the lens of race, class, and gender. That is a recipe for the repression of knowledge through campus thought police, as opposed to the warrant for which universities exist: the quest for truth.

The demand for conformity is what is most striking. If I recall correctly, the counterculture revolutionaries of the 1960s, who are now the Left in this country, named conformity as their greatest enemy. They would not conform to their parents' customs, traditions, values, morality, religion, or authorities.

What has happened is, they have replaced one system of conformity with another. The older system expected people to find a mate for life, get married, stay married, and raise a family together; to work hard, save money for a rainy day, and generally eschew buying things on credit; to not have babies out of wedlock nor kill them during gestation; to keep their perversions to themselves; to go to church, read the Bible, obey the law, be a patriot, love God and country; to frown on divorce, adultery, and fornication; to know your neighbors, join free associations, and better your community, and not to envy or covet what others have. Naturally, people being people, not everybody conformed—but most did, and the radicals of the Sixties hated them for it.

Blinded by Science

"God created man in His image. He wants us to recognize and know His design for the Universe: The chief aim of all investigations of the external world should be to discover the rational order and harmony which has been imposed on it by God."
~ Johann Kepler

Every day on Facebook I encounter people who tell me they won't believe anything unless a scientist says it. Science has become their religion, and scientists their priests who convey ultimate truth to their disciples. The problem is that scientists are wrong much of the time, and their 'truth' is fleeting and ever-changing.

For instance, scientists are easy targets for hoaxes, if the hoax seems to prove their presuppositions (what they suppose, assume, or take for granted as true in advance). The gullible scientific community touted Piltdown Man as the 'missing link' for forty years before it was exposed as a fraud. We seem to forget that everything men do is flawed because men are flawed. Scientists are not exempt.

The truths of science come and go, change in part or entirely as time goes by. Each generation of scientists rewrites its textbooks to select from the past what they still have faith is accurate. But more than that to suppress the enormous pile of errors, hoaxes, lunacies, and falsified results—that to dispute the veracity of would once have, in the not too distant past, gotten you kicked out of the scientific community.

Studies show that the bias of researchers often distorts the results of scientific research. And yet, there are those among us who, if a scientific expert told them arsenic was good for you, would take their word for it—and admonish any doubters they are 'science deniers' who 'hate science.'

I love science. I cherish all human knowledge and wisdom. All Christians should appreciate science because it enables us to see the glory and majesty of God's creative power. Some want to believe science can measure everything, but we simpletons know it cannot do so. The study of consciousness, chaos theory, and quantum physics tells us some things cannot be measured *if anything* can truly be.

Scientism, a.k.a. scientific materialism is the view that only science has anything important to say about the human condition. It specifically rejects belief in God and the supernatural; it rejects boundaries for science. It is scientism—not science itself—that leads some people to think that Christ and science are at odds. Scientific materialism will pass away.

The word 'truth' is used fifty times by the Apostle Paul in his epistles. Many scientific facts have changed in the last ten years. And even scientists in the same field today dispute many 'scientific facts'.

Science was founded as a means to know God, not as an end in itself. "The greatest myth in the history of science and religion holds that they have been in a state of constant conflict," contends the historian of science Ronald Numbers. That pernicious myth continues to be promulgated in science magazines and textbooks.

According to Michael Keas of *Salvo* magazine, science and biblical religion have been friends for a long time. Judeo-Christian theology has contributed in a friendly manner to such science-promoting ideas as discoverable natural history, experimental inquiry, universal natural laws, mathematical physics, and investigative confidence, balanced with humility.

Since the medieval university, Christian institutions have often provided a supportive environment for scientific inquiry and instruction. David Lindberg, a leading historian of medieval science, has concluded, "no institution or cultural force offered more encouragement for the investigation of nature than did the Christian Church."

The Scientific Revolution only happened in Christendom, a society immersed in the Christian worldview, which is that a creative, rational intelligence is behind the Cosmos and its natural laws. Only Christianity had taught man that God's Creation is orderly and designed for discovery by His human image-bearers. Only in the Christian view did Creation have a definite beginning, experience unique stages of development, and is moving towards a purposeful end.

It was solely in medieval Christian universities that science was first institutionalized and taught generation after generation. Many Catholic priests made significant discoveries over the centuries, including Georges Lemaitre, the proposer of the Big Bang Theory. The foundation of science rests on truths that cannot be discovered scientifically. The scientific enterprise cannot stand alone in providing comprehensive answers to life's ultimate questions. It takes a certain kind of world for the study of it to even be possible, and it was only the Christian worldview that enabled science to emerge and flourish.

Science does not have all the answers. Scientists believe in energy and consciousness, but they do not know what they are. Genesis tells us who we are, and from whence we came. The more science has examined the world, the more it agrees that the Genesis account is the correct sequence of events. What Genesis says happened is real, even though it was written 3,400 years ago by a man who was no scientist, but a conduit through whom God speaks to us.

Life never emerges from non-life. Science cannot explain the existence of life. Science says that the Universe came into being from nothing in less than one minute. And all of a sudden, here is a million billion miles of space, with ten billion degrees of heat. And within three minutes, all matter that will ever be was created. Science has no idea how that happened. Moses knew.

Even atheists agree that the Cosmos and everything in it can be traced back to an ultimate creation event - that the Universe and all its space-time dimensions had a beginning. That IS evidence for a Creator; some refuse to see it. They have no other explanation.

The Holy Bible teaches us that YHWH is the only uncreated Being that exists. He created our Cosmos, bringing into existence space and time, establishing physical and moral laws, enduing inanimate matter with life, and endowing human beings with spiritual capacities.

The Bible, thousands of years ago, taught us that Creation continues to expand; that it operates by fixed laws; that one of those laws is a pervasive 'Law of Entropy' or decay. In the Bible, life appears as a procession from simple to more complex, culminating in Adam. Life progresses from merely being alive to 'soulish' (having intellect, will, and relational capacity) to spiritual (creative, cultural, morally aware, worshipful). Men wrote it down millennia before modern science emerged, which is evidence that they had received revealed wisdom from YHWH. According to the Holy Bible, the Creation began when God created all matter, energy, space, and time—instantly and subject to physical laws. He made the Cosmos as our home.

Science says that the Big Bang was an enormously powerful yet perfectly fine-tuned burst, in which time, space, matter, and energy all came into existence in an instant, along with the physical laws that govern them, from a source beyond our Universe. In other words, the Bible and science agree. The Bible gave us this knowledge thousands of years ago. Scientists predominately disputed the idea until relatively recently. Score one for the Bible.

In the same sequence, with which science agrees, God made plants, then animals, and His last move was to create a single pair of human beings—male and female He made them. Adam and Eve were given free will to obey or disobey Him. They only had one thing they could not do. They did it anyway. Man has had a rebellious nature ever since. The presence of sin in our world has brought untold pain and suffering, not to mention death. God sent His Son to redeem us, to atone for us, to save us. All redeemed persons will live forever in a new paradise God will create for us.

Using common-sense science, we can see how incredible it is that Earth is just right to be our home. If we see a conflict between scientific truth and biblical truth, we misunderstand one or the other. Science agrees that where we live, on Earth, our home, exhibits more than 500 unique characteristics that are exquisitely fine-tuned to allow life to exist. If gravity were a trillion trillion trillionth weaker, there would be no planets or galaxies; if it were stronger by that same minute amount, the Universe would collapse.

What kind of cosmic accident is it that Earth happens to be in the perfect place in the Milky Way? If we were closer to its edge, there would be no planet Earth; if we were closer to its center, radiation would kill us. We are just the right distance from the Sun for life to exist, with just the right orbit, and just the right moon to stabilize our tilt and, thus, our temperatures. Earth would not be able to sustain its atmosphere and protect us from cosmic rays if it were a wee bit smaller. If Earth were a hair bigger, gravity would be too strong.

Scientists say the human race appeared on Earth at the perfect time in the scientific history of our planet. The light and heat from the Sun have been exceptionally stable for about 50,000 years—the same period when scientists see man burst onto the archaeological record. Before man appears, the Earth was rotating much faster, producing winds of thousands of miles per hour over days shorter than our current 24 hours—and 24-hour days are perfect for us. If our days were just one hour longer, the temperature extremes would cause widespread mortality, and agricultural production would be severely hampered.

I find that much of the skepticism regarding the Creator is the result of a misunderstanding about what science has discovered about the Cosmos in which we exist. The Copernican Principle is a mistaken conclusion drawn from the Copernican Revolution. The Earth *is* the center of God's Universe regardless of whether it is physically dead center. To understand this, we must first come to grips with the difference between Earth and any other place in our Universe.

The Universe is utterly hostile to life. We have searched the heavens at minimum 78,000,000,000,000,000,000,000 miles away (if I calculated correctly) without finding any evidence of any life anywhere else whatsoever. Meanwhile, the Earth is teeming with an incredible array of living creatures with more than two million species named by taxonomists thus far. That ought to show us something important.

What are the scientific facts that tell us how rare the Earth is? Mostly, these have to do with how exquisitely God designed the Earth and placed it in the Universe. There would be no Earth filled with life if any of the following were changed by approximately 3 percent: The magnetic field; the size and proximity of the moon; the depth of the Earth's crust; the level of oxygen and nitrogen; the temperature; and the atmosphere and atmospheric pressure.

Those who believe in the Copernican Principle fail to see that Earth is the perfect observatory for human beings to view the heavens. On no other planet we have found, does there exist the combination of 'coincidences' that provides us with a clear view of the Universe. Why such a great view from Earth? God is granting us knowledge of the heavens so that we might see His glory.

One would think that a field such as science would always be open to new ideas. But there is one idea to which the men who hold the commanding heights of the official scientific organizations cannot abide, and that is that there is, or even might be, a God. For one example, the Royal Society of London claims that the Theory of Evolution is supported by evidence but that the idea that the Universe might be designed and therefore have a Designer is not supported by evidence. They refuse to even look at the proof of the latter, which is quite plentiful.

Our government schools are urged to teach and only teach atheistic evolution as the only possibility of the origin of life. Really? A godless universe *is the only possibility*? That is a pretty strong statement that reveals more about the people who made it than it does about the Universe.

If you do see Intelligent Design mentioned in a science journal it is generally accompanied by scoffing ridicule, paired with terms such as "an intellectual virus, pseudo-science, insidious, terrifying, threatening, and a return to the Dark Ages." These people yearn for scientific research to disprove the possibility that God exists, but I've got news for them: It hasn't and never will because God is alive and well.

Intelligent Design is not a religious movement, as its enemies shriek. It is a theory based on evidence, and it makes more sense to interpret our Cosmos as the product of intelligent design, not a cosmos that appeared out of nothing by chance. In other words, mind created matter. Matter did not develop minds. That is a scientific argument, not a religious one. More and more scientists are becoming convinced that the Universe is designed. Some very famous former atheists now believe there must be some sort of Designer, even if they have not become religious.

Orson Scott Card has said that the reaction of Darwinists to the very idea that our Universe *could be* designed is "illogical, personal, and unscientific, resorting to credentialism and expertism. Real science never has to resort to credentialism. If someone with no credentials at all raises a legitimate question, it is not an answer to point out how uneducated or unqualified the questioner is. It is pretty much an admission that you don't have an answer, so you want the questioner to go away. Expertism is the 'trust us you poor fools' defense. Essentially the Darwinists tell us we are too dumb to understand."

William Rusher observes how nasty Darwinists can get: "One can't help being a little surprised at the sheer savagery of the evolutionists' attack on Intelligent Design. One thinks of scientists as calm, intelligent people, perhaps wearing white smocks, who take on questions to which we don't know the answers, think about them carefully, and test various explanations experimentally until they come up with one that solves the problem."

But that hasn't been the reaction at all of the evolutionists to Intelligent Design. They have all but bitten themselves in two trying to drive it straight out of the realm of serious discussion. The haters of God declare that Intelligent Design is not in any 'peer-reviewed science journals.' But they control those journals! And any article submitted that presents Intelligent Design Theory is not published. It's a neat trick. Anyone who challenges their worldview is either ignored or ridiculed. It is a rigged game. Some of the most important discoveries in scientific history have come from men who were not peer-reviewed.

Ann Coulter writes, "No one disputes that organisms can develop small improvements on something that already exists. Otherwise, there would be no health clubs." Charles Darwin said that, according to his theory, hundreds of mutations would be necessary to produce the first wing or nose gradually—and each one of those mutations would have to itself prove beneficial to the critter. As Ms. Coulter points out, "The first mutations toward a nose would make you look funny, and no one would want to reproduce with you."

The godless will answer that we must admit it is *possible* evolution is true. Coulter responds, "It's also possible that the galactic ruler Xenu brought billions of people to Earth 75 million years ago, piled them around volcanoes, and blew them up with hydrogen bombs, sending their souls flying every which way until the landed on the bodies of living humans, where they still invisibly reside today—as Scientology's L. Ron Hubbard claimed."

Evolution cannot be observed or tested in a science lab. Therefore it is not science. As Coulter explains, "Imagine a giant raccoon passed gas, and perhaps the resulting gas might have created the wide variety of life we see on Earth. And if you don't accept the giant raccoon flatulence theory for the origin of life, you must be a fundamentalist Christian who believes the Earth is flat. That's basically how the argument for evolution goes."

After the Piltdown Man fraud, for forty years hailed as a peer-reviewed scientific FACT that proved Darwin right, came the peppered moth, what atheist evolutionist Jerry Coyne called the prize horse of natural selection. It was taught to every schoolchild for fifty years as *scientific fact* that proves the Theory of Evolution is a *scientific fact*. But it was trickery.

The famous photos were staged by gluing dead moths to tree trunks. The phony pictures still appear in some textbooks, as do Haeckel's bogus embryos that were proven fraudulent a hundred years ago. Despite being a known hoax, schoolchildren are taught that the peppered moth is "the most striking evolutionary change ever actually witnessed in any organism," and "the most spectacular evolutionary change ever witnessed and recorded by man."

One of the greatest deceptions is the story of the Scopes Monkey Trial. It is taught to schoolchildren through the fake film, presented as historically accurate, *Inherit the Wind*. According to leftists, as Ann Coulter says so well: "A brave high school biology teacher named John Scopes tried to educate his illiterate, toothless students in backwater Dayton, Tennessee, by teaching them 'science.' For his trouble, he was nearly lynched by fundamentalist Christians, who stormed his classroom and arrested him on the spot for teaching Darwin's Theory of Evolution," and threw him into prison.

All lies. The ACLU hatched the whole prank in New York to recruit a southern teacher who would agree to be prosecuted by backwoods hicks, all of which the *New York Times* would breathlessly report to make them look stupid, and to demonize Christians.

Scopes was a gym teacher who never taught evolution and was not a biology teacher. He did not spend one minute in jail. At the real trial, the most famous atheist in the world, Scope's lawyer Clarence Darrow, would compare Christians to rabid dogs who ought to be killed to protect the citizenry, and repeated one of the most terrible of all atheistic lies that Christianity was the cause of the bitterness, hatred, war, and cruelty in the world.

The basis for the Scopes Trial was a 1925 law passed by the Tennessee legislature that made it illegal for children to be taught they descended from apes, i.e., that denies the divine creation of Man revealed in the Holy Bible. The jury found Scopes guilty and levied a $100 fine.

There are fourteen significant discrepancies between the movie and the real-life events. For one, the film does not show that the crux of the godless case was Piltdown man and Heidelberg man—both shams. For another, the two attorneys were supposed to have the chance to interrogate the other on the witness stand. Darrow interrogated the Defender of the Faith William Jennings Bryan, a three-time Democrat candidate for president, under oath. But when it came time for Darrow to take the stand, Scopes suddenly pled guilty in a canny move to keep the press from hearing Bryan poke holes in Darrow's atheism and Theory of Evolution.

It was the New York newspapers that made it appear to have been a contest between backwoods religious nuts and cosmopolitan educated scientists, when in fact, just as many scientists shared Bryan's Christianity as agreed with Darrow's skepticism.

Piltdown Man was said to be 500,000 years old. It was exhibited in the British Museum so schoolchildren could see their 'ancestor.' It would become the subject of the doctoral theses of 500 scientists. It was deliberate deceit. The skull was soaked in potassium dichromate, which fooled the world's best scientific minds into believing it was 500,000 years old—not its actual age of about 300 years. It featured an orangutan jaw and ape fangs glued inside.

Then there was Beijing Man, and others, all frauds, but believed and taught to schoolchildren as 'proof that evolution is a scientific fact' because atheists used old bones to create imaginary scenarios. Nebraska Man was yet another con that was used to prove 'evolution is a fact.' From a single tooth, scientists decided they had found the missing link. Illustrators created a half-ape-half-human creature complete with his wife and children for our textbooks. Well, it ends up it was a pig tooth. The President of the Natural History Museum in New York, also a prominent member of the atheist organization known as the ACLU, perpetrated the bamboozlement.

Richard Dawkins says that if you teach children about Jesus, it is child abuse. He also describes the New Testament as a sadomasochistic doctrine, and says Christians are fascists of the American Taliban. But from Marx to Hitler, the men responsible for the greatest mass murders of the twentieth century were avid Darwinists, like Dawkins, not churchmen like Billy Graham. As Darwinism gained currency, humanity sank into degradation and brutalization.

Often the godless assert that science has debunked God. No evidence in any real science debunks God. The irreligious put out a laundry list of grievances against the God they say isn't there. They do not want Him to be there. Richard Dawkins agrees with Adolf Hitler that Christianity is like a pox on humanity. Instead of seeking the truth, both of them wanted to justify evil because it is what they wanted to do.

In 1850, virtually all scientists were Christians, exploring God's thrilling Creation. It was the followers of Darwin who wanted God eliminated from science. Today, of all the colleges in the country, a mere 1 percent teach from a godly worldview, and virtually all museums espouse the Darwinist view. The new American is being molded into an atheist or pagan, sexual deviants immersed in the Occult.

A majority of scientists are not atheists. However, atheists now control almost all scientific institutions. Of all scientists, four out of ten believe in the Creator; only one-sixth are atheists. But among members of the National Academy of Sciences, only 7 percent believe in the Creator, and two-thirds do not think there is a God at all.

Many unbelievers have testified that it was Darwinism that led them away from belief in God. Thus Satan used this phony Theory of Evolution to separate Man from his Creator. That would enable him to easily tempt men and women into sin, unmoored from moral law, fearing no judgment, wanting no salvation.

Science is part of the dominion our Father has given us over the Earth. To use it against Him is to misuse this great gift. You can make a god out of science, but science is littered with a graveyard of discarded ideas that people now laugh at, and are indeed incredulous that anybody ever believed them.

The scientific materialist teaches that every human action or feeling is due to evolution—and nothing else. Any scientist who suggests otherwise, such as that we have minds apart from our physical selves, and the Cosmos appears, based on the evidence, to have been designed the way it is, risks being fired and blacklisted from further employment.

Worshipers of science love to claim that they follow facts while Christians have blind faith in fairy tales. But the Bible teaches that real faith is built on reason and evidence. The Bible, in both Testaments, shows us that it is essential to test any truth claim. The scientific method, in fact, has its origins in Scripture.

Belief in God and Jesus is rational, not blind faith. It is based entirely on evidence. The opposite of knowledge is not faith but ignorance. The opposite of faith is not knowledge but unbelief. Spiritual growth involves increasing our understanding of God and Jesus, and of the Cosmos in which we find ourselves.

Science and faith are not opposed. Science cannot exist without faith, without trust in the comprehensibility of reality; trust in the laws of reason, logic, and mathematics. Faith simply means 'confident belief in the veracity, value, or trustworthiness of a person, idea or thing.'

It would be funny to observe atheists trying to take credit for science. The leading lights of atheism never set foot in a laboratory: Marquis de Sade; Nietzsche; Bertrand Russell; Marx; George Bernard Shaw; Lenin; Stalin; Mencken; Sartre; Mussolini; Clarence Darrow; Ayn Rand; Christopher Hitchens; Larry Flynt; George Soros; Warren Buffett.

On the other hand, it is easy to count off the devout Christian men who really advanced science: Copernicus; Galileo; Kepler; Newton; Bacon; Descartes; Mendel; Boyle; Faraday; Maxwell; Pasteur; Kelvin; Werner von Braun—just to name a few.

Instead of being against science, modern science is the brainchild of Christianity. Almost all the great scientists who discovered real things were devout Christians until recent decades. Only in Christian Europe, full of Bible believers who went to church regularly, did the systematic study of nature take place that led to the Scientific Revolution. Almost every one of the scientists who founded each of today's scientific disciplines was a devout Christian.

All human beings do what Douglas Axe calls 'common science,' which he connects to common sense. We all observe the reality around us and form ideas, concepts, and theories about it. When a college professor says something that doesn't make sense to you, and you express doubt about the veracity of some scientific theory, you might be called ignorant. But there is no fundamental reason why we should not be skeptical of scientific theories. Scientists should be skeptical and willing to admit they *could be* wrong, too. They are far from infallible.

Not only is it unlikely that Darwinism explains the origin of new life forms, but it also cannot even explain the production of the necessary proteins required to do so. Anything that ever supposedly evolved had to exist first. It seems like lunacy to assert that *it must be true* that primordial soup suddenly begat life. Nothing is created without knowledge. You cannot do anything constructive unless you know how.

Axe writes: "The reason we perceive purpose in inventions is precisely the reason they can't occur by accident: they exhibit an organized, functional coherence that can only come from deliberate, intelligent action. They are conceived from the top down and constructed from the bottom up. They may *operate* by nothing more than physical causes, but they certainly don't *originate* that way. Functional coherence makes accidental invention fantastically improbable."

We make robots, but they only do what we program them to do. A dog does what he *wants* to do. A dog is obviously something greater than its parts. Even single-celled creatures are vastly more sophisticated than a robot. Every single cell in a dog is devoted to being a dog, both sustaining and being sustained by the dog.

Furthermore, even the lowly bacteria only comes into being from other bacteria—never from anything else is bacteria born and never do bacteria give birth to anything else. Even the great atheist Richard Dawkins must confess: "You may throw cells together at random, over and over again for a billion years, and not once will you get a conglomeration that flies or swims or burrows or runs, or does anything, even badly, that could remotely be construed as working to keep itself alive."

During human history, there have been zero new species of mammals created. When Adam and Eve lived, it is estimated that there were 8,000 different kinds of mammals. Half of them have now become extinct. By all scientific evidence, after God created Adam and Eve, He ceased making new life forms.

While evolution implies that the Cosmos becomes more and more organized, the Second Law of Thermodynamics says no: the Universe becomes more and more unorganized over time. The Universe is decaying and disordering, which is called the Law of Entropy.

If living creatures evolved from simpler to more complex life forms, we would see that process taking place around us all the time. Evolutionists claim this happens by way of mutations. But mutations rarely occur, perhaps in only one in a million individuals. The majority of mutations are harmful if not lethal. For every beneficial mutation, there are at least a million that are detrimental.

The odds against a mutation ever creating a new species are astronomical. There is no evidence that an animal ever even generates a new organ, nonetheless a new kind of creature. Since human beings' appearance, not a single new species of mammal has been observed to come into existence.

Philosopher Thomas Nagel, who is certainly no Christian, says of evolution: "It is *prima facie* highly implausible that life as we know it is the result of a sequence of physical accidents together with the mechanism of natural selection. My skepticism is not based on religious belief or a belief in any definite alternative. It is just a belief that the available scientific evidence, despite the consensus of scientific opinion, does not in this matter rationally require us to subordinate the incredulity of common sense. This is especially true with regard to the origin of life."

Dutch botanist Hugo DeVries explains: "Natural Selection may explain the *survival* of the fittest, but it cannot explain the *arrival* of the fittest." Not only can evolution not explain any new species coming into being, but it also cannot even show how new genes could come into being. Evolution assumes the prior existence of living entities before its explanations start. As the Swiss evolutionary biologist Andreas Wagner observed, "Natural Selection can *preserve* innovations, but it cannot *create* them."

Of the trillions of living creatures of incredible variations, natural selection explains not one of them. But evolutionists try to tell us that their theory has astonishing *creative powers*. Evolution cannot even show how an enzyme evolves, nonetheless a complex living creature.

Why do we not see evolution going on all around us now? Where are the new features being created all by themselves before our very eyes? Now we are told we can't see it because the process is finished and no more life forms may be expected. So we would have to go back in time to see evolution work in the real world. How convenient. William James correctly foresaw that evolution would become a religion and its adherents would seek for it to replace faith in Christ.

Democrats claim to be the party of science and love to portray Conservatives falsely as anti-science. But science reveals that a genetically complete and unique human being is formed at the moment of conception—which Democrats reject. Science says that a pair of sex chromosomes—X and Y—determines one's sex, which Democrats refute. When science measures the qualities of human beings, it finds them to be patently unequal—born physically and mentally unequal, and always they remain so—which Democrats say is not so. The very foundation of science is that objective truth exists and that humankind can find it—which Democrats deny is real. Democrats, as a matter of course, deny essential scientific facts that do not fit their ideology.

Valid science is based on replicability and falsifiability. The former means a given experiment can be done over and over again, yielding the same results. The latter means any theory that is beyond being proved wrong is not genuinely scientific.

There is no halfway point between something and nothing. 'Nothing' cannot be examined by science. Scientists will say that Creation exploded onto the scene 13.4 billion years ago. Now that is something. Before that, they will say, was nothing. So nothing exploded into something. How do you get something from nothing when 'nothing' does not exist?

Usually, Americans who work for the Devil are a secretive lot, making it difficult to pin down precisely what they are up to. But scientist Carolyn Porco, featured prominently by PBS, National Geographic, and Discovery Channel, has written a manifesto:

"The confrontation between science and formal religion will come to an end when science's role in the lives of all people is the same played by religion today. Every culture has religion. It undoubtedly satisfies an obvious human need. But the same spiritual fulfillment and connection can be found in the revelations of science. One day, the sites we hold most sacred just might be the astronomical observatories, the particle accelerators, the university research installations, and other laboratories where the high priests of science — the biologists, the physicists, the astronomers, the chemists — engage in the noble pursuit of uncovering the workings of nature herself. And today's museums, expositional halls, and planetaria may then become tomorrow's houses of worship, where these revealed truths, and the wonder of our interconnectedness with the Cosmos, are glorified in song by the devout and the soulful."

On the wall of a university classroom for Evolutionary Biology is a display of the timeline of man coming from an illustration of an ape. At 400 BC, it shows Buddha; at Zero, it shows Julius Caesar; at AD 600, it shows Mohammed. But no mention of Jesus: He by whom those dates are set. No bias there.

On a BBC Documentary about creationism, the show opens by describing anyone who believes in a Creator as a religious fundamentalist, obviously meant as an insult. Then Professor Donald Prothero, an ardent and seasoned anti-creationist, asserts: "If you don't start with naturalism, then you can't be a scientist." That is an incredibly biased statement. The BBC only presents one side of the story. Even though the documentary is about creationism, when the show's producers are asked how many creationist scientists are being interviewed about their own fields, they replied, "None."

The documentary is entirely unbalanced. On the aired show, the host states the popular myth, "We share 99 percent of our DNA with chimps," trying to encourage the viewers to see ourselves as close cousins to chimpanzees. However, that percentage has long been known to be highly exaggerated. It could be as high as 84 percent, but it is not our bodies as much as our minds that differ so from them.

The producer then takes a group of creationists to a gay church, as if that is somehow related to the issues at hand. A young creationist handles it well, saying, "From a Christian perspective, all human beings are sinners, not merely those who give in to homosexual lust, and all need to repent and accept Jesus Christ as Savior!"

A Professor of Astrophysics informs us that the Universe has a will and that he worships the Universe. Our creationist replied, "I would say that people who want to explain life without God want a godless universe because they don't want the baggage of Jesus Christ, they don't want the sin, they don't want the judgment, they don't want the other aspects of God in their life, so they can live whatever way they choose."

Evolutionary biologist William Provine claims that Darwinism is the most significant engine of atheism ever created by man. Richard Dawkins agrees: "Darwin made it possible to be an intellectually fulfilled atheist." That is what the Theory of Evolution is for—to promote atheism.

There is no doubt that a consistent understanding of evolution does lead to atheism, even among those who were once professing Christians. Scientist Jerry Coyne proclaims, "Evolution is unique amongst the sciences because it strikes people on the solar plexus of their faith directly, it strikes them in the idea that they are specially created by God; because evolution says you are not, it says that there is no special purpose for your life because it's a naturalistic philosophy. We have no more extrinsic purpose than a squirrel or an armadillo, and it says that morality does not come from God, it is an evolved phenomenon."

Every person either sees reality as a naturalist or as a supernaturalist. The public schools only teach naturalism—the theory that matter and energy are the only objects existing within the Universe, and that mental and spiritual phenomena are explainable as functions of the nervous system. That is the proposal of the Antichrist: Man is nothing more than an animal and belief in our Father nothing more than a psychological or sociological tool—a crutch. Communists agree, as do the Secular Humanists, whose ideas are indoctrinated into your children in compulsory state schools.

Darwinism is the theory that all living creatures descended from a common ancestor. A theory is a proposed explanation for something that exists. The alternative account, that God created life, should not be excluded from science just because it involves God.

There are at least twenty different definitions of the word 'species' used among various scientists. The term 'kind' in the Bible is roughly equivalent to our scientific description of 'genus' or 'family.' Species in the modern sense is a much narrower word than kind.

The most significant change we see in the animal kingdom is not in the wild but as a result of human beings' intentional action with pet and livestock breeding. Even then, after centuries of it, dogs, cows, and horses are still just dogs, cows, and horses.

The Theory of Evolution states that it is common for living creatures to depart from their original type, limitlessly, by accumulating new features on a road that leads to new species, genera, families, and orders. But the Augustinian friar Gregor Mendel formulated the strict, fundamental laws of heredity that are the foundation of genetics. Mendel's Law shows how spectacularly stable species are. Its offspring do not necessarily inherit traits acquired by one creature's adaptation to his environment. Mendel opposed Darwin's theory, and his work undermines macroevolution.

Neo-Darwinism was formulated in the 1940s, which made random mutation the engine driving evolution. This meant that *genetic mistakes* were responsible for the incredible complexity and diversity of living things. But mutations are an irreversible loss of excellent and needful information, a degeneration of proper functioning—not improvements. Nonetheless, the Neo-Darwinist slogan became, *Man is the result of a purposeless and natural process that did not have him in mind.*

In 1959, the famous atheist Julian Huxley used the pulpit in the chapel of the University of Chicago to announce that Christianity was a fraud. In response, a group of scholars founded the Creation Research Society. Its mission is to reconcile modern science with the Bible. Right away, 650 scientists joined. And right away, atheist scientists began attacking them. But one of its members, J.W.G. Johnson, debunked all of the supposed links between apes and human beings, including Piltdown Man. He also showed how the Second Law of Thermodynamics makes it impossible for a simpler creature to evolve into a more complex one.

The Intelligent Design movement started in the 1990s and today includes Protestants, Catholics, Jews, Buddhists, and agnostics. In 2001, the Discovery Institute published a document that was subsequently signed by more than 800 scientists, all of whom possessed doctorates from famous universities worldwide— from America, Russia, China, and Israel, and other countries. It read: "We are skeptical of claims for the ability of random mutation and natural selection to account for the complexity of life. Careful examination of the evidence for Darwinian Theory should be encouraged."

Evolution is based on circular reasoning. It claims genes, organs, and limbs are similar because creatures have a common ancestor. How do they know beings have a common ancestor? Genes, organs, and limbs are similar. There is no evidence for the truth of the thing. Similarly, the argument is that common ancestry explains genetic similarities we have with animals. How do we know we have common ancestry? Genetic similarities with animals. There is zero evidence of evolutionary transitions, and without those, it is a lie to call evolution a *fact*.

The evolutionists used to claim our ancestors were apes, such as in the famous classroom illustrations. Now they have changed it to "humans and apes share a common ancestor," because after all, we have been observing apes for thousands of years, and they are still the same apes they have always been. That is a shrewd rhetorical trick because the common ancestor of humans and apes would also be an ape—at best.

Protons decay, and atoms dissipate into radiation. The Universe is slowly burning out and will die of heat death. It is not evolving but disorganizing—devolving. We see in nature the extinction of species, not the conception of new ones due to the Law of Increased Entropy.

When we see primitive people living today in remote parts of the world, we do not doubt their humanity. We can see that human nature is a defined and permanent feature of humanity. But evolutionists see primitive people from the past, of which all we have is bones, as less human, less evolved.

As Cardinal Ratzinger, the future Pope Benedict, affirmed: "Evolution has been exalted above and beyond its scientific content and made into an intellectual model that claims to explain the whole of reality and thus has become a sort of first philosophy." Some admit this publicly, such as evolutionist philosopher Michael Ruse, who says, "For many evolutionists, evolution has functioned as something with elements which are, let us say, akin to being a secular religion." It has become the belief system of atheists.

Pope John Paul II emphatically rejected the evolutionary idea that matter evolved into human consciousness. He rejected atheistic evolution entirely, which rejects Man as a spiritual being. The fact is that humankind's existence is no accident because God wanted us to exist: Beings who can think of Him and know Him. That is what defines a human being ultimately.

John Paul II also wrote, "A theory's validity depends on whether or not it can be verified," which evolution cannot be. "Evolution has become something more than a hypothesis," meaning it has become a pseudo religion. But the leftist press twisted John Paul's words with these headlines: "The pope said we might have descended from apes, Pope backs acceptance of evolution, Papal confession: Darwin was right about evolution, The pope backs natural selection, The pope made peace with Darwin"— all of which are lies.

John Paul II always and roundly rejected the theory that human beings were descended from lower life forms and firmly affirmed that humans were created directly by God, as the Bible says. He defined the theory as an "intellectual construct independent from the results of observations." Secular philosopher Karl Popper, who is adored by atheists, has also stated that Darwinism is intrinsically untestable and therefore non-scientific.

Cardinal Schonborn asserts, "Many people today are very sensitive and act hurt—even aggressive—whenever anyone doubts the Theory of Evolution. But nothing is worse for science than forbidding questions and inquiries. Can the greater thing have arisen from the less? Can lower things bring forth of their own power, higher and more complex things? Nothing in our experience suggests that something lower can give rise to something higher."

As theologian Andreas Laun has written, evolutionists assume "an elephant would climb out of a pond containing frogs, if one only stood for long enough—for millions of years—at the water's edge waiting." And yet our courts have made it against the law for a government school to tell students that the Theory of Evolution is not the only theory explaining the origin of life and species.

The Bible says the world was created out of nothing. All non-biblical creation myths begin with a being forming our world out of pre-existing materials. Only the Bible presents a God who can create all that is out of nothing.

PBS produced a show for schoolchildren telling them that the Theory of Evolution is a fact. The program says that up until 1957, Darwin seems to be locked out of America's public schools, but then hallelujah! "Long-neglected science programs were revived in America's classrooms." It doesn't teach the kids that before 1957 American public schools produced more Nobel Prize winners than the rest of the human race combined and twice as many in the fields that Darwinism *should have* affected most but didn't, physiology and medicine.

Marc Kirschner, a biologist from Harvard, admitted, "Over the last 100 years, almost all of biology has proceeded independently of evolution. Molecular biology, biochemistry, physiology, have not taken evolution into account at all." Here I thought it explained the whole world!

Chemist Philip Skell says antibiotics research ignores Darwin. He asked more than 70 eminent researchers if they would have done their work differently if they had thought Darwin's theory was wrong and their responses were all the same. No.

Two well-known scientists calculated the odds of life forming by natural processes. They estimated that there is less than one chance in 10 to the 40,000th power that life could have originated by random trials. 10 to the 40,000th power is a 1 with 40,000 zeros after it!

Chemist Dr. Grebe: "That organic evolution could account for the complex forms of life in the past, and the present, has long since been abandoned by men who grasp the importance of the DNA genetic code. "Researcher and mathematician I.L Cohen: "At that moment, when the DNA/RNA system became understood, the debate between evolutionists and creationists should have come to a screeching halt. The implications of the DNA/RNA were obvious and clear. Mathematically speaking, based on probability concepts, there is no possibility that evolution is the mechanism that created the approximately 6,000,000 species of plants and animals we recognize today."

Current generations are not taught the biblical worldview. Just the opposite, they are indoctrinated with the Theory of Evolution's worldview, the ultimate aim of which is to do away with right and wrong by doing away with God. Its first job is to get rid of Adam and Eve. If they do not exist, and sin does not exist, we have no need of Jesus Christ as our Savior.

Its teachers deny or manipulate known facts to rob tens of millions of little boys and girls of their simple faith in God and the Bible. Part of the idea is to devalue the past, denigrate our ancestors by making them look dumb, deprecate our heritage, and make the only frame of reference ourselves—how we *feel* and what we feel like doing.

Evolutionists describe a strictly mechanical universe with no room whatsoever for the spiritual and supernatural. There is no place for our Creator in the Theory of Evolution, no Savior or Resurrection, no Heaven or Hell (Imagine it, John Lennon says)—no Sin and no Judgment Day (which is the part people like)—no Eternal Life. It is an invention of Satan.

Please consider that not one person living now, or who lived in the past, or who will live in the future has the exact DNA blueprint that created YOU—unless you are an identical twin. Some scientists estimate that well over 100 trillion humans have lived on this planet. I doubt that. How ever many there have been, you are unique among them. There has never been anyone exactly like you and never will be.

Many scientists are now convinced that cells containing such a complex code and such intricate chemistry could never have come into being by pure, undirected chemistry. No matter how chemicals are mixed, they do not create DNA spirals or any intelligent code whatsoever. Only DNA reproduces DNA.

So what do you think? Are you up from primordial slime? Or did God design you and the world you exist in at this moment? And if He did intend you: What for? For a reason and a purpose of His.

As James M. Kushiner has observed, "science and faith are both found together inside man and nowhere else in the Cosmos." Scientist William Bragg says, "Sometimes people ask if religion and science are not opposed to one another. They are: In the sense that the thumb and fingers of my hands are opposed to one another. It is an opposition by means of which anything can be grasped." Like many things, science can promote good or promote evil by men, based on their motives and what spiritual power they serve.

God did not create humans capable of discovering all of this astonishing scientific knowledge, so we would turn into atheists and make man a deity. God is granting us scientific understanding, so we might glimpse His Glory and praise His Name.

Freedom vs. Tyranny

Christianity is the most marvelous force for good that the world has ever seen. It is from the Christians that humanity derived protection for children, rights for women, the right to own property, and limited government. By applying their faith to public life; the Christian religion has bequeathed incredible benefits in innumerable ways to Western Civilization.

Even Friedrich Nietzsche, who famously said, "God is dead," admitted Christianity was the only source of the idea that "all men are created equal." The very freedoms that the godless Left are using to tear down the Christian faith came from that same faith. As Dinesh D'Souza insists: "This modern concept of freedom we inherited from Christianity. Christianity emphasizes that we are moral agents with the right to express your own opinions, the right to choose a career, the right to travel where you want, and the right to own your own personal space. The right to live your own life."

The state will define all public space as governmental space if we let it. While our Founding Fathers saw Church and State working separately but towards the same ends, if that balance is not maintained, the state will take over everything because only it can call in the police and military. As Stalin once asked, "How many divisions does the pope have?"

Men can only be as free as they are willing to self-regulate their conduct. Something in every society must control behavior so as not to let anarchy reign. If men do not, or cannot control themselves, the state must step in to do it for them, for the betterment of society. The more virtuous the men of a nation are, the more free society can let them be. Immoral men cannot be at liberty to follow their impulses.

The reason secular humanists work so hard to ban Christ from the Public Square is that only Christians among competing groups in America claim to possess an authority that transcends the state—a higher power than the government. The secularists acknowledge no morality except power. To them, the personal is political; all reality is political; what is political is all that matters. That is their religion. And that is why they are firmly ensconced on the Left Wing because Christianity is decidedly conservative, by which I mean it favors *conserving* the traditions of our forefathers about good versus evil, right versus wrong, truth versus falsehood.

At the heart of traditional values is sacrifice for others, in monogamous marriage, stable families, good manners, and charity. Socialism involves forcing people to do what they do not want to do, from above. It also creates irresponsible individuals who refuse to take care of themselves and gradually lose the ability to do so.

I continuously see leftists complaining that conservatives or Christians are 'trying to legislate morality' and 'shoving your morals down our throats.' And yet, the atheist socialists constantly legislate what they see as 'moral' and try to prohibit what they see as 'immoral.' Surely all leftists think their holy trinity of racism, sexism, and disapproval of homosexual behaviors are all 'immoral.'

So-called 'same-sex marriage' activists argued before the Supreme Court that it was 'immoral' to oppose what they wanted. Leftists all the time say it is 'immoral' to deny 'global warming' schemes to redistribute trillions of our dollars to the Third World. MLK said segregation was 'immoral.' The other day a prominent Democrat said it was 'immoral' for a nation as wealthy as ours not to feed all its children. Even the Republicans' fight against slavery, which was defended by Democrats, was because it was 'immoral.'

The secular humanist is working to exclude belief in God from public life and exclude all who hold a Christian worldview—and to punish them if they cannot get them to shut up. The fact is that secular humanists are planning an intolerant utopia for your descendants, which will not contain a trace of Christ Jesus, in the name of sexual liberation from any moral limits. Reverend Charles Finney once said, "God will bless or curse America depending on the course Christians take in politics."

Secular Humanism degrades Man into nothing but a product of chance and denies us the dignity of being created in the Image of God. It denies the plain fact that if you have no fellowship with God, you are destined for the Lake of Fire. It cannot correctly diagnose or relieve man's real problem, which has tragic consequences.

Western Civilization was born from the Christian Faith and a Christian Way of Life. Only from Western Civilization emerged the Scientific Revolution; capitalism & free enterprise; the Industrial Revolution; the middle class; near-universal literacy; the town school; the university; hospitals; hospice; the very ideas of equality, representative government, and individual freedom; virtually all modern machines and technology—incredible levels of prosperity and a hitherto undreamed of standard of living. No civilization can afford to neglect the very foundation that produced its highest achievements—or allow that foundation to be purposely undermined by its enemies from within.

Culture is the way of life of a particular people, as defined by Christopher Dawson. You may judge the strength of culture by its institutions and the quality of its achievements. America, built on an astounding new idea of self-government and self-determination, produced by far the most extraordinary advancements and explosion of wealth ever witnessed in the 200 years or so following its founding, mostly due not to scientists but from *inventors*. Many people confuse the two or give credit to science for what inventors create. Inventors create new products and services that people need or want; scientists usually follow along later to explain how they work.

Now comes leftist ideology to ravage Western Civilization and demolish its traditional institutions, leaving no roots to its past, unleashing parasites to plunder its treasures as it descends into decadence. Decay comes. Stability is shattered, along with spiritual decline, as we begin to emulate primitive cultures that are devoid of faith and wholesomeness, and barely rise above the level of beasts.

Unity is ruined as the community of thought is splintered, discipline discouraged, language ignored or distorted, and all we held dear is deprecated. A new concept of existence is spread that disparages our intellectual tradition but propagates bogus mythology denuded of significance, and often absurd and grotesque.

The fact is, real religious experience is a reality of profound depth. But to the thinkers of the French Revolution, the Church was seen as a negative force, like ignorance, superstition, or tyranny. They closed their eyes to the positive influence of Christianity on the course of human events. They denied that progress owed anything to Christians, despite the extraordinary progression history bore witness to in their own society—its whole life had a religious orientation.

God enormously blessed the West. The Left extolls the primitivism of Third World peoples and their religion of Pantheism—worshiping the Earth and everything that lives on it.

All of the major ancient world religions linked with some high historical culture except for Judaism, the religion of Israel, which belonged to a tiny nation on a minute piece of land, not wealthy or technologically advanced, but with an extraordinarily high degree of literacy. Hostile empires more highly developed and much more powerful surrounded tiny Israel. And yet, the great I AM chose Israel to whom to reveal His divine laws that govern the moral life of the individual. The Father of the whole world, who hates sin and loves good, proclaims that human history has a moral purpose and what each person does has cosmic meaning and consequences—and what villages, cities, states, and nations do, has immense implications. Now, this was a revolutionary idea: THERE IS A DIVINE PURPOSE FOR THE WORLD!

The Christian faith is founded upon the historical personality of Jesus the Christ—divine life entered the human race and the natural world. Man, the craftsman, and artist; builder of cities and sailor of ships; the scientist and the philosopher, is the channel through whom Creation acquires consciousness, becomes spiritual, and participates in the divine life. Man is the point at which the spirit world touches the world of the senses. Man is bound to matter in this life, and this puts him in constant danger of being dragged down to the purely animal life of the senses and passions.

Christianity became a dynamic moral and social force. Western Civilization was a religious entity based on spiritual unity, not political unity. European Man was a member of the Church of the Living God and had a far deeper loyalty to Him than to any state. Christendom was a magnificent religious commonwealth, a society based on membership in a spiritual community.

The Church took care of the sick and the poor and provided social welfare and education. The Reformation kicked off modern progress, launching a scientific revolution of experimentation and applied knowledge. Protestantism is a religion of action.

By the time of the Enlightenment, the Christian faith had so molded the thoughts and feelings of Europeans for over one thousand years that some of them no longer recognized the origin of their ideas. Thinkers arose who disparaged the supernatural but could not divest themselves of the Christian teleological concept of life.

The fertile brain of Abbe de St. Pierre created most of the social projects to come: free education, including for females; the abolition of war and poverty; the unlimited possibilities of government action to establish paradise on Earth, which he likened to the Kingdom of God.

The French Revolution was meant to refashion society from its foundations, a clean break from the past, complete with a new revolutionary calendar for a New Age of Humanity. But no Utopia was forthwith. Instead, what eliminating God produced was the atrocities of the Reign of Terror, failure and disillusionment, a grim commentary on the main idea of Rousseau that Natural Man is intrinsically good.

Revolutionary persecution of the Church failed to extinguish its light as planned. And this made men realize that Theophilanthropists and the Decadary Cult could not so easily replace Christendom's historic faith.

Skeptics arose who wanted to kill the supernatural aspects but keep the moral teachings of the Christian Faith. Among them was the atheist William Godwin, the father of modern anarchy, who foresaw a New Age: "In that blessed day, there will be no war; no crimes; no administration of justice, as it is called; and no government. Besides this, there will be neither disease, anguish, melancholy, nor resentment."

So, socialism was formulated to substitute social science for Christianity. But America boomed without it, based on progress that was not due to government action but government inaction—due to individualism, strict moral discipline, religious optimism, and enthusiasm for Christian social reform. It had been free enterprise that launched the Industrial Revolution of 18th century Britain and used the mathematical achievements of devout Christian men such as Galileo and Newton to found the modern Science of Mechanics—Machines!

The initiative came from the religious traditions of English society, in which industry and thrift are virtuous, and self-indulgence discouraged. A man had to work hard, be abstemious, and conscientious because work is your religious vocation. A very high degree of social discipline and organization made it all possible. Production, standardization, manufacturing, communications, and transportation were revolutionized.

Great cities grew in America with millions of inhabitants, where 100 years earlier, savage tribes were still living in the Stone Age. 19th century Christians abolished the slave trade for the first time in the world. Christians also abolished torture and cruel penal codes, while they systematically fought disease and famine and hunger and social ills of all sorts around the globe. Yes, progress proved fatal to the survival of some primitive peoples, mostly due to disease unknowingly carried, but that was never the intention of those who believed nothing but good could come from the substitution of books, modern products, and knowledge of God for nakedness and cannibalism.

Modern civilization is entirely a product of European Man. The Left is bent on undermining the foundation of this incredible accomplishment—the most remarkable happening in human history—by destroying its spiritual traditions.

No society survives without moral and spiritual harmony and cultural unity. The mind of our age is divided against itself, dividing the common conception of reality. The Left teaches an existence that is merely a product of blind chance. But the clock of the Cosmos moves in an irreversible direction. The Story of Man had a beginning; it will have an end.

Science has served humanity well, but since it is entirely indifferent to moral considerations, it is no substitute for religion. The Left refuses to acknowledge a hierarchy of habits. It promotes living for the moment in the chaos of pure sensation. A spirit of destruction and spiritual alienation animates it. It is because the Christian faith is the foundation upon which Western Civilization rests that it is under demonic attack.

The religion of society expresses its dominant attitude toward life and its ultimate conception of reality. The destruction of Christianity by the Antichrist is not progress. It is social disintegration; supposed humanitarianism divorced from the historic religious beliefs from which it comes. Science needs to be directed by a moral purpose it does not possess.

Europe owes its very existence to the shared spiritual society of Christianity. As Nietzsche philosophized: "Let us not forget, in the end, what a Church is, and especially in contrast to every 'state'; a Church is above all an authoritarian organization which secures to the most spiritual men the highest rank, and believes in the power of spirituality so far as to forbid all grosser appliances of authority. Through this alone, the Church is under all circumstances a nobler institution than the state."

The Left has pushed Christianity and spiritual convictions out of the mainstream, wrongly claiming they must be the source of strife when the Antichrist is the real cause of conflict. This has impoverished our entire culture and society. Leftists love centralized power because they want to use it to reach down into every village of America to force people to change their habits, customs, conventions, speech, thoughts, and beliefs. It is harder to persuade decent folks to support killing babies or glorifying perverts than it is to find one judge who will decide for hundreds of millions of people new rights and new wrongs.

Patrick Henry argued against giving courts the power to strike down laws made by elected legislatures because if you allow that, the courts can run amok, as if "there is no power above them to control their decisions. Then the laws cannot control them. They are independent of the people, of the legislature, and of every power under heaven."

As Americans have lost their Christian faith, they are no longer a people of virtuous character. That automatically has led to less freedom because only an upright people can be genuinely free. Vice undermines liberty. As Os Guinness says, "Freedom is not permission to do what we like but the power to do what we should."

The terrible liberal vice is pride; pride in the belief that no people who have gone before us, and certainly no supernatural being, knows better than we do. The noble conservative virtue is humility; we conserve the wisdom and experience of the past and place ourselves below eternal truths to which we should strive to obey. Conservatives have their minds most in tune with the Cosmos as it is.

The godless spend a lot of time and energy making sure no tiny hamlet anywhere in our colossal land has a crèche on public property. What is it about the baby Jesus they find so offensive that to see Him drives them mad?

The Supreme Court made a grave error, but an intentional one, when it elevated Atheism to the level of Christianity by fiat. By this ruling, the godless have not only driven God out of the government schools, but they also work diligently to push Him out of public life, and Atheism rules where God has been driven out. The vast majority of parents did not want to fund schools that teach an anti-Christian ideology, but they are forced to by taxation, which is so high most do not have enough money left over to send their children to a proper school.

The anti-Americans who loathe their own country have been at it for quite a while. Those in academia and the media used to write about the Soviet Union as America's moral equal, an outrageous thing to consider—that a murderous, totalitarian nightmare was similar morally to the best and most generous country ever. To do so is to deceive by presenting a false reality. It is to lie.

Chesterton made clear that the godless "introduce their horrible heresies under new and carefully complimentary names. But beware of every euphemism. Every one is used in favor of bad morals. When someone wishes to wage a social war against what all normal people have regarded as social decency, the first thing he does is find some artificial term that shall sound relatively decent." So whoring around becomes 'sexually active' and perverts become 'gay.' The Devil also uses dysphemisms such as 'racism,' 'sexism,' 'homophobe,' and 'bigot.'

Beware the Left and its schemes to engineer a new utopia. They create bloodbaths and enslavement instead. Even when they don't, they still do great harm. Take the Great Society of President Johnson: We are going to try to take all the money from the 'haves' and give it to the 'have-nots.' So trillions of dollars were spent. The result is not less poverty but a new permanent welfare-dependent class never seen before in human history: generations of people who proudly live off of the labors of others. The insidious byproduct is that the federal government has become ten times larger in what Roche calls "insane centralization, this reckless overthrow of the American constitutional heritage."

All utopian schemes are based on hatred. The object of this hatred is those who stand out by their own efforts; those with superior achievements, be they individuals or groups; those who do most to supply our wants and needs; the 'bourgeois,' the 'capitalist,' the morally good, the innocent—meanwhile, the utopian preens about how caring and compassionate he is with other people's money. That is why socialist political/economic systems are so dehumanizing. The evil ideology of the Left creates a profound psychological change and horrendous damage to men's souls.

Economic freedom is a moral good because it is right for each person to grow up into an individual who can provide for himself at least the necessities of life. Socialists promise a dream and deliver a nightmare, again and again, by, as Benjamin Wiker writes, "micromanaging the details of everyone's life with all the blundering inefficiency, confusion, unintended consequences, and plain idiocy that have made the name 'bureaucrat' a term of infamy."

The welfare state nefariously sabotages community bonds, the natural ties and local affections. We won't need husbands and fathers because the state will provide. We won't need wives and mothers because the state will nurture your children. Instead of depending on your immediate family, extended family, friends, acquaintances, and neighbors, you will rely on bureaucrats.

That is what Alexis de Tocqueville called *soft despotism*. I'll let Tocqueville explain what that term means:

"An immense tutelary power is elevated, which alone takes charge of assuring their enjoyments and watching over their fate. It would resemble paternal power if, like that, it had for its object to prepare men for manhood; but on the contrary, it seeks only to keep them fixed irrevocably in childhood; it likes citizens to enjoy themselves provided that they think only of enjoying themselves. It willingly works for their happiness, but it wants to be the unique agent and sole arbiter of that; it provides for their security, foresees and secures their needs, facilitates their pleasures, conducts their principal affairs, directs their industry, regulates their estates, divides their inheritances; can it not take away from them entirely the trouble of thinking and the pain of living?

"So it is that every day it renders the employment of free will less useful and more rare; it confines the action of the will in a smaller space and little by little steals the very use of it from each citizen. Thus, after taking each individual by turns in its powerful hands and kneading him as it likes, the sovereign extends its arms over society as a whole, and finally reduces a nation to being nothing more than a herd of timid and industrious animals of which government is the shepherd."

Tyranny comes to America through the federal government bureaucracies when they take the authority that was once reserved for parents, families, churches, local school boards, towns, counties, states, and legislatures. This development makes the politically connected powerful at the expense of those who aren't; makes politics a vastly outsized power that should be tempered by other institutions of society; gives total control to people with totalitarian designs.

Bureaucracies naturally look to preserve and expand their own power not to serve the people. As the Anti-Federalists put it, this is a natural tendency: Every man, and every body of men, when invested with power, is ever disposed to increase it.

New World Order

In 1993, a World Parliament of Religions gathered in Chicago to champion a new unified global religion. It concluded with a mission statement that focused on earth worship but never once mentions God.

In 2004, Europe's elites agreed that the new European Constitution would omit any reference to the Christian roots of Western Civilization. Makes one wonder from whence came those thousands of still-standing and quite magnificent cathedrals. They proclaimed that the public square would be neutral - but at the same time eliminated moral arguments informed by Christianity. Some neutrality that is. Methinks they spoketh with forked tongue.

It is noteworthy that Rocco Buttigione was chosen to be Commissioner of Justice for Europe, but subsequently disqualified for his personal views on the nature of marriage and the immorality of homosexual acts—his thoughts, that is, not any action he had ever taken. That represents a new totalitarianism that flies under a false flag of 'tolerance.'

Europe today is in the throes of Christophobia. Most of its inhabitants, without spiritual roots, live with an inner emptiness and no hope of a future for their civilization. They sink into loneliness, selfishness, nihilism, narcissism—and all of that leads to a sharply declining birthrate.

So lost are they that they deny their Christian heritage. That Christianity had anything to do with the formation of their free, law-governed, prosperous European societies is disacknowledged. They can only do this by falsifying their past. And then the truth no longer has any role in governance and public policy.

It was after Europe stopped going to church that Europeans stopped reproducing themselves. Europe was once the greatest of all civilizations that ever appeared in our world. To willfully depopulate is an expression of a crisis in civilizational morale—a spiritual catastrophe. "The height of its spiritual aspirations determines the magnitude of a people's cultural achievements," teaches theologian David B. Hart.

It should be evident to all but the blind that atheistic states have birthed incredibly horrible persecution, slavery, and mass murder. And don't tell me about the Inquisition again. When was the last time Christians massacred people for rejecting God's authority? Every godless experiment has the same bloody result from the French Revolution to the Soviet Union to Red China to Pol Pot. It is terror and slaughter based on faith that there is no God to whom you will have to give account for your deeds.

Is it a coincidence that the Bible says the Antichrist will rule the whole world—and the Illuminati was formed expressly for that very purpose? The main impediment to the New World Order is the Christian faith. The founder of the Order of the Illuminati vowed to destroy Christianity. Adam Weishaupt was his name. Like Rousseau, he said that life would be harmonious if people just gave up owning things—private property. It is from those two men that Karl Marx got such an idea.

Weishaupt did not believe you should love your country or your community or your family or your wife or your children or your parents or your brothers and sisters. He felt that these loves impede what should be the correct aim—to love everybody. Here we had the Marxist message in 1776—abolish marriage, the family, religion, property, and nations.

To get the ball rolling is always first to subvert morality, because immoral people, by and large, shun God, for the apparent reason that none living in darkness wants the light shone on their evil deeds. We all know how hard-core sinners shudder at the suggestion they come with you to church.

The hardest to convince would be women. To recruit women, they would be sold *liberation*, which would include abortion. To break up families, women would be persuaded that Holy Matrimony was itself mistreatment of women. The Illuminati men had other motives: they wanted as many women as possible to have sex with them, a common theme of secret societies and oddball cults.

The grand conservative truth is this: Government should not exist to control us. It should secure our safety and protect our freedom. Period.

The Carnegie Endowment, the Ford Foundation, and the Guggenheim Foundation selected twenty historians to found the American Historical Association in 1928 and provided its funding. That association aimed to rewrite history and promote Secular Humanism and collectivism in the United States, with the ultimate goal of destroying it and preparing the way for the New World Order.

Paul C. Vitz, in his book *Censorship,* informed us "Public school textbooks exclude the history, heritage, beliefs, and values of millions of Americans. Those who believe in the traditional family are not represented. Those who believe in free enterprise are not represented. Those who are committed to their religious heritage—at the very least as an important part of the historical record—are not represented."

Leftists yearn to make all schooling illegal except the schools they bring to heel, to be run by their godless governments. The Left's desire to police our habits is a tremendous assault on our liberty, vetting every aspect of our social lives to force conformity to political correctness. Democrats yearn to control everybody and everything, to compel compliance with their worldview on every person in America. To that end, they want everything subsumed in an Almighty State with them in charge: Totalitarianism.

The horrors of the 20th Century were brought to you by leftist ideology, which inspired and condoned them. It should not continue to surprise us, if we are acquainted with history, that the schemes of the Left are based on destruction, and will lead, in the end, to enslavement.

Free people are free to own things, including their time and labor. Whatever is theirs, they can freely trade with others of their choosing. Free people can choose whether to buy, sell, save, share, give, or accumulate. They can elect to do nothing with their time or to work around the clock. A socialist would take away all that freedom, and compel people to work for terms that they have not freely accepted, as well as confiscate all their property. That is slavery, my friends. And it is demonic. The horrors of a world without God were entirely on display behind the Iron Curtain—a living Hell for a billion souls.

In 1950, James Warburg, son of the 'Father of the Federal Reserve,' unabashedly told the U.S. Senate in a public hearing: "We shall have world government, whether or not we like it. The question is only whether world government will be achieved by consent or by conquest." Four years earlier, John D. Rockefeller had provided the funds to build the United Nations in New York.

Many Americans have wanted to bring about a New World Order. President Franklin Delano Roosevelt probably did more to bring it about than any other single person. Rex Tugwell, part of FDR's Brain Trust, wrote a new constitution in 1974. It would abolish freedom of speech, control all communications and travel, eliminate the right to free assembly, and, most importantly, stamp out the Free Exercise of Religion, even making worship a 'privilege' granted by the state. The Bill of Rights would be thrown out, and private ownership of guns prohibited. The Ford Foundation spent $25 million promoting Tugwell's new constitution.

Why would the wealthiest men on the planet want socialism to be the New World Order? It seems counterintuitive to think the rich would want to share the world's wealth. As explained by Gary Allen, "If one understands that socialism is not a share-the-wealth program, but a method to consolidate and control the wealth, the seeming paradox of super-rich men promoting socialism becomes no paradox at all. Instead, it becomes logical, even the perfect tool of power-seeking megalomaniacs. Communism or more accurately socialism is not a movement of the downtrodden masses, but of the economic elite."

W. Cleon Skousen instructed us: "It was almost inevitable that the super-rich would one day aspire to control not only their wealth but the wealth of the whole world. To achieve this, they were perfectly willing to feed the ambitions of the power-hungry political conspirators committed to the overthrow of all existing governments and the establishments of a central world-wide dictatorship."

The intention of the Council on Foreign Relations, formed in 1921, is to gradually cede the power, authority, and sovereignty of the United States to the United Nations, all the while desensitizing Americans by implementing socialism and totalitarianism progressively. In the end, the CFR wants to rule or help rule humankind through a global socialist government.

Admiral Chester Ward, Judge Advocate General for the United States Navy in the 1950s, and former member of the CFR wrote that the goal of the organization is "submergence of U.S. sovereignty and national independence into an all-powerful one-world government." He also explained how the CFR influences our government today: "Once the ruling members of the CFR have decided that the U.S. Government should adopt a particular policy, the CFR prepares propaganda both to sell the changes to the public and to demonize any opposition." Edith Kermit Roosevelt (granddaughter of TR) wrote in 1961 about the CFR's plans for "a One World Socialist State governed by experts like themselves. The result has been policies that favor the gradual surrender of United States sovereignty to the United Nations."

The Solicitor General for President Obama admitted before the Supreme Court that citizens could be *forced* to eat broccoli under Obamacare. And that eventually, everyone might be forced by our government to embrace the homosexual agenda, including all Christian schools, universities, charities, and finally churches.

To bring about Satan's New World Order, America must be disintegrated from within by first getting rid of Americans' shared identity, their mutual religion, values, customs, traditions, associations, and language. Psychopolitics have been employed to bring this to fruition. Christianity is the wall blocking the New World Order. After all, the New Testament told us of its plan nearly 2000 years ago.

As the book *Crimes of the Educators* shows us, the Common Core movement "is a jobs program for bureaucrats, educationalists, think tanks, experts, administrators, counselors, textbook writers, and publishers, who will all rake in millions." The new Common Core standards are, in part, a new massive data collection program on America's families, which has nothing to do with education. It is being smuggled into government schools, and its purveyors are lobbying for private schools and homeschoolers to be forced to participate.

Among other things, the globalists want to know the religious views and political views of your family and medical history, including the mental health of your household. Children will be the only ones questioned, and they will be asked to squeal on their parents if they know of any illegal activities or drug use or politically incorrect opinions held.

Why would the federal government want private information gathered about every child in America and their families? By what authority do they gather it? The National Center for Education Statistics will receive massive dossiers on every student. Do we want the government to have our children tell if they or their parents hold any politically incorrect views? Why would federal bureaucrats even want such information? Why would the government spend billions of dollars collecting it? Only a police state keeps gargantuan files of personal, private information of law-abiding citizens.

The 'father of global education' and 'the philosopher of the United Nations' and its 'prophet of hope' was Robert Muller (1923-2010). He said that his 'spiritual master' was the former head of the United Nations U Thant, an atheist Buddhist, and communist. Both men wanted to globalize education; wanted children around the globe to be taught the same lessons "to bring about lasting peace." What would these lessons be? The Gospel? No. U Thant said, "I would attach the greatest importance to spiritual values. I would deliberately avoid using the word 'religion.' I have in mind faith in oneself as the highest virtue of all."

Robert Muller is the author of the *World Core Curriculum*, from which is derived *Common Core*. Muller spent nearly 40 years creating his *World Core Curriculum*. Its purpose is to teach children worldwide that what is best for their future is a one-world education system, a one-world government, and one-world spirituality that includes a one-world religion.

A One-World Religion? Isn't that what Christianity already is? Muller's religious beliefs were something entirely different, coming from an occult spirit guide he said was named Djwal Khul. The preface to *World Core Curriculum* reads: "The underlying philosophy, upon which the Robert Muller School is based, will be found in the teachings set forth in the books of Alice A. Bailey by the Tibetan teacher, Djwal Kuhl, and the teachings of M. Morya as given in the Agni Yoga series books."

In her book *Education in the New Age*, Alice A. Bailey admitted: "One of our immediate educational objectives must be the elimination of the competitive spirit." She devoted her life to the destruction of Christianity so that a path is clear for her single global religion in the Age of Aquarius. Attacking individualism and establishing a global collective is a considerable part of her program. She was most assuredly anti-freedom and anti-America.

The first president of UNESCO, Julian Huxley, said the goal of that organization was "to help the emergence of single world culture, world humanism," which is atheistic socialism. UNESCO has been plotting to cram the *World Core Curriculum* down the collective throats of the human race, which will "install radical new values in children"—views decidedly opposite Christian values. Robert Muller called it "a curriculum of our universal knowledge which should be taught in all schools of the earth."

A big part of the scheme is to "combat family attitudes," to annihilate the values parents pass on to their children. The United States must go, along with its Constitution. All nation-states should dissolve; individual liberty is to become a thing of the past. Agenda 21 will take over every detail of our lives. The UN declares, "Rights and freedoms may in no case be exercised contrary to the purposes and principles of the United Nations."

Advocates of the New World Order hate Christ Jesus more than anything else. That is why they fought to remove any reference to Him in schools. The Christian faith has been the most efficacious opposition to communism. The schools instead substitute a disguised form of Satanism they call Secular Humanism, which naturally teaches kids there is no such thing as morals. If there are no morals, then the ends justify the means for individuals—and more importantly, for the state. As Karl Marx said, "We make war against all prevailing ideas of religion. The idea of God must be destroyed."

The Bible says that the Antichrist will bring all of Mankind under a single global government. There is a great plan to eliminate national boundaries and usher in a New World Order in the service of evil. The primary public reason given will be to end all wars. And to end world hunger. To make the world FAIR.

The Antichrist

Research into the attitudes of 'progressives' shows they have no intention of seeking compromise with Christians. Few of them have any Christian friends because they reject Believers as potential friends and do not wish to have any interaction with them. They only view Christians as their enemy. Carefully consider that it is Satan who is the ultimate enemy of Christ.

Progressives dehumanize Christians much as Nazis dehumanized Jews. They also believe that prayer should be banished from the world outside of a private home or church. In their view, churches should be eliminated from participation in adoptions, orphanages, and charities. Christians should have no say in social and political issues, the Left asserts, and companies should be able to discriminate openly against Christians in employment.

While being on God's side is being punished, being against being against God is as well. A Kentucky t-shirt company declined to print shirts for a 'Gay Pride' festival; because of the sinful message it was asked to create on them, which was that people should be proud of evil behavior. The owner was sent, by the state, to a re-education camp for 'diversity training' and told that Christians in business must "leave their religion at home."

The owners of a Christian bookstore in Knoxville, Tennessee, were dumbfounded after the *News Sentinel* rejected their advertisement because it included an offensive word – 'Christian.' The ad read: "Store closing sale – Cedar Springs Christian Store – Clinton Highway location – All merchandise, fixtures, slat walls must go. Sale through August 13, phone 865.947.XXX." The classified advertising department said the ad did not run because it contained an offensive word, and that ugly word was *Christian*.

Catholic Charities are a favorite object of progressive hatred, whether they are running a soup kitchen, foster home, adoption agency, food pantry, hospital, or nursing home; whether they are assisting immigrants, battered women, fatherless kids, the disabled, or helping the homeless. In progressive ideology, helping the helpless is no excuse for those who believe in Jesus not to be hounded into the closet. Catholic Charities serve ten million Americans each year through 2,500 offices, spending billions of dollars donated by individual members of the Body of Christ. Where is the comparable Atheist outfit?

Attacking Christian charities is attacking the poor people they help. Animated by spite and malice, the secularists forge on against the common good. They drain the quite limited funds that charities receive in donations to help the needy into prolonged court battles.

Protestant Gospel Rescue Missions use hundreds of thousands of volunteers, living out their faith, to serve sixty-six million free meals to hungry people each year, while also providing twenty million nights of safe shelter, helping 45,000 unemployed people find jobs, graduating 16,000 addicts from recovery programs, placing 36,000 families into subsidized homes. Each of its three hundred missions is open 24/7/365. Does not the Left grasp how all this charitable work, delivered with the personal touch of kindness and love, reduces the burden on taxpayers?

The most egregious example of Satan moving on the hearts of men and women is the case of the Little Sisters of the Poor. Surely its work should soften the hardest heart of anyone who is still fully human. They take care of the lowest of the low; those the world has thrown away—the old, sick, and dying—and they love them and live with them as a family. In the charity field, the Little Sisters are spoken of with hushed tones. Trying to hurt them ought to be the equivalent of slapping babies. But here we are, with the God-haters demanding they break with 2,000 years of Christian teaching about the nature of the God-ordained family, or be fined by the federal government to the tune of millions of dollars—money that would be better used to feed the hungry, clothe the naked, and house the dying.

The Devil uses the world system to oppose Christ and the Church. When you see human governments work against the spread of the Gospel and the Church's growth, you know the Devil holds sway. Lucifer and his demons can control entire nations by taking control of their governments; they can influence political officials to persecute and even murder believers. The political leaders of various countries have visited every cruelty and indignity Satan could devise upon Christ's followers.

A battle rages between good and evil for influence over governments—and each life on earth. Satan promotes false progress that proves detrimental to the moral character and opposed to the genuine interests of our better nature. As evil progresses, individual life becomes coarse and vicious. But God's Word is above human legislation. We are to obey the human government—unless it contradicts the laws of God.

The French Revolution sought to stamp out belief in God and faith in Jesus, and every socialist since has had the same goal because the Body of Christ creates a realm of value that transcends the state. We truly value the things we can attach no price, those things we do not wish to trade: our life, love, children, beauty, wisdom, and religion.

Christianity played a decisive role in American history, with its ideas of the sacred spread all across the traditions and ceremonies of life. Christian Civilization ingeniously endowed our institutions with religious authority without demanding faithful obedience from all Americans. Love your neighbor applies no matter what his beliefs are and does not command conformity from him. Christians are obligated to tell others about Jesus but never to force others to follow Him. We do not demand our critics be silenced. We declare our faith without threatening violence to those who scoff.

The traditional family has been the target of all socialist revolutionaries, especially Vladimir Lenin, whose idol Karl Marx devoted a book to the demolition of the family. The 1960s New Left radicals hated the 'bourgeois family, ' and the feminists loathed it. They have succeeded, with their sexual revolution, the 'liberation of women,' and the homosexual movement, in placing the traditional family of mom, dad, and children in peril.

Since the color red has fallen out of favor among political movements, after red socialists murdered 100 million innocent souls, green is the new color of the Left. The greens worship not God but the environment. They laugh and call themselves watermelons, green on the outside but red on the inside. They want central planning for the whole world with them in charge, to "save the planet." However, history proves that central planning—besides the death, terror, famine, starvation, suffering, and misery it has caused—*always devastates the environment*.

The lunatic environmentalists claim that human concerns are no more important than those of the snail darter or spotted owl. That has its roots in Pantheism—that God IS nature, not its Creator who is transcendent over it. The truth is that our Creator made everything in Creation *for us*.

The greatness of Western Civilization rests on virtue and truth, according to George Orwell. That is why what disturbed him most about Socialism/Fascism/Communism was its war on objective truth, *even more than its murder and brutality*. Pope Benedict XVI said: "One cannot build a humane, just, prosperous, free society on the foundation of radical skepticism about the human capacity to know the truth of anything."

The Left in America today cares not one whit about the truth. Story after story that gets them amped up into mob action proves to be false—Tawana Brawley, Duke Lacrosse, Rigoberta Menchu, accusing the Tea Party of shouting the N-word on the steps of the Capitol, the Virginia Rape case, "Hands up, Don't shoot!" at Ferguson—but even after these stories are proven to be hoaxes the Left never apologizes for them or for the damage they caused. In fact, they double down and cause more damage while claiming that even if that particular story is big fat lie, it reveals a 'larger truth.'

At the bottom of every plank in the platform of the Left is a big fat lie. They claim guns cause crime and death when in fact studies show conclusively that the carrying of concealed handguns, and armed property owners, are the most significant deterrent to crime of which we know. When evidence such as this is presented, many American newspapers delete them from the comments section and Leftist writers attack—not the data but the person posting the data, which is their strategy on every issue. Nearly every mass shooter and assassin in American history has been a leftist. About the only exception was the Charleston church massacre, which the Left blamed on Fox News and conservatives in general, but the killer said he did it because *no one shared his views*.

The Left never stops hating on Israel and justifying Muslim terrorism. Palestinians do not want their own state nearly as badly as they want all the Jews massacred in their beds. Israel is the only democracy with a free press and a prosperous economy based on free enterprise in the Middle East. The Arabs who live in Israel are freer and more affluent than any other Arabs on this planet.

The Left ignores the apparent historical link between Jews and Judea and Jerusalem, while promoting a false narrative that Arabs have some natural right to Judea, and that Jerusalem is some kind of holy city to Muslims, which is as ridiculous as it would be for Jews to claim Mecca was their holy city. Mecca is the holy city of Islam. Jerusalem is not mentioned once in the Koran. But appears 787 times in the Holy Bible.

The Left does not hold the so-called Palestinians to the same standard of conduct as any civilized people. They hold Israel to a higher standard than any other country. The Left lets Arabs openly claim that there never was a Jewish Temple in Jerusalem without calling them out on what is unquestionably a blatant lie.

As Hannah Arent said so well back in 1950: "The building of a Jewish national home was not a colonial enterprise to exploit foreign riches. Israel was a poor country, and whatever riches it possesses are exclusively the product of Jewish labor which is not likely to survive if ever the Jews are expelled from the country." The Jews took a barren wasteland and made into one of the most modern, prosperous countries in the history of our planet, with fabulous achievements in science, technology, industry, and agriculture.

Another lie at the foundation of leftist ideology is that human beings are unable to provide for themselves and unwilling to work together towards common goals all by themselves without the Almighty State. But look at where leftist ideology has ruled unimpeded for decades: America's inner cities, where trillions of dollars have disappeared in one corrupt leftist boondoggle after another. Democrats have ruined what once were the most prosperous, vibrant cities in the world. Now they are cesspits of sad people, violent crime, dependency, poverty, and broken homes.

That abominable Obama was vile enough to preach to Americans not to "get up on your high horse" about Islamic terrorism—that is, about the blatant murder of innocent men, women, and children—because of the Crusades! Which were not only 800 years ago, but indeed did not involve America.

He went on to blame Christianity for slavery and Jim Crow Laws when, in fact, it was Christians who abolished both. While Obama blamed the Crusades on Christians, they were, in fact, a response to Islamic invasions and the brutal rape and murder of innocent Christian pilgrims by Muslims.

As Dinesh D-Souza has written, what is distinctively Western and Christian is not slavery but the movement to end slavery. Abolition is a uniquely Christian Western institution. "Never in the history of the world, outside of the West, has a group of people eligible to be slave owners mobilized against slavery." People were willing to expend considerable wealth and, ultimately, blood to get rid of slavery, not for themselves but for other people.

Slavery has existed from the dawn of human history, in the most primitive of human societies and the most civilized. The Chinese, the Indians, and the Arabs all had slaves. Slavery was widespread in Africa, and American Indians had slaves long before Columbus came to the New World. Christians were the first group of people in world history to start an anti-slavery movement.

At bottom, the Devil's real target is Western Civilization, in particular, America. His servants have fought for decades to dismantle the norms, conventions, customs, morals, values, and institutions at the heart of the Christian world, attacking the family, the church, and the education system. It is presented to the Useful Idiots as the 'liberation' of an endless stream of victims: blacks, women, animals, the environment, Atheists, sexual deviants, Latinos, Muslims. In each case, the dastardly deeds of Democrats result in more laws and less individual freedom.

What the leftist does is reduce the victim of real or imagined oppression to an excuse for his heroic posturing. And he enlists the vague term 'Social Justice,' which, at bottom, means to cut down the tall poppies, to prevent any individuals from gaining more property, privileges, income, and wealth than others because they are intelligent, wise, diligent, ambitious, energetic, disciplined, strong or good-looking.

The endgame of 'scientific socialism,' as Marx called it, is communism: the end of private property and end of unequal incomes, with all things being owned in common by a Global Government. As George Orwell brilliantly predicted, those guided by the Evil One might not erect concentration camps and Gulags at first but instead create a prison for the mind, a Devil's Matrix one could say.

By using words. Orwell called it NewSpeak. Part of it is to create labels to demonize those who stand in your way so that you do not have to justify your arguments and actions that are unjustifiable in the real world. By calling people racist, sexist, homophobes, Islamophobes, etc., you deflect rational arguments that poke holes in your evil ideology.

NewSpeak involves subverting the truth for the sake of power, sometimes called 'the politics of truth.' That is used to delegitimize truth since it does not match up with what Cultural Marxists want. The truth must be silenced by total hostility and ritual profanity towards those who will not accept being dominated by the Left. The troops will be led into the heart of darkness not by the intellect but by appeals to the emotions and feelings. That is how you get American kids of unparalleled abundance to become fiercely loyal to evil mass murderers such as Chairman Mao, Ho Chi Minh, and Che Guevara.

Intellectuals want to rule the world, so they are naturally attracted to a totalitarian scheme, with them, experts that they are, in charge. They are against Free Association; the myriad ways people come together organically, on their own. When the socialists laid down the Iron Curtain, one of their first moves was to stamp out any associations not created by the Almighty State: groups for collectors of stamps, coins, etc.; theatre troupes, choirs, orchestras, bands, sports teams, tournaments, Scouting, clubs, societies for this or that, charities, guilds, unions, professional associations, schools, mosques, churches, synagogues, chapels, churches, and so forth. All must be brought under the watchful eye of the all-powerful state to ensure political correctness.

Let us ponder the words of Richard John Neuhaus: "The state is not the whole of society but is one important actor in society. Other institutions - notably the family, the church, educational, economic, and cultural enterprises - are at least equally important actors in the society. They do not exist or act by sufferance of the state. Instead, these spheres have their own peculiar sovereignty, which must be respected by the state."

The Left believes in violence, especially mob violence. It is animated by hatred from those who would take revenge on the world God made. For those who have turned their backs on God, being a leftist provides psychic therapy. It will probably worsen for Christians, who can expect to see their faith hated, their charities closed down, their children ridiculed, their social standards deprecated, their employment opportunities shriveled up, and their love for Jesus forced into the closet.

Every day, Christians make America a better place. As the forces of darkness have taken control of America, they have deconstructed truth, meaning, and reality itself. All that remains is power. The power to gain more powers. The powers to distort the truth and declare that evil is good and make everybody agree with you or not be able to buy or sell what he or she needs to survive. It is the power to annihilate and to achieve worthless aims. It is the negation of all that is good, beautiful, right, and responsible. A culture that disdains judgment is incapable of imparting wisdom. That is the Devil's dream. The Antichrist comes to power through politics.

The Antichrist culture in America loves abortion because it negates the sacredness of unique and unrepeatable human life. It uses social science as a weapon of cultural warfare. Philip Rieff says that Sociology is "a deathwork against the sacred order" that phonily claims neutrality while partisan to the Antichrist culture. It offers the therapist as a substitute for the priest. It promotes "specialists without spirit" and "sensualists without heart." Life without soul.

The dynamics of lying dominate the Antichrist culture, Rieff writes. For instance, America—the freest country ever—is presented as a vast penal colony in need of liberation. The freedom offered by the Antichrist is freedom from morals, but it does not make us free. It makes us slaves to our desires. It promotes lives devoted only to entertainment and pleasure. It supports the joys of transgression as a means to alienate people from the sacred order. The goal is anomie. The result is the state as lord and master.

A godless culture cannot lead to higher humanity—a change in a downward direction unmistakably marks it. In place of commanding truths from God, we substitute human rules about minutiae. The godless culture celebrates its talent at ruining what is sacred. The Antichrist denies and mocks the Bible, not because it is not true, but because it is true.

To the Antichrist, a human being is no more significant than an insect, a mosquito as sacred as a person. The goal is to empty human beings of their identities in the sacred order. Leftists babble produced Franz Fanon, Stalin, and Pol Pot, all of whom celebrated in blood the destruction of the sacred order.

Antichrist culture seeks to separate man from his spiritual nature, leaving him an animal enslaved to appetites, without moral compass points, in a destabilized society. That is an immense disorder of truth—God is not the author of chaos—disorder brings death. Discard the sacred; make God out to be a fiction; ravish the truth; worship at the altar of the supreme fantasies fathered by Marx and Freud.

Mein Kampf is about imposing a fictional new order on a disenchanted reality. Kulturkampf sought to disarm moral authority through law and politics, to shift the moral imagination from Church to State. Both Nazis and Marxists invented substitute religions to supplant Christianity. The Antichrist argues that faith in God involves the abnegation of intellect but then demands faith in its human substitute—as if that signifies you are smart.

To destroy a crèche in a public space but promote transgression in a public space—as in lewd conduct—passes for tolerance. 'Values neutrality' always means taking the side of Antichrist culture. The truth is treated as obsolete. It is replaced by "Everyone is entitled to his or her own opinion."

Obedience to God is presented as the ultimate in boredom, with disobedience portrayed as exciting. The Antichrist demands ever-growing rights to transgressive behaviors. We are left with a land without civility, a nation without grace; full of anti-Christian militants that no one has the balls to stand up to. But Utopia will never come. God is not mocked.

The truth is the truth whether you believe it or not. Marx was a hater. The moving force behind the Antichrist is pure hatred. You can see it in Hitler, Lenin, Stalin, and Picasso, Mapplethorpe, and Madonna. The last three turn their animosity toward the audience.

Antichrist culture aims its arsenal at the dignity of civilization. Nothing is sacred, especially not human beings. Leftist culture does not imagine itself on the road to truth. Its milestones are the destruction of the holy truths others hold dear. Taxpayers are forced to fund works of sacrilege. *Piss Christ* puts Christ in urine because the Christian faith holds as sacred that Christ lives in the Believer. So the 'artist' is saying, "You are piss."

Jesus said that false messiahs would come with plans to save the planet (and perhaps the whales too) and bring about a utopia (the word means nowhere). But He warns that the false saviors will be in league with the Devil. They will make predictions that are just plausible enough. The Antichrist will not come as a seemingly evil person but as an angel of light. He will appear to be a fantastic man who pulls off miraculous feats that help people.

Satan will rule humankind through the Antichrist, a global leader of high charisma, a messianic figure who will form a one-world religion and one-world government promising to save us from war, poverty, and pain. He will have a hypnotic magnetism. No one will be able to buy or sell anything without pledging eternal loyalty to him. Those who resist will be intimidated, starved, and murdered. Most people will yield to him, valuing their bodies more than their souls.

This world has a happy ending, however. Jesus the Christ comes back to vanquish the Devil and his demons forever to Hell, ushering in a New Heaven and a New Earth for all those who have believed on His Name. Only a personal faith in Christ can save you.

As Darkness Creeps Across Our Land

"In every culture, guides are chosen to help us conduct ourselves through those passages from one crisis of choice to another that constitutes the experience of living." ~ Philip Rieff

A Christian believes that we know moral truths about human nature. They have been revealed to us by our Creator, yes, and then by experience and common sense. Everyone can understand the moral truth about humankind. Because of this, the Founding Fathers attested that a people who believed in virtue and strove to be virtuous could govern themselves with a minimal governmental authority over them. People who behave themselves do not need much of a state. The godless do not believe any of that, so they always desire a leviathan state run by themselves—the self-appointed experts.

G. K. Chesterton observed that while free will includes the freedom to do things, it most importantly appears as the freedom *not to do something*—because it would be wrong to do so. Our ultimate happiness often depends on what we choose *not to do*. That is the heart of morality. And why traditional Christian morality is hated by the godless because they prefer to posit that we cannot help what we are or what we do.

It was also Chesterton who said, "Tradition is democracy extended through time." As Benjamin Wiker explains, "Tradition means giving votes to our ancestors. It is the democracy of the dead. Tradition refuses to submit to the small and arrogant oligarchy of those who merely happen to be walking about. It is merely the respect we owe to the wisdom that has collected over time."

The American Left despises and seeks to destroy everything good: America, individual freedom, free enterprise, marriage, family, life, and truth. It especially loathes Christian women. As those who execrate Jesus gain control over more and more of our culture, the persecution of Christians increases. Those who serve the Devil become bolder and more open about the fact that they aim to prohibit any influence on our society by Him. They seek to silence the Body of Christ, one way or another.

There is no question that America is awash in sin and the resultant loneliness and depression (along with mental, emotional, physical, and spiritual problems). Since the 1970s, social science shows we have become less and less happy people, less trusting of our neighbors and our institutions, suffering a decline of true friendship, and the fracturing of families.

We are all sinners who are depraved and would be lost if not for God's saving Grace. We all deserve eternal damnation. Not one of us is good. But one of the worst problems in our postmodern age is making excuses for bad actors. With the collapse of permanent standards came the unwillingness to call deeds evil. Even if someone does something that we once called wrong, we are now instructed to say it is not their fault, because surely they had a bad childhood or have been mistreated by somebody somewhere or oppressed by the anonymous 'society.' People who do terrible things become victims!

Let me tell you, a culture of self-pity and narcissism shows a nation running off a cliff into the abyss. Man is the maker of his own tragedy. The problem is not in our genes or the stars but our spiritual condition. When we choose to reject God, we hurt ourselves and hurt those around us.

The words 'discrimination' and 'judgment' used to represent beautiful virtues before the transvaluation of values turned the world upside down. To have good judgment and discriminating taste was considered part of being a person of good character, a person who had developed the ability to discern what is right, good, noble, and beautiful. And what is not.

What we need today is a prophetic voice. As Richard John Neuhaus explicated, "Prophecy, if it is real prophecy, is an exercise of love. Amos, Hosea, and Jeremiah employed such harsh language in criticizing the children of Israel precisely because they thought more of the people than the people thought of themselves. The prophets were in love with, were possessed by, a vision of the dignity and destiny of those they addressed. The outrageousness of the sin and failure was in direct proportion to the greatness of God's intent for his people."

Without a doubt, the Devil's favorite Bible phrase is, Judge not! But of course, whenever Satan quotes the Bible, it is to twist the meaning. Christians MUST discern between right and wrong, and speak the truth about it. We must exercise right judgment, not based on feelings or opinions, but God's Word.

We are not to stand in judgment of individual souls, as in; YOU are going to Hell Bob! But we are never to approve of sin, and we are never to stand silently by while others mock God, mock the Bible, mock Jesus, or call sin good. We are God's representatives on Earth. We are not the judges of an individual's final destiny, but we are the judges of SIN ITSELF.

Philip Rieff has written of how we sacrifice the authority of the past. We profane sacred history and reduce human beings from sacred selves to social roles. People have always committed transgressive acts, but only today do they demand that transgressive acts be called 'good.' The body is the temple of God, and so it must be violated and defiled. Made into mere meat. 'It is forbidden to forbid' is the motto of our times.

Rieff says that a covenant is an agreement to observe the most precise and most distinct ideas of all—the only truly clear and distinctive ideas—the commanding truths of revelation that ought to guide our conduct. The authoritative truths have been replaced with systematic mendacity. Society kills itself when it develops its lies and deceptions to the point at which it is widely admired. We are in spiritual warfare between truths and strong delusions.

We can see it now; the more the Left wins victories for its worldview, the more open they are about their visceral hatred of God-fearing people. There has even been a lawsuit filed against a Christian for praying for someone else. What harm can there be if someone prays to a God that you think is a fairytale character anyway?

Believers are hated, but for what? Even charities staffed by volunteers who are 38 percent minorities and serve in the worst slums are targets for secularists. They cannot abide any group that believes in Christ. There is only one word for that, and it is satanic.

Another target is homeschooling, even though it produces the most excellent citizens of all schooling options. Parents' freedom to educate their children is met with seething hatred by the Left, as one of its leading lights admitted: "Homeschooling amounts to allowing the faith-deranged to infect their young with their disorder."

Either you will master sin or sin will master you. We must walk in the light or be overcome by darkness. The Devil wants you to reject God's authority—to become a rebel against your Maker, as he is. But temptation is an excellent opportunity to demonstrate loyalty to our Creator. The higher the temptation, the higher the victory.

Atheists love to throw the Inquisition in the face of Christians, to make some moral equivalency between Christianity and Islamic terrorism. Or to make some moral equivalency between Christian history and Secular Humanism's murderous crimes. That is just a criticism of man's inhumanity to man—not the Body of Christ's cruelty to man.

The atheists love to claim that a poor peasant's faith in Jesus is only based on gullibility, but who has been more gullible than a true believer in socialism? Some people had faith that the Soviet Union was a new model of equality and progress. It was, in fact, a prison for not only the body but also the mind. Allow me to set the record straight for you: In 300 years, the Inquisition killed fewer people than did the militantly atheist, socialist regime of Josef Stalin on any given afternoon.

Dwelling in the dark heart of the Left is acrimony for their fellow man and enmity of the Lord. That is why anyone who does not applaud sexual perversions is, not just someone with a different opinion about such matters, but a 'hateful bigot.' And the entire white race must be demonized as racists. Demonization is part of the leftist ideology. Deviants are heroes, and people who believe in the Bible are villains.

It is the Left that is animated by a mean-spirited drive to control others, but they project that onto conservative Christians. It is the Left that openly hates those who disagree with them, but they project that onto conservative Christians. If you do not agree to turn morality upside down, you must undergo 'sensitivity training,' reminiscent of Chairman Mao's ignoble 'reeducation camps.' They have changed the meaning of teaching from dispensing knowledge and wisdom to using government schools as a political weapon.

Bigotry is a negative bias towards people because of the group to which they belong. It runs rampant today—bigotry against white men, against Christians, and against conservatives, who are demonized continuously as being collectively deleterious people.

It is not enough to allow Christians to believe as they wish; their views must be annihilated from the face of the Earth; they must be made to renounce their most sacred convictions. People with power use their authority to silence, intimidate, punish, or criminalize those who hold differing views. They will not stop until they have the state criminalize public utterances that align with biblical morality.

The Left is not reaching out to persuade others with their marches. They mobilize a mob mentality, tapping into the most base of emotions, the most animalistic of passions, to gear people up to hate others so that they can gain power over them. They make war on reality itself and nature itself and wisdom and morality, and knowledge. The Left is hostile to the traditional family and wants it destroyed. They spurn the Rule of Law. They have an aversion to the truth.

There is a seemingly ever-spreading conviction that each individual's moral standards are to be arrived at by no more instructive means than looking into his own heart. Small wonder, then, that this process so often results in an understanding not of what is right but what some person wants to do. The latest excuse for an abortion is, "You have no right to speak about my personal choice." Well, going to Hell is a personal choice. To rape and murder is a personal choice. There is nothing glorious or sacred about 'making a personal choice.' Many personal choices are wrong and immoral. Nearly all of the terrible things human beings have done have been 'personal choices.'

Everybody falls short, but the difference is some are forgiven for their sins, and some are not. The difference between them is that some are sorry for the sins they have done; humble themselves and acknowledge to their fellow man and confess to God that what they did was wrong, and ask Him to forgive them for what they did.

Others stand up and shake their fist at the sky and say, "I am not sorry for my behavior; I am PROUD! I intend to do it again and again and to tell the world that God is wrong, and the Bible is wrong." Such a person is CHOOSING to go to Hell.

The Bible is relevant today; it was in all days past; and will be in all future days. It presents timeless, eternal truths that are not subject to fads, fashions, or trends.

If a person chooses to wallow in habitual sin—whether they call it a lifestyle or not—they elect to separate themselves from God and live in rebellion against Him. God will punish all sin *unless it is forgiven*. To be forgiven, the offender must first apologize, if you will, to God—they must repent, which means to *change*, or at least admit you need to change and try your best to improve.

I am not basing my opinions on any old book, like *Harry Potter* or *Twilight*, as some imbeciles like to claim. The Bible is a sacred book, authored by God Himself, and in it, HE tells US right from wrong—not the other way around.

Some write to me and say, "I believe in a god who loves everybody, and he would never send anyone to hell." Well, they are just making up their little god through fantasy. There is no god like the one they imagine.

Many people are very hostile towards Christ, but not towards Islam, Buddhism, or even Wiccan. At root, this is hatred of Jesus. To hate Jesus—a beautiful person if there ever was one—is not natural for a man. This hatred is being channeled through men and women but has its origin in dark supernatural forces. This rage is usually rebellion against God for issuing moral commands that one wishes to violate.

Hell exists to exterminate sin so that after Hell has done its job—after Christ Jesus judges the quick and the dead—Heaven will be free from sin. God doesn't make anyone go there or even want anyone to go there. People choose to go there by letting the Lord know they have no interest in Him; they hate His plan of salvation and don't want to go to Heaven under His terms.

We all want crime punished. We want Hitler punished, and Jeffrey Dahmer punished, and the monster punished that kidnapped a ten-year-old girl, raped her, sodomized her, sawed both her arms off while she was conscious, and left her in a ditch to die by the side of the road. God says there are *higher crimes* than rape, pedophilia, and murder—namely idolatry, blasphemy, sacrilege, disbelief, and far worse than disbelief: spending your time on Earth preaching and teaching others to doubt.

God loves people, but he does not love sin. He cannot stand sin. But you cannot stand above God, look down at Him, and tell Him He must define sin according to your particular opinions. You are not in a position to judge God.

We were made to worship. As Bob Dylan said, "You're gonna serve somebody." The question is who or what. Human beings, throughout time, have always worshiped. The word *worship* means to show reverence or pay homage to one who is worthy and honorable. The term expresses extreme humility and recognition of the infinite superiority of the one who is worshiped.

Some folks ask, "What kind of God needs and wants to be worshiped? It sounds as though He might be very proud, arrogant, or insecure. Why would He need affirmation from us if He's God?" These are childish questions. As James MacDonald has written, "God is not a human being, and He doesn't function like one. We will not understand Him if we demand he act like a human being. We think it's arrogant for one human being to want the adulation of another because we recognize that most people are not qualitatively very different from one another. God is not some exalted human being at the top of the humankind pyramid—He's in an entirely different category, where He is the only member. He's not like us."

Now, religious freedom doesn't give you the right to tell other people what to do. But the irreligious DO want to tell everyone else what to do. They want people silenced who believe in godly morality. They want them to be rendered unemployable—taking away a man's right to earn a living if he believes in traditional marriage.

I always hear the argument that a Christian should have no say when it comes to social issues. But an atheist should have a say. I read the usual nonsense on social media: Christians want a theocracy! Really? Was America a theocracy in 1960? 1930? 1900? 1870? 1840? 1810? 1780? WHO has said they want a theocracy? NO ONE. So why do atheists keep saying it? They know it is a lie. I am very suspicious of any movement that feels the need to couch itself in lies.

Christians are not on the offensive—we are playing defense. The godless never run out of evil ideas, and they are always wily to any opposition. They might say, "Let's kill 55 million unborn babies!" A person who loves the Lord might say, "No. That is not a good idea." The audacious response? "YOU are divisive!"

The godless might even claim that two men sodomizing each other should have equal societal approval as the God-ordained family, which is a father, a mother, and their mutual children, in case any have forgotten. If anyone objects, "YOU want to impose your beliefs on others!" So an idea is put forth to CHANGE our society in a way that promotes evil, but any defense of what is right is met with a false charge that the defenders of uprightness are the ones on offense.

The godless always want to throw around the silly old saying, "Don't shove your morality down my throat." The implication is that the godless are not doing the same thing. Every society has a moral environment about how people should be, what is acceptable or not, admirable or shameful, what others should do for us, and what we should do for others.

Shame has always been one of the most potent sanctions by which a community's moral life sustains itself. Shame stems from a need to be well regarded by others and is usefully distinguished from guilt, which involves our personal sense of wrongdoing. Shame disciplines the transgressor of boundaries and makes an example of him to others. Thanks to the therapeutic revolution, shame is now thought to be nothing more than a pleasure-squelching product of ignorant religious beliefs. We have a culture beyond shame: shamelessness. Having universal permission to not give a damn about what anybody else thinks has weakened our social bonds. Cheating on one's spouse, lying about one's past, consorting with underage interns, conceiving children out of wedlock, falsifying one's resume, and flat-out lying in public are all now excusable.

Spiritual warfare requires knowledge of the truth, and understanding of the truth comes from the Word of God, and the Word of God is in the Holy Bible. I am not saying that truth does not also make appearances outside of the Bible; of course, it does. But you can know truth when you see it by comparing it with the Word of God.

Any doctrine, belief, idea, concept, behavior, or statement that contradicts the Bible comes from the Devil. Primarily this is true of any theory that denies the Bible is true; that God exists; that He created Man and the Universe and is the Creator of all living things; that God is a Person; or that Jesus was resurrected from the dead.

What we see is the denial that all men and women are sinners. With this comes belligerence toward any restraint of sinful activities if they relate to sexuality. It is at bottom a flight from reality. It is a sanctioning of raw impulse. It is to be ruled by one's appetites rather than ruling your cravings.

As rectitude has decreased, sin, selfishness, and violence have increased. And some call it 'progress.' Cancer progresses. What we see here can only be called 'progress' in the same way terminal cancer is 'progressive.' If you have no sense of direction, and demand no sense of responsibility; if you do not see that man's destiny should be spiritual growth but instead think the purpose of life is only to avoid pain and seek pleasure, we have made progress indeed.

From the decade when God, prayer and the Holy Bible were kicked out of our schools, violent crime has increased 500 percent, along with every other terrible thing. My friend, any doctrine that approves sinful behavior; or ignores the necessity of repentance; that promotes self-gratification, or creates the perception that you are missing out on the good things of life unless you pursue sin; that teaches sin is simply innocent enjoyment or tells you that sin is cool—is from Satan. Any church that lowers standards to accommodate sin is under the sway of the Devil. You can tell true doctrine by discerning if it promotes loving God, serving God, and purposes nothing contrary to His Word.

Another essential point is how Satan's minions, such as the writer of *The Da Vinci Code* Dan Brown, invent an enormous lie that some people want to believe. One such lie is that the Church ripped many 'other gospels' out of the Bible at some point; these banned books have been hidden for centuries, but now your guru will show them to you. It is an outrageous lie in every way possible. What truth is it that the Church has supposedly hidden from everybody? Women should rule the world; God considers homosexual behaviors awesome; Jesus was not crucified but instead had sex with Mary Magdalene while his Apostles watched, moved to France, and had a bunch of kids who became the future kings and queens of that nation.

Another of the dumbest ideas making the rounds of the Internet is that Christianity is the source of the world's continual wars. If you want to prevent the horrors of the bloodiest battles in history, you will separate the godless from the state. Anti-Christian socialists caused the blood-bathed horrors of the 20th century: Hitler, Stalin, Lenin, Mao, and Pol Pot.

Between Alexander the Great, the Persian Wars, and various Roman wars, ten million people were killed in battles that had nothing to do with religion. In China, hundreds of millions of people have died in wars stretching back nearly 2,000 years that had nothing to do with religion. Millions of Indians died in wars before the white man ever set foot in the Americas. It had nothing to do with religion. Genghis Khan's men killed tens of millions, but it had nothing to do with religion. Tamerlane slaughtered 17 million—not for religious reasons.

Most European wars were fought for reasons other than religion, too. The atheistic French Revolution killed millions of noncombatants; the atheistic revolutions in Russia and Red China killed up to one hundred million innocent civilians. And in Africa, at least 12 million people were killed in wars in the last 200 years that had nothing to do with religion.

The religious wars fought in Europe killed maybe ten million—not even one percent of the dead from all wars. Less than 5 percent of all war deaths in human history can be attributed to conflicts having to do with religious differences, and Islam waged most of those. Ninety-five percent of all deaths of innocent civilians in human history have been perpetrated by man's political rulers, man's *governments*, not only for reasons that had nothing to do with Christianity but most often for godless purposes. Keep the godless way from the levers of power, and you will have far less war and death.

We learn from the Bible that we are not to have secular courts decide what is ultimately right and wrong. We are to JUDGE based on Scripture. But no matter what the Father declares is wrong (sinful and immoral), the offer of forgiveness is always there for those who are remorseful, confess their sins, and ask for forgiveness. Only one sin is not forgivable, and that is refusing to accept this offer, e.g., by being proud of your crime and not seeking forgiveness because you refuse to confess that what you did was wrong.

It is true, as the godless charge, Christians are against sin. Everyone is against things that violate their core beliefs. The godless may rail against greed, sexism, racism, capitalism, carbon footprints, and Indian mascots. To a Christian, abortion, hedonism, sexual perversion, sacrilege, and blasphemy are offensive.

The godless may find the Creation story in Genesis hard to believe, as well as the Resurrection of Christ Jesus. The godly find it hard to believe that all life happened by accident because two enzymes ran into each other in primordial soup billions of years ago. Both sides have faith in what they think, but neither can prove it beyond a shadow of a doubt.

The godless love to claim, 'Jesus was a socialist.' That is a gross misrepresentation of Him. He never implied that the government should confiscate our wealth and give it to others. He said we should be generous with those in need by acts of charity, donating out of the heart, giving to charities of our choosing, or choosing individuals. Jesus would certainly not vote for progressive ideology today.

When Russell Kirk listed the 'canons of conservative thought,' first on the list was "belief in a transcendent order, or body of natural law, which rules society as well as conscience. Political problems, at bottom, are religious and moral problems." Jesus would agree. No socialist does. G. K. Chesterton called Original Sin the only part of Christian theology that can be really proved. The sinful nature of humankind is readily apparent to all honest observers.

It is not true that you can't legislate morality. We do it all the time. We have laws against stealing, rape, and homicide, a long list of traffic laws, and a million other laws we call regulations, all of which can be summed up by, "We believe these actions are wrong and if you do them you will be punished."

As author Mark Davis writes in his book *Upside Down*, conservatives are trying to turn back the clock and unring a bell. We do want to return to a time when America was not sacrilegious and publicly blasphemous; when promiscuity was at a low, perverts in the closet, abortion illegal, illegitimate births rare, crime low, national debt low, federal government small, work ethic strong.

Fight the Good Fight

"It is cultural suicide to demand all space and no walls." ~ Robert Bork

When I was a wee lad, I was taught that there was a God who created the Universe and the people in it. He expected a particular code of conduct from people. Virtue was to strive for and vice to avoid. All persons would have their failings in this regard, but what was important was to recognize what was right and what was wrong; to do one's best; to be repentant about one's shortcomings, and ask God to forgive us for our moral failures.

I never heard any of the 100 members of my extended family use profanity or speak with filthy language when I was a boy. I watched television, but I do not recall any hint of vulgarity or overt sexuality. I ventured out in public countless times in my youth and never heard foul words. I did observe a high level of civility, as in men and women addressed as Sir and Ma'am, and innumerable forms of polite social courtesies.

A concerted effort has been made, since the 1960s, to destroy the social habits of the American people. All institutions of authority that might set limits on acceptable behavior, the 'intermediate institutions'—families, churches, schools, private associations—that stand between the individual and the national government and its bureaucracies have been weakened. Equal acceptance has been assigned to the opinions of the most foolish among us. The result has been societal chaos—the necessary precondition for an all-powerful government to step in and take control, with not only the permission of society but upon its pleading.

Critical to any life worth living is the ordering of our loyalties— accepting responsibility for deciding by what we will be bound. The life without obligations that are freely taken and faithfully observed is life in bondage to chaos, a life without meaning.

Freedom is found in obedience to moral standards; all other liberations are nothing but different ways of becoming lost. We bind ourselves in friendship, in marriage, vocation, and most profoundly, in our religion. For those who do not believe in God, their faith—that to which they are devoted—might be a political program. All of us are bound to some worldview that we profess and to which we hold ourselves accountable.

Religion could be described as what people ultimately believe to be true, in which case everybody is religious because everyone has some belief system about the reality in which they find themselves. The secular humanists have pulled off a diabolical trick by making those whose ultimate beliefs about the Cosmos include our Maker, are somehow excluded from the public square. That, of course, leaves the square only fit for the expression of their views, which is totalitarianism, not to mention evil.

What the Church cannot do is force people to do what it wants by calling in the police. When Jesus says, "Give to Caesar what belongs to Caesar, and give to God what belongs to God," He is not saying the world is divided between the two. The Kingdom of God encompasses all of existence; Caesar's role is temporary.

Secular humanists demand that those who believe in God change their views and accept behaviors that God always has condemned. If the godly must deny what their holy writs say, they must reject that Scripture represents eternal, universal truths. That makes the Word of God worthless.

No one is more religious than a devout leftist. They are devoted to destroying the free market economy, private enterprise, individual freedom, national sovereignty, the rule of law, the free exercise of religion, and traditional morality. Along with the very idea that your life is yours and what you do with it is your responsibility—not that of the Almighty State. They police your speech and thought to force adherence to politically correctness. Why do they want to destroy everything worthy, good, noble, virtuous, pure, and beautiful? Because the master they serve loves to see human beings suffer in misery.

Since few people would volunteer to go to Hell for Eternity, a Grand Illusion must be created to tempt us sufficiently by making us think lies are true and evil is good. Propaganda and brainwashing are among the chief tools used. As George Roche writes in *A World Without Heroes,* the leftist is an anti-hero. He or she operates in bad faith, twists words, assaults liberty and religious belief, showers contempt on America, denigrates traditional propriety, denies the goodness of our history, "to make bearable his or her own intellectual and spiritual barrenness." It is the work of such anti-heroes that has changed America from "a serene, joyful, proud, free nation to a vast, suffering bureaucracy, consumed by its 'guilt.'" The anti-heroes are lost souls, "the slavering servants of the Dark Lord, in dread of a just God. *The world* flatters our vanities and feeds our lusts, to enslave us, and pulls us into darkness."

To escape our unhappiness, we sate our senses, as *the world* provides the illusion of happiness through sensual delights, vicarious thrills, and carnal urges. Our civilization cannot maintain itself when the people no longer believe in it. Moral relativism dissolves the bonds that hold together our communities. Malcolm Muggeridge maintained, "When mortal men try to live without God, they infallibly succumb to megalomania, or erotomania, or both. The raised fist or the raised phallus." Roche adds, "Unhappy the country that loses its moral bearings! Unhappy the many, bereft of spiritual leadership, who are doomed to cling to the self as the only reality in an unfathomable existence. Small wonder we fling ourselves on the treadmills of sensation."

Politics is about getting, using, and keeping the power to make people do what you want, and not do what you don't want. Those on the Left want politics to rule every tiny aspect of your life— totalitarianism. Their main thrust is to scrub America clean from any mention or influence of our Creator. The ways of these progressives are, in fact, entirely hostile to God and His People. And the oddest ducks of all are the so-called liberal Christians, who side with the Left at every turn, thereby allying themselves with the very people who snarl with contempt at Christ.

By rejecting God's Laws, we leave the making of law to the whims, fads, and fashions of self-interested men. We make access to political power the most valuable thing in the land. Those with access can lobby politicians to advance their causes. The populace can vote to line their own pockets with the taxpayer's money. All legislation is someone's morality, and those who serve Satan will impose their morality on you if you let them.

Think about it. The views and values held by the vast majority of *We the People* have been excluded from public policy for decades, only because those views and values come from God, not from the heads of some men. And no Christian has suggested the same exclusion go the other way; no Christian suggests that the views of the godless, as demonic as they might be, ought to be excluded from the public landscape. Politics is about people deciding what is wrong and how to make it better. These are *moral judgments*, and for most Americans, moral judgments come from the Moral Judge.

The law, by definition, deals with standards of correct behavior. It is, therefore, more than just a set of rules. The law derives its legitimacy and authority from the perception that it tries to express what the people under it believe to be right and wrong.

Laws are based on what lawmakers vote to be codified as right or wrong, good or evil, which means laws are the *moral judgments* of men and women. The moral truths of Christianity are valid and universal and therefore, should at least have a place in the table.

The Free Exercise of Religion demands that the Christian point of view not be banished to private conscience. You cannot exercise in a closet. When the moral judgments of people who believe in God are excluded from the legislative arena, what is left? Only the views of the godless, which is precisely how they want it.

Once Christianity is obliterated from the public square, all that is left is the individual with political or bureaucratic connections, the identity politics grievance groups, and the Almighty State. The godless Left has gradually changed the purpose of legislation in America, from an organic law that reflects the fundamental beliefs, values, customs, conventions, and traditions of our nation, to an instrument of social engineering.

The law is supposed to reflect the morality of *We the People*. But the Left has ruled traditional morality—that held by the majority of Americans today and was held by 90 percent of Americans down through the course of history until the use of the law for social engineering began by the Left in the 1960s—is meaningless where the law is concerned. Right and wrong no longer matter.

Godless revolutions always revoke the Rule of Law. The Rule of Law means that laws are not made to favor any particular individuals or groups in advance. Think of it as the rules to baseball: you have fair balls and foul balls, a book of rules about how the game is to be played, even rules by which you might get kicked out of the game for flagrant violations. But the rules are decided before the players take the field and no one knows before the match begins who will be helped or hurt by them, who will hit a ball that barely clears the fence or hit one that falls one inch short.

Notice how the Left uses the law in a far different way to advance their agenda. Affirmative Action obviously favors some individuals and groups and disfavors others. That is a flagrant violation of the Rule of Law: to grant privileges to some but not others; to use the law to redistribute assets that have been legally earned; to employ the law for social engineering; to use it to further your political agenda and punish any who would oppose you.

After a godless revolution of socialists, the state and its leading representatives stand above the law, which is why a Lenin, Stalin, Hitler, Mao, or Pol Pot can massacre millions of his own citizens without being arrested for murder. Leftist regimes always bring about this type of government.

In our times, the Supreme Court has decided on who the final arbiter of morality and culture should be: Itself. The Court continues to weaken the power of *We the People*, and their elected representatives, to govern themselves. What should be a legal institution has become the adjudicator of political, cultural, and social issues. It is noteworthy that since the Sixties, decisions of the Supreme Court are announced in the media as victories for someone's moral position, rather than a determination based on the law.

Hardly anything has been more deceptively misrepresented to Americans in recent decades than the 'Establishment Clause' of the First Amendment. It is not there to keep the Church out of State business. Quite the opposite: It is there to keep the State out of Church affairs. The First Amendment to the Constitution never says religion must be separated from society. Today a child cannot read the Bible in school but can read the *Communist Manifesto*, which Stalin and Mao held to be their bible when they murdered 100 million people.

In 1980, the Supreme Court ruled that it was illegal for a school to display the Ten Commandments. Even though they are engraved on the Supreme Court itself. Twenty years later, the Court ruled that it was unconstitutional for high school students to publicly pray at a football game, in a trial that opened, as all do, with the words, God save the United States and this Honorable Court!

The American Civil Liberties Union (ACLU) leads these efforts to censor acknowledgment of God, even though the vast majority of Americans favor God being revered in public. So much for *We the People*. With a budget of $50 billion, the ACLU files suit after suit to financially intimidation municipalities.

There has been no more anti-Christian organization that the ACLU. For decades it has fought to remove every nativity scene in the country from public view, while at the same time, fought for the rights of artists to be paid by taxpayers to display Christ Jesus in a bottle of urine publicly or the Virgin Mary covered in feces.

The ACLU views Free Speech and the Free Exercise of Religion as enemies of their agenda for America. In public schools, children have had Valentine cards confiscated that mentioned God; wall tiles for a fundraiser removed because two said God Bless on them; clergymen banned from school property; students prohibited from praying at graduation; football teams stopped from praying together before a game; invocations and benedictions outlawed. The ACLU sued two school board members for reciting the Lord's Prayer at a public meeting (The ACLU lost that case). In Iowa, a valedictorian was told he could not mention Jesus during his speech. The Alliance Defense Fund came to his aid, and the school learned what they did not know: It is your constitutional right to thank Jesus for your success in your speech.

America, as envisioned by the ACLU, will not sing 'God Bless America,' 'My Country 'Tis of Thee,' or 'The Star Spangled Banner' in public; will remove the Ten Commandments from all public buildings including the Supreme Court; fire congressional and military chaplains; remove 'In God We Trust' from our currency, public documents, and National Motto; and excise 'Under God' from the Pledge of Allegiance.

The ACLU will demand that crosses and Stars of David removed from the military cemetery at Normandy, and all other military cemeteries, and Arlington National. They may require their removal from all citizens' graves—since they are obviously in public view. Finally, the Declaration of Independence must be changed to remove those offensive words 'God' 'Creator' 'Supreme Judge' and 'Divine Providence.'

Costly lawsuits have been filed by the ACLU against public schools over gospel concerts; a teacher who taught Bible lessons for 30 years off school property; teachers meeting on their own time to pray together; and prayer at a high school baseball game—which the ACLU called "immoral," while demanding prison time for the school officials.

The ACLU has filed many suits over public displays of the Ten Commandments, some of which had been there for more than 100 years. They seek to eradicate public acknowledgment of Christianity. They sued the National Park Service because of a cross in the Mojave Desert to honor veterans of World War One. In countless cities, the ACLU demanded tiny crosses be removed from city seals. They all caved in to save legal expenses except Los Angeles. The ACLU spokesperson, Ramona Ripston, says the cross, which is so small you can hardly see it, makes "non-Christians feel unwelcome in Los Angeles."

Catholic Charities has been sued by the ACLU, who demanded that their employee health insurance pays for contraceptives, in direct violation of Catholic doctrine. The ACLU sued the Salvation Army to force them to hire non-Christians. They sued Yeshiva University to demand that two lesbians be allowed to live together in student housing against their Jewish Faith. They sued the Virginia Military Institute to stop cadets from saying grace before their meals.

The ACLU pockets millions of dollars from taxpayers in these lawsuits. When they win or settle they use the Civil Rights Attorneys Act to collect their attorney fees, which means schools and municipalities have to pay the ACLU for the pleasure of being sued. The ACLU could not care less how much it costs taxpayers to demolish the history, heritage, and faith of America.

None of these cases are about genuine violations of the First Amendment clause that states plainly the federal Congress shall not establish a national religion. The First Amendment was never intended for the government to censor public religious expression.

What has been the result of all this demonic activity by the ACLU, and their cohorts, the atheist progressives? Have their ideas reduced crime, improved society, or strengthened families? Have their actions reduced suicide, drug use, alcoholism, perversion, and deviant behavior? Have their ideas made for a more civil, polite, courteous society, and made America a better nation?

The ACLU is Lucifer personified. Incredibly, they will sue a Christian hospital because it won't kill babies, and sue Catholic shelters for children because they do not provide contraception or abortion. *We the People* never voted for this takeover of America by God-haters.

Militant atheists will eventually come for place names that honor our Christian heritage in America. The most obvious one would be in Texas, Corpus Christi (Body of Christ). Sacramento is named for the Christian Sacraments, Los Angeles means 'City of Angels,' Sante Fe 'Holy Faith,' Santa Cruz 'Holy Cross.' Providence is a Christian term.

But the largest group is the cities named after Christian Saints. They include Saint Paul, Saint Louis, St. Petersburg, St. Augustine, San Francisco (St. Francis), San Diego (St. James), San Antonio (St. Anthony), San Jose (St. Joseph), San Bernardino (St. Bernard), Santa Monica, Santa Barbara, and the town I am from, St. Joseph. California alone has sixty municipalities named for Saints, while Texas has 27.

There are also rivers, islands, lakes, bays, canals, peninsulas, points, parkways, roads, bridges, tunnels, townships, and counties named either for Catholic Saints or Protestant Christians or Christian terms. And plenty of places with biblical names such as Bethlehem, Goshen, Canaan, Zion, Antioch, Bethany, and Trinity. Not to mention three named Christian County. Changing all these names to suit the secularists will require many new maps. Do not the godless people who live in these places feel affronted and unwelcome by the very names?

The New Testament commands Christians to care for the poor, especially widows and orphans; to feed the hungry, give drink to the thirsty, clothe the naked, shelter those without shelter, visit the sick and the prisoner, AND tell them the GOOD NEWS—the GOSPEL.

That is Christian charity (love), and Christians have done an incredible job of it for nearly 2000 years. But nowhere in the Bible do you see it commanded that this be done by government—by Caesar. There are one hundred places where the Bible talks about the poor, but not once is any government involvement mentioned ever.

Nothing has created more deprivation that the twisted idea that the primary job of the government is to redistribute all the wealth of a nation, which the Left sees as its best idea—to take property from one who has earned it and give it to others in exchange for their votes. What government welfare is is counterfeit Christian charity. It mimics Christian charity, except it leaves out the most critical part—the Good News, the Gospel, which it has made illegal.

One Trillion Dollars spent each year for the redistribution of wealth under a scheme that makes the Gospel against the law. If that trillion dollars remained in our pockets, that could be one trillion dollars of Christian charity that includes the message of Jesus—that is genuinely 'inclusive.'

Instead of having a client dependent on the government teat for life, perhaps the REAL problems underlying the incapability to take care of oneself regarding physical needs—often a symptom of a spiritual disease—could be healed.

I am all for private Christian charity for the deserving poor but not for state welfare checks indiscriminately mailed out to everybody regardless of circumstances. Welfare makes more of what it purports to remedy. Studies show that there are hardly any illegitimate babies where there is no government aid given for illegitimate babies. When you offer a government benefit, more and more people will queue up to get it. It is the welfare state that has led to 80 percent of the urban poor having babies out of wedlock. It has destroyed the families in the inner cities, leaving them devoid of fathers. Left behind are children who are unnurtured, underfed, unwashed, undisciplined, and unloved.

Christian charity should distinguish between honest poverty and laziness. It should work to reclaim the intemperate, counsel the erring, and stimulate the indolent whilst easing suffering - changing the person, not just temporarily adjusting worldly conditions - to transform individuals while we feed their bodies.

Efficacious help should be personal and conditional, bringing the giver and receiver together, with love, yes, but also with discipline. When the recipient is responsible for her plight, a willingness to change must be present. Because material deprivation is usually the tip of the iceberg, to indeed help, we must remove the evil that causes the hardship, which is moral, spiritual deficiency. Those with habitual sinful tendencies should be made to work or left to the consequences of their misconduct.

The horrors of the 20th century show us the insanity of the socialist, atheist dream that makes a god of science and lowers man to the status of a beast. Still, the madness persists, being indoctrinating into our children. What is the legal definition of insanity? The inability to distinguish right from wrong.

Atheists love to claim they are merely against religion. But make no mistake about it—they mean Christ Jesus. He represents the only religion with enough sway in Western Civilization, and its morality, laws, and government, worth fighting against. You might wonder what they hate about Jesus so much. They see Him as the obstacle to building a secular utopia. They want absolute power.

The people who serve Satan will never be satisfied until they banish our Father and the Holy Bible to the closet. The goal is total submission. They want preaching and teaching against abortion, sexual perversions, and occult religions prohibited as 'verbal violence' or 'hate speech,' even in Christian schools, homeschooling, churches, radio, and television.

Once God and His People have been banished from the Public Square, decisions about values become contests between opinions, instead of contests of truth claims. The secularists do not claim to have any truth—and they deny that anyone else has any either. If one person or group believes incest should be legal, and another believes it should not, the state will probably rule for incest because, after all, those committing incest aren't hurting you any. That is the result of removing transcendent moral truth from our society. As Aristotle said, it is impossible to discuss virtue with people who are handicapped by an incapacity for virtue.

It is right that we are better off today regarding creature comforts, the march of technology, the advance of medicine, and so forth. But it is not a wise man who fails to comprehend that by every social pathology America is ten times worse—literally—than it was before God was banned from public schools in the 1960s where he had resided comfortably for three hundred years in America—and before the rest of the Cultural Revolution, which was the fruit of a deliberate, demonically inspired Cultural Marxist strategy—whether we look at the levels of violent crime, killing babies, suicide, mental problems, spousal abuse, child abuse, sexual abuse, drug addiction, obesity, sexually transmitted disease, public profanity, lack of civility and manners, promiscuity, adultery, divorce, broken homes, sexual perversions, sacrilege, idolatry, blasphemy, and just plain old loneliness and unhappiness and misery. It is evident *for all who do not refuse to see* that SIN causes most of the world's problems.

There is no doubt that the Bible declares *the world* is against God. That is because this world is ruled by Satan, who rules it through a creature-centered philosophy, which is often pushed by governments under his control. This philosophy rejects God and sets up a substitute life and counterfeit religion with Man as its object of worship.

The enemies of God are fallen men and fallen angels—as well as fallen nations—separated from Him and organized to serve the Devil. The Prince of Darkness influences the desires of the flesh—his toehold to your heart—to accomplish his devilish schemes. It only takes a drop of cyanide to poison a whole glass of wine.

Unclean spirits will whisper that you should depend on man's knowledge and technology; seek firstly to pleasure yourself; try to find happiness through sex, wealth, or fame; lie, cheat and steal to get ahead; there are no rules and no morals; be proud of your sins! The world works to destroy you by appealing to your senses, enticing your appetites, coercing you to conform to its standards, and ridiculing your faith. Do not love the things of this world, which are of no lasting value.

As the Apostle Paul has taught us: "Run in such a way as to get the prize. Everyone who competes in the games goes into strict training. They do it to get a crown that will not last, but we do it to get a crown that will last forever. Therefore I do not run like someone running aimlessly; I do not fight like a boxer beating the air." Finish your race with joy. Fight the good fight of the faith.

The Devil's Matrix

Man is the Crown Jewel of Creation, and far different from the rest of it. Man is a unique presence in the Cosmos, the only creature who bears the Image of God; can become a child of the living God; is a joint heir with Christ Jesus, and partaker of the divine nature through the indwelling of the Holy Spirit. Man is God's masterpiece, the climax of His creative effort. Everything in the Cosmos was created before man and *for man*: trees, mountains, rivers, fields, plants, and animals. That is the opposite of what 'the world' is teaching our children.

The Devil is tricky. I was reading what at first appeared to be an innocent enough book review, in which the writer slipped in a few things for his boss.
 1) For 2500 years, the Bible account of Adam and Eve was taken seriously. [Was? It is taken seriously by hundreds of millions of people right now!]
2) Adam and Eve were once viewed as actual human beings. [Were?]
3) Before Adam and Eve, other cultures had developed their own origin stories. [There was no 'before' Adam and Eve.]
4) The writer of Genesis borrowed the Great Flood story from other tales. [As if God has to 'borrow' mankind's stories.]

5) All this was before scientific discoveries were making the discrepancies in Genesis and other claims of the Bible seem more and more absurd. [Excuse me? No examples are given.]

Underlying everything is something scientists will never get to the bottom of or the top of, and this truth, they are loath to admit. A cosmos created by a Creator would be that way. Scientists do not know what life is; only that it animates our bodies. If we seek the ultimate truth, we must supplicate God and His Word.

Some say that God's plan is true but boring, while the Devil's Matrix is exciting but false. I know this, it is hard to create good things, and the process might take a long time, but they are easy to demolish quickly. People following a wicked master, whom they do not see, are working to destroy Western Civilization.

To those without spiritual discernment, the fictions of the godless can be more persuasive than the truth. Traditional values are scorned and ridiculed by vandals, who are also hostile to any suggestion that America might be a splendid place of high achievement. We should fight against them, for the Lord, and with His help.

With the loss of faith in Jesus, souls were swept clean and ripe for infestation by the dark side, because men and women must have faith in something—be it New Age nonsense or leftist political movements—to drown the grief of solitude, and the dread of death. They are often marked by sentimentality, where feelings that should be focused on the 'other' are focused on the self. It is not the object of their emotions that is important, but themselves. So, *I stand up for the poor*, is not really about the poor, who only serve as objects for their noble gestures. Virtue signaling.

304

The godless materialist tries to *reduce* everything to explain away what matters most, thereby trivializing all of substance. In this sick worldview, there is no self-control because there is no self to control. And no ethics, because one must have free will to behave ethically. Even rationality is an illusion imposed by some neural network to another if we only have brains but no minds. This worldview matches that of Carl Sagan: "My fundamental premise about the brain is that its workings - what we sometimes call 'mind' - are a consequence of its anatomy and physiology, and nothing more."

Let's listen instead to John Richard Neuhaus: "The person who insists that my experience of a Mozart piano sonata is not an encounter with beauty, but nothing more than a neurochemical response to physical vibrations has said nothing of consequence about my experience; he has said a great deal about his own poverty, if not perversity, of mind. "

To me, scientific materialism such as this is superstition without rational foundation, dogmatic religious beliefs confusing science with religion. It seems silly to me to suppose that this Universe somehow created itself. And if God created this Universe full of physical laws, it makes sense that God also reveals moral laws.

One goal of the Enemy is to substitute 'facts' for 'truth.' The idea is indoctrinated into our youth that *facts are what are proven by science*, while the *truth is a matter of opinion*. After being under this ether for a dozen years or so, it is easy to move them further down the Path to Perdition by telling college students that whatever is not a scientific fact *is not true*. 'There is no truth outside of scientific facts,' being the final philosophy. But that is a lie. Facts are part of the truth; the truth is more massive than facts. The truth decides which facts are correct. Having lost our grip on reality, is it any wonder our milieu is famous for its mental problems?

The Devil encourages the corruption of every facet of a man's life. He works to derail the young man from a life of faith by winning him over gradually by the systematic, persistent corruption of all he believes and enjoys. Gerald McGraw put it this way: "A single quarter lifted to the eye can obscure the blazing light of the Sun, a star whose diameter is 865,000 miles. Just so, if we let him, Satan can cause us to block out our vision of God."

Once the diabolical scoffers have rid the world of traditional values, all that remains is *I want*. But the idea of a life well lived is to seek the truth, not to invent it. Those who have set about debunking the idea that there is any such thing as objective truth must have a goal in mind. They have their own set of subjective truths that they will defend. The godless ideologies all contain pieces of veracity wrenched from their proper context. Any accuracy in these ideologies comes from objective truth. As C. S. Lewis maintained, "The human mind has no more power of inventing a new value than of imagining a new primary color."

David Brooks' article in the *New York Times* 'If It Feels Right' is quite revealing: "The eminent Notre Dame sociologist Christian Smith led a research team that conducted in-depth interviews with young adults from across America. Smith and company asked about the young people's moral lives, and the results are depressing. The interviewers asked open-ended questions about right and wrong, moral dilemmas, and the meaning of life. In the rambling answers, you see the young people groping to say anything sensible on these matters. When asked to describe a moral dilemma they had faced, two-thirds of the young people either couldn't answer the question or related problems that were not moral."

"Not many of them have previously given much or any thought to many of the kinds of questions about morality that we asked," Smith writes. When asked about wrong or evil, they could generally agree that rape and murder are wrong. But, aside from those two crimes, moral thinking didn't enter the picture. The default position, which most of them came back to again and again, is that moral choices are just a matter of individual taste. "It's personal," the respondents typically said. "It's up to the individual. Who am I to say? I would do what I thought made me happy or how I felt. I have no other way of knowing what to do but how I internally feel. I mean, I guess what makes something right is how I feel about it."

Dennis Prager writes: "From the time long before the United States became a country, until well into the 1950s, the Bible was the most widely read book in America; it was the primary vehicle by which each generation passed on morality and wisdom to the next generation. Since that time, we have gone from a Bible-based society to a Bible-ignorant one; from the Bible being the Greatest Book to the Bible being an irrelevant book. Ask your college-age child, niece, nephew, or grandchild to identify Cain and Abel, the Tower of Babel, or the ten plagues. Get ready for blank stares. I recently asked some college graduates to name the four Gospels. None could."

Prager concludes, "But what we have today is worse than ignorance of the Bible. It is contempt for it. Just about anyone who quotes the Bible, let alone says it is the source of his or her values, is essentially regarded as a simpleton who is anti-science, anti-intellectual, and sexist. Whenever teenagers call my radio show or I meet one in person, I can usually identify—almost immediately—those who are receiving a religion-based education. They are far more likely to act mature and have more wisdom than their Bible-free peers."

Only human beings consider God, the Creation, the afterlife, meaning, purpose, and morality. Man alone is cognizant of the past, present, and future. Uniquely, men and women wear clothes, adorn themselves, and create music, art, books, technology, and science. Exclusively, humans are spiritual beings who pray and worship and realize a transcendent reality. Man is the singular being that is both good and evil.

I love science, but it is limited to what can be measured and observed. The things that matter most are beyond science: Love, beauty, honor, sacrifice, worship, faith, hope, virtue, meaning, and purpose. Science has undoubtedly given us far greater control over the physical world, but it has not made men and women happier, and it has not led to social harmony.

The only thing keeping the Theory of Evolution alive is bigotry against the Creator on the part of scientists and educators. Real science can be investigated and repeated in experiments—evolution cannot. It is a religion, not actual science. If you put your faith in science instead of putting your trust in God, you become a sitting duck for the craziest, zaniest chicanery, as long as it presented as 'scientific.'

Alexander Solzhenitsyn affirms, "Truth eludes us if we do not concentrate with total attention on its pursuit. Destructive and irresponsible freedom has been granted boundless space. Society has turned out to have scarce defense against the abyss of human decadence, against the misuse of liberty, such as motion pictures full of pornography, crime, and horror. This is all considered to be part of freedom and to be counterbalanced, in theory, by the young people's right not to look and not to accept. ... How did the West decline from its triumphal march to its present debility? Secular Humanism: the proclaimed and practiced autonomy of man from any higher force above him. We turned our backs on the Holy Spirit. The new way of thinking did not admit the existence of intrinsic evil in man. A total emancipation occurred from the moral heritage of Christian centuries. Man's sense of responsibility to God, and society has grown dimmer and dimmer, and humanity has found itself in a harsh spiritual crisis. All the celebrated technological achievements of progress, including the conquest of outer space, do not redeem the twentieth century's moral poverty, which no one could have imagined even as late as the nineteenth century. We have been deprived of our most precious possession: our spiritual life."

Satan personifies sin. Sin is what he continuously does or plans to do, and what he deceives, persuades, and inspires others to do. Sin changes your heart. It ruins the purity of your thoughts. Sin alters the way you see yourself. It destroys anything life-giving, beneficial, and peaceful. Most tragically, it ruins relationships—one's relationship with God and relationships with other humans.

Overall, God's instruction in the Holy Bible smashes the false notion that many have: Sin is of minor concern as long as nobody gets 'hurt.' There is no such thing as a sin that does not harm. It *always* devastates. The damage may not be visible. The consequences might not immediately appear to the perpetrators. Most do not wait around to see the injury.

The flesh is a willing participant in sin. The 'flesh' here means that we are born sinners, and it is in our nature to rebel against God and want to go our own way. This sinful nature can only be neutralized by the Holy Spirit, which comes to dwell in those who believe in Jesus. The flesh wants to fornicate, think nasty thoughts, live for the senses, distract itself through entertainment, and put other things ahead of Christ as our focus of attention, all of which is idolatry.

The flesh wants to be selfish, refuse to forgive others, envy and covet what someone else has, and lead other people onto the Highway to Hell so that you won't be lonely there. Lust is a sin of the flesh. Sure, demons can entice you, with objects of desire to lead you into vice, but *the Devil made me do it* is no excuse. He cannot force you to do anything.

Everybody is going to sin, but not everybody is going to make a habit of it. A Christian wants to escape sin. An unbeliever only wishes to evade the consequences of sin. The worst advice in the world is: *Just follow your heart!* From the human heart, come evil thoughts of sexual perversion, adultery, pride, deceit, theft, murder, and all sorts of wickedness. It is not a sin to have such ideas bubble up in your mind, but it is a sin not to say no to such thoughts. There is an old saying: You can't stop a bird from landing on your head, but you can stop it from building a nest in your hair.

Speaking of *the world*, the Bible talks about 'the world' being against Him and His People. Here He refers to popular culture, entertainment, sensual pleasures, politics, science, and education. It is indeed not that God is against any of those things, per se. It is that they are quite often arrayed *against Him*.

Lucifer weaves a matrix for you to live in, a compelling illusion that takes you away from a relationship with your Father. And into thinking only about this world and what it puts in His place. Who cannot perceive the breakdown of moral standards in our day? Look at our movies, music, art, advertisements, immodest dress, ribald public behavior, crude manners, and dirty books, magazines, and websites. Killing babies is called 'choice,' and disgusting perversions called 'gay.' The abomination of witchcraft is foisted on innocent children as if it is harmless fun. Murder and cannibalism are themes for cinematic enjoyment.

One of the Devil's big lies in fashion right now is that it isn't your fault if you do bad things because your circumstances made you do it. Perhaps you were mistreated as a boy, grew up poor, or in a messed up family; maybe you are not white.

That has been the theory behind progressive social programs since the 1970s; if only 'society' improved your circumstances and self-esteem, everybody would become equally law-abiding, productive citizens. They built brand new apartments for the 'disadvantaged' across the nation only to be shocked that those given free housing tore it up.

Darwinism helped break down the idea of 'free will' because, under that ideology, we are compelled by our genes to do what we do. Marx said we do what we do for reasons of economics. Nietzsche said we do what we do for power, or ought to. Freud came along to tell us everything we do is because of sex.

The Cultural Marxists that sought to annihilate America, Western Civilization, Capitalism, and Christianity put it all together. They taught the whimsical notion that words have no real meanings at all. So they could make words mean whatever they wanted them to mean. For confusion and propaganda, they did, including making some words mean the opposite of their definitions. Dewey and his educationists took over our schools to brainwash the young. And here we are living in an abyss of darkness and sin.

Freud was wrong that man only lives for pleasure and self-gratification. Man seeks meaning in his existence. Men and women are not robots but human beings with free will; free to choose our attitudes, morals, and actions, for which, having free will, we are then responsible. Satan tries to tell you that men only invent values and mores. It is our job to seek and find what is right. God has a unique purpose for each person, but Man has the freedom to reject that purpose. As Victor Frankl explained, "Man does not simply exist, but always decides what his existence will be, what he will become in the next moment."

The diabolical idea that a man is nothing more than the result of conditioning by biology, psychology, and society, i.e., that man is nothing more than what his genes and environment have made him, is nihilism: the belief in nothing. Each individual *is capable* of rising above his conditions. We see this all the time, the man who overcame the odds stacked against him. In the end, we each become what we have made of ourselves, or better yet, what we have been transformed into by the Lord. Even in horrible concentration camps, some individuals acted nobly, and others did not. They acted how they chose to act. They became whom they decided to become.

At the same time, I believe many Christians with good intentions do harm when they more or less blame God for evil. Some people have become ex-Christians after a horrible event in their lives, such as the loss of a child; the rape or murder of a loved one; the death of a young wife to cancer; a young man wheelchair-bound for life from a diving accident; after which some Christian pronounced, Well, it was God's Will!

The Holocaust nearly killed Judaism. Many Jews, and even more so their children and grandchildren, came out the other side as atheists because they could not believe YHWH was there if such a thing happened. Why do people blame God for what diabolical men like Adolf Hitler, Josef Stalin, or Chairman Mao do? I certainly hope it is not because Christians often say; It was God's plan.

I think we need to stop that. Since we have free will, when men do evil, it is not God's plan but *men's plans*. The Devil's schemes. God hates evil. He is holy—and evil is evil *because* He hates it. All people who love the Lord are called to hate wickedness, too. Evil people act *against* God's will. I believe that God has a blueprint for every life, but Man has the will to go his own way, and usually does. God commands us to recognize evil and fight against it—an odd command indeed if He wills it.

Notice that Jesus and His disciples did not attribute evil to the Father. They saw suffering all around them, and every time Jesus gave it a spiritual dimension, He said it came from Satan and his army of demons. They prayed that God's will would be done on Earth *as it is in Heaven*, which shows me that it ofttimes isn't.

A central problem is the overall promotion of irresponsibility, which has produced a vast decline in holding individuals responsible for their actions, allowing for massive scapegoating by blaming society, fathers, mothers, childhood trauma, former lovers, genes, or brain chemistry. All of that is against God's prescription: Fill up that God-shaped vacuum in your heart with gratitude for God's blessings; study the Bible; join a church; and most of all, habitually hit those knees.

The idea of liberty that our Founding Fathers made famous was *freedom combined with moral responsibility*. They did not mean libertinism (being devoid of moral restraints on sexuality). Postmodernism rejects absolute values and asserts that nothing but personal taste should decide our behavior. Refusing to recognize that evil exists in every man—Original Sin—has had dire consequences for our society. As Aleksandr Solzhenitsyn says, "Alas, truth is seldom sweet. It is almost invariably bitter."

One significant movement of our day is to absolve people from moral blame for whatever they do. That started with the idea that being an alcoholic, and later a drug addict, was not a moral failing but a disease. You could no more overcome it with willpower than you could cancer.

Drunkards by the millions, and those who love them, have made 'alcoholism is a disease' an accepted truth in our society. But is it true? Plenty of doctors and scientists have concluded that *it is not* valid. But their books don't sell well, because they are 'negative thinkers.'

One example is Herbert Fingarette, who writes, "This myth, now widely advertised and widely accepted, is neither helpfully compassionate nor scientifically valid and, in fact, has never had a scientific justification. A mass of scientific evidence accumulated over the past couple decades challenges every major belief associated with the phrase 'alcoholism is a disease.'"

To the trained eye, there is a gigantic difference between societies built on the Christian faith and all others. If the secularists succeed in banishing Christ from our country we will see people making excuses for not doing what Christian society does, e.g., spouses personally caring for sick, incontinent, perhaps demented wives and husbands, possibly with help from other family members, versus just dumping them in institutions staffed by strangers that do not love them. That is only one example of the millions of small Christian deeds that we take for granted in charity, honesty, and kindness.

Charity is not innate in Man. To defer instant gratification is not inherent in humanity. For men to take responsibility for the women who bear their children is not intrinsic in men. For men and women not to steal, when entrusted to guard someone else's valuables, is not inborn in us. Without a belief in God, what good is an oath or a sacred vow? Where is the scientific reason for monogamy? If you want to see the real fallen state of the human race, look no further than the atheistic socialist countries that men set up in the 20th century.

Ralph Waldo Emerson contended that the corruption of language follows the corruption of man. Those who work for Devil love to corrupt our language. It gives them power for propaganda. Notice how powerful words are. Gifted speakers are often either revered or feared. People use words to bless and to curse, to supplicate to God, and to summon demons. Look at the legal force given to oaths. Those entering college with the most mastery of words do best *in every field*. Most of what each of us knows about our Cosmos came from words, written or spoken. Just try to think without words.

Consider how God told Adam to *name* all the animals. Whatever he called them, that is what they'd be. And ponder this: "In the beginning was the Word, and the Word was with God, and the Word was God." And this: "The Word was made flesh and dwelt among us."

Those who believe the Word of God will live forever in paradise. Think about how God tells us He created all of Creation by *speaking it* into reality. God said, "Let there be light." And there was light.

Even though few of the most influential people in our culture are Christians anymore, we still swim in a sea of 'social capital' that is the result of a Bible-based civilization, even as our schoolchildren are taught not to believe in Christianity. As belief declines, so will that capital. As people bend the rules more and more, and as personal and public morality go into steep decline, the government has to pass more and more laws to stop people from doing what it once went without saying people would not do.

We see all around us the deterioration of relationships, the loss of real family, and genuine friendships. We see it in our poor regard for the oldest and youngest of our human race. Those who do not care for their ancestors will not likely care for their descendants—if they even produce any. There was a time in America when our aging parents and other elderly relatives and even strangers were a cherished part of our communities.

Our country is plagued by ingratitude. Our people live with material comforts their ancestors could not have dreamed about, and freedom to pursue pleasures that our ancestors had not imagined. Yet rarely does one hear gratitude expressed for this.

Irresponsible behavior is no longer publicly frowned upon. Decadence abounds. Freedom naturally leans towards evil if Man is master of the world and has no responsibility to his Maker for what he does. It is no wonder we have so much crime when we hesitate to call any behavior wrong.

The problem is anthropocentricity: Man as the center of the Cosmos with no God above him. Man worshiped by man—and his evil denied. Without Christianity, "Man is the measure of all things—imperfect man, who is never free of pride, self-interest, envy, vanity, and dozens of other defects," says Solzhenitsyn. Our most precious possession is our spiritual life.

Every plank in the ideology of the Left today rests on lies and deception. That is why leftists hate the truth. And they hate the country in which they were born. We are reaping what these evil men and women have sown. Every 33 minutes, there is a murder in America. Every week, 10,000 kids run away from home.

Arguments against God do not generally make much sense. Those who make them instinctively know this, which is why they resort to *ad hominem* attacks and other insults in nearly every discussion of moral issues. I have heard it said that if God is good and God is all-powerful, why does He let this world of sin go on? He wants to impress upon us the gravity, the enormity, and the cost of sin.

Doesn't everybody want to be happy? As political scientist Charles Murray has discovered in his research, happiness does not come from passing pleasures but from deep satisfaction with the way your life has been lived; to be generally pleased with who you are and what you have done and "to reach old age generally pleased with who you have been and what you have accomplished that has been important through your own efforts over an extended period of time."

In every study ever done, sociologists have found that Christians are much happier than unbelievers and far less likely to drop out of school, be unemployed, or commit a crime. In other words, going to church promotes good habits.

Regular churchgoers are healthier, earn more money, finish college more often, and live longer than the lost. People who attend church regularly exhibit better mental and physical health; have more stable marriages and fewer disabilities in their old age. They feel better about themselves, are less depressed, and use fewer drugs and alcohol. And their children have better outcomes, too.

If we ruminate over the technological advances of the last sixty years, including the increasing medical care capabilities and longer life spans; the spread to people of all stations of what once were considered luxuries and unheard-of personal comforts; the new welfare state to prevent utter poverty; and the social revolutions of the 1960s that promised to make us all happier, you might think that Americans are far more happy today than in the 1950s. You would be dead wrong. Americans have grown continuously more depressed and miserable over the last fifty years.

The reasons lie in a matrix of falsity promoted by our educational institutions and various forms of media, as to what will make you happy. It is not how many sexual partners you have and how wild you swing. It is not even how much money you make, and material possessions you accumulate. Besides people in abject poverty, the results of happiness surveys are not affected by income level.

What does sociology say about happiness? The happiest Americans are housewives. Married people are far happier than those who are not; children raised in traditional families are far happier than those who are not, and people who attend church regularly are way happier than those who do not. Having been a good parent produces happiness, as does having a good marriage. Having done your job well can make you happy, as can to be a faithful adherent to your religion. Being a good friend and a good neighbor enhances happiness. That is about all there is to it.

True happiness nearly always involves some combination of God, family, vocation, and community. Kind of makes me wonder why they don't teach that in school. And should make all of us wonder why Faith, Family, Vocation, and Community have been enfeebled by our government since the 1960s, at the behest of Democrats.

Hardly any factor promotes happiness as does a good marriage. It makes me curious why kids aren't told this. They are not getting married these days, so this information must not be getting through. The happiest people in America are married—43 percent of whom say they are very happy. The unhappiest group is those never married—less than one out of ten are very happy! In the middle are widows and divorcees. The happiest people in America as far as how they spend their time are homemakers! Fifty-seven percent of whom say they are very satisfied. Only 44 percent of people who work outside the home are very satisfied with how they send their typical days.

American men used to be known the world over as men who said what they meant and kept their word. That is why deals on a handshake used to be so common—men were only as good as their word, and everybody understood that. That is a far cry from today's litigious society.

Integrity means doing the right thing—not because you might suffer consequences if you don't. But because your principles are such that you do the right thing even when there are no negative consequences for doing the wrong thing—such as if you won't get caught.

To take advantage of another person was considered dishonorable under the Christian ethic that once upon a time dictated behavior in America. That does not mean it was wrong to out-negotiate someone, buy something for less than it might have been worth, sell something for more than it might have been worth, or write a contract that gave you favorable terms. It meant that it was dishonorable to lie, cheat, steal, or defraud someone else.

By the 1990s, after decades of public school brainwashing against the Lord, the level of Christian faith among Americans began to wane. Contrary to some public pundits' opinions, it has declined more among the working class than the upper class. America was at its most Christian in 1963—just before Satan attacked. That same year, the Supreme Court kicked God, the Bible, and prayer out of the public schools and started to brainwash children into Secular Humanism. It makes the state the highest authority in the world instead of God.

1963 was the highest year of church building, church membership, and church attendance in American history. Only one out of a hundred Americans had no Christian faith. By 1972, 4% had left the Christian faith. By 1980, it was 10%. By 2010, 20%.

Six out of ten of working-class Americans have not stepped foot in a church more than once in the past year, double the number from fifty years ago. Despite liberal elites who sneer at the ignorant folks who go to church, better educated, upper-class Americans go to church more often than the high school dropout poor people.

Americans were once far neighborlier. Only in the United States, among nations, was the sense of community once so influential that unrelated people who happened to live near each other routinely volunteered to assist their neighbors regularly. People used to watch each other's kids, drive neighbors to the doctor, loan tools or groceries, and key an eye on nearby houses for those on vacation.

It used to be that Americans were the most engaged of all the world's people in civic affairs. During my lifetime, voting in the presidential election is down 22 percent. The number of folks who attend public meetings, belong to a national associations, serve as an officer in a club, work for a political party, or serve on a local committee has declined by half. Parents with children belonging to the PTA is down 61 percent. People have civically disengaged.

Even the percentage of people who have entertained friends in their home has dropped by almost half. Those who say that their whole family usually eats dinner together is down 69 percent. Membership in bowling leagues is down 73 percent. But bowling alone has increased. And people now have lower trust that the people around them will do the right thing, which is known as 'social trust.'

The famed political scientist Francis Fukuyama has found that social trust determines prosperity in a culture. The percentage of Americans who agree that other people generally can be trusted, people generally try to be fair, and others are generally helpful, has slowly but steadily declined since the 1970s from 64 percent to 44 percent.

Social trust is eroded by ethnic diversity in all neighborhoods—the opposite of what liberal elites predicted, who do not practice it themselves. The communities with the most diversity have the lowest trust in local government, and trust neighbors less—even those of the same ethnicity. They are less likely to give to charity, work on projects for their community, perceive that they have a good quality of life, and have fewer close friends. A neighborhood with weak social capital is more vulnerable to crime. Social welfare bureaucracies or the police must solve most of its problems.

The more often you attend church, the happier you are! According to the results of the General Social Survey, when asked how happy they are, half of the people who attend church more than once a week are very happy. Four out of ten who go to church weekly self-describe as very happy, while one-third who attend church once a month do. The less you go to church, the less the odds are that you are very happy. The least likely to be very happy, 23 percent, are those who never go to church. And the most joyful of all Christians are 'Fundamentalists.'

People need food and shelter—no doubt about that. Beyond that, they need self-respect, and it is only earned by achieving something where failure was possible. Knowing that you have responsibility for the consequences of your actions is a significant part of what makes life worth living. It is far less satisfying to have the welfare state take care of your children than to know you have taken care of them yourself when you could have failed. It is much more deeply satisfying to receive a raise you know you have earned than to get one just because you are in a labor union.

A man holding down a menial job supporting his wife and children is doing something authentically meaningful with his life. If that same man lives under a system that tells him his wife and children will be taken care of, whether he contributes or not, is diminished in status. Taking possible hardship out of the way for people also robs them of being able to look back and say they made a difference.

Americans lost confidence in the rightness of our traditional principles. There was a time when America did not practice all she preached. Somehow, it came to be that America no longer preached what she practiced. The only thing preached now is the devilish notion of nonjudgmentalism. So nobody is lazy, nobody is a whore, and nobody is a criminal. The only people you can criticize are Christians and heterosexual white males.

The American moral code that applied to everyone across all lines of race, class, or background is gone. Replaced with nothing. This code had the power to restrain unseemly behavior— unbecoming behavior, unfitting, indecent—as in not in keeping with established standards of taste, indecorous in appearance, improper in speech or conduct. Unseemliness is prevented not so much by laws and regulations as by mutual understandings; upon an allegiance to behave by these shared understandings.

Sadly, so many of my fellow men and women have been duped, as I once was, by the Devil's Matrix into believing that happiness is being gratified and entertained. Real joy comes from making wise decisions and taking proper actions that accumulate over time. It is to delay instant gratification for long-term benefits.

The Devil's Matrix in which our country is now immersed has turned morality upside down. Those without scales on their eyes can see the fruit it produces is rotten. That means its source is evil. It hides knowledge, scoffs at wisdom, looks for innocents to despoil, revels in filth, makes grotesque art, dumbs down our children, uses language to pervert, feeds on our darker urges, plays on our pride, envy, and covetousness. It makes war on the good, the true, and the honorable. Spread the Word.

"The masses have never thirsted after truth. Whoever can supply them with illusions is easily their master; whoever attempts to destroy their illusions is always their victim." — Gustave Le Bon, *The Crowd*, 1895

Bibliography

Axe, Douglas. *Undeniable: How Biology Confirms Our Intuition that Life is Designed*. New York: HarperCollins Publishers, 2016.

Barton, David, https:wallbuilders.com

Barzun, Jacques. *Darwin –Marx –Wagner –Critique of a Heritage*. University of Chicago Press, 1941.

Bethell, Tom. *Darwin's House of Cards*. Seattle, Washington: Discovery Institute Press, 2017.

Blumenfeld, Samuel & Newman, Alex. *Crimes of the Educators*. Washington, D.C.: WND Books, 2014.

Breitbart, Andrew & Ebner, Mark. *Hollywood, Interrupted: Insanity Chic in Babylon—The Case Against Celebrity*. Hoboken, New Jersey: John Wiley & Sons, 2004.

Buckley Jr., William F. *God and Man at Yale*. Washington D.C.: Regnery Publishing, 1986.

Buchanan, Patrick J. *The Death of the West*. New York: St. Martin's Griffin, 2002.

Byfield, Ted. *Why History Matters*. Edmonton, Alberta, Canada: SEARCH, 2008.

Chaberek, Michael, O.P. *Catholicism and Evolution: A History from Darwin to Pope Francis*. Kettering, Ohio: Angelico Press, 2015.

Coulter, Ann. *Demonic: How the Liberal Mob is Endangering America*. New York: Crown Forum, 2011.

Coulter, Ann. *Godless: The Church of Liberalism*. New York: Crown Forum, 2007.

Dalrymple, Theodore. *In Praise of Prejudice: The Necessity of Preconceived Ideas*. New York: Encounter Books, 2007.

Davis, Mark. *Upside Down: How the Left Turned Right into Wrong, Truth into Lies, and Bad into Good*. Washington, D.C.: Regnery Publishing, 2016.

Dawson, Christopher. *Progress and Religion*. Washingto, D.C.: The Catholic University Press of America, 2001.

De Lubac, Henri. *The Drama of Atheist Humanism*. Paris: Spes, 1944.

De Marco, Donald, and Wiker, Benjamin. *Architects of the Culture of Death*. San Francisco: Ignatius Press, 2004.

Eberstadt, Mary. *It's Dangerous to Believe: Religious Freedom and Its Enemies*. New York: HarperCollins, 2016.

Erickson, Erick & Blankschaen, Bill. *You Will Be Made to Care: The War on Faith, Family, and Your Freedom to Believe*. Washington, D.C.: Regnery Publishing, 2016.

Fiorazo, David. *The Cost of our Silence: Consequences of Christians Taking the Path of Least Resistance.* Abbotsford, Wisconsin: Aneko Press, 2015.

Flitton, Dave. *The Occult History of the Third Reich.* New York: The History Channel (documentary), 1991.

Frankl, Victor E. *Man's Search for Meaning.* Boston: Beacon Press, 1959.

Frum, David. *How We Got Here.* New York: Basic Books, 2000.

Hedges, Chris. *Empire of Illusion: The End of Literacy and the Triumph of Spectacle.* New York: Nations Books, 2009.

Hirsen, James. *Hollywood Nation.* New York: Crown Forum, 2005.

Hitchens, Peter. *The Abolition of Britain: From Winston Churchill to Princess Diana.* San Francisco: Encounter Books, 2000.

Hitchens, Peter. *The Rage Against God.* London: Continuum International, 2010.

Holmes, Kim R. *The Closing of the Liberal Mind: How Groupthink and Intolerance Define the Left.* New York: Encounter Books, 2016.

Horowitz, David. *The Professors,* Washington, D.C.: Regnery Publishing, 2006.

Johnson, Paul. *Intellectuals: From Marx and Tolstoy to Sartre and Chomsky.* New York: HarperCollins Publishers, 1988.

Kengor, Paul. *Takedown: From Communists to Progressives, How the Left has Sabotaged Family and Marriage.* Washington, D.C.: WND Books, 2015.

Kjos, Berit. *Brave New Schools*. Eugene, Oregon: Harvest House Publishers, 1995.

Kimball, Roger. *The Long March: How the Cultural Revolution of the 1960s Changed America*. New York: Encounter Books, 2000.

Klinghoffer, David. *The Unofficial Guide to Cosmos: Fact and Fiction in Neil Degrasse Tyson's Landmark Science Series*. Seattle: Discovery Institute Press, 2014.

Leaf, Jonathan. *The Politically Incorrect Guide to the Sixties*. Washington, D.C.: Regnery Publishing, 2009.

Lennox, John C. *Seven Days that Divide the World: The Beginning According to Genesis and Science*. Grand Rapids, Michigan: Zondervan, 2011.

Lewis, C.S. *The Abolition of Man*. New York: HarperCollins, 1944.

Lewis, C. S. *The World's Last Night*. Orlando, Florida: Harcourt, 1960.

Lichter, S. Robert, Lichter Linda S, and Rothman, Stanley. *Prime Time: How TV Portrays American Culture*. Washington, D.C: Regnery Publishing, 1994.

Lind, Bill. *The Origins of Political Correctness*. Washington, D.C.: Accuracy in Academia, 2000.

Lutzer, Erwin W. *Hitler's Cross*. Chicago: Moody Publishers, 1995.

Marsden, George M. *The Soul of the American University*. New York: Oxford University Press, 1994.

Medved, Michael. *Hollywood vs. America*. New York: HarperCollins Publishers, 1992.

Morris, Ham, Cuozzo, Morris, Wieland, & Henry. *When Christians Roamed the Earth*. Green Forest, Arkansas: Master Books, 2002.

Murray, Charles. *Coming Apart*. New York, Crown Forum, 2013.

Myers, Jeff and Noebel, David. *Understanding the Times: A Survey of Competing Worldviews*. Colorado Springs: David C. Cook, 2015.

Neuhaus, Richard John. *The Naked Public Square: Religion and Democracy in America*. Grand Rapids, Michigan: William B. Eerdmans Publishing Company, 1984.

Olasky, Marvin. *The Tragedy of American Compassion*. Wheaton, Illinois: Crossway Books, 1992.

Pipes, Richard. *Communism: A History*. New York: Random House, 2001.

Pollak, Joel B. *See No Evil: 19 Hard Truths the Left Can't Handle*. Washington, D.C.:, Regnery Publishing, 2016.

Rana, Fazale and Ross, Hugh. *Who was Adam: A Creation Model Approach to the Origin of Humanity*. Corvina, California: RTB Press, 2015.

Ravitch, Diane. *The Language Police*. New York: Vintage Books, 2004.
Rieff, Philip. *My Life Among the Deathworks*. Charlottesville, Virginia: University of Virginia Press, 2006.

Ritenbaugh, John W. *Leadership and Covenants*. Charlotte, North Carolina: Church of the Great God. www.ccg.org.

Roche, George. *A World Without Heroes: The Modern Tragedy*. Hillsdale, Michigan: Hillsdale College Press, 1987.

Ross, Hugh. *A Matter of Days: Resolving a Creation Controversy.* Corvina, California: RTB Press, 2015.

Schaeffer, Francis. *How Should We Then Live?: The Rise and Decline and Western Thought and Culture.* Wheaton, Illinois: Crossway Books, 1955.

Scruton, Roger. *An Intelligent Person's Guide to Modern Culture.* South Bend, Indiana: St. Augustine's Press, 2000.

Scruton, Roger. *Fools, Frauds and Firebrands.* London: Bloomsbury Continuum, 2015.

Scruton, Roger. *How to be a Conservative.* London: Bloomsbury Continuum, 2014.

Shapiro, Ben. *Primetime Propaganda: The True Hollywood Story of How the Left Took Over Your TV.* New York: HarperCollins, 2011.

Shiflett, Dave. *Exodus: Why Americans Are Fleeing Liberal Churches for Conservative Christianity.* New York: Sentinel HC, 2005.

Skousen, W. Cleon. *The Five Thousand Year Leap.* Franklin, Tennessee: American Documents Publishing, L.L.C., 1981.

Solzhenitsyn, Aleksandr. *A World Split Apart.* New York: Harper & Row, 1978.

Sommers, Christina Hoff. *One Nation Under Therapy.* New York: St. Martin's Press, 2005.

Still, William T. *New World Order: The Ancient Plan of Secret Societies.* Lafayette, Louisiana: Huntington House Publishers, 1990.

Sunquist, Scott W. *The Unexpected Christian Century.* Grand Rapids, Michigan: Baker Publishing Group, 2015.

Swanson, Kevin. *Apostate: The Men Who Destroyed the West*. Parker, Colorado: Generations with Vision, 2013.

Sykes, Charles J. *Dumbing Down Our Kids*. New York: St. Martin's Press, 1995.

Tsakiris, Alex. *Why Science is Wrong . . . About Almost Everything*. San Antonio, Texas: Anomalist Books, 2014.

Walsh, Michael. *The Devil's Pleasure Palace: The Cult of Critical Theory and the Subversion of the West*. New York: Encounter Books, 2015.

Vance, J.D. *Hillbilly Elegy*. New York: HarperCollins, 2016.

Vitz, Paul C. *Censorship: Evidence of Bias in Our Children's Textbooks*. Ann Arbor, Michigan: Servant Books, 1986.

Weaver, Richard M. *Ideas Have Consequences*. The University of Chicago Press, 1948.

Weigel, George. *The Cube and the Cathedral: Europe, America, and Politics Without God*. New York: Basic Books, 2005.

Wells, Jonathan, Ph.D. *The Politically Incorrect Guide to Darwinism and Intelligent Design*. Washington D.C.: Regnery Publishing, 2006.

Wiker, Benjamin. *Moral Darwinism: How We Became Hedonists*. Downers Grove, Illinois: InterVarsity Press, 2002.

Wiker, Benjamin. *10 Books Every Conservative Must Read*. Washington D.C.: Regnery Publishing, 2010.

Wiker, Benjamin. *10 Books that Screwed Up the World*. Washington, D.C.: Regnery Publishing, 2008.

Wildmon, Donald E. *Speechless: Silencing the Christians*. Minneapolis, Minnesota: Richard Vigilante Books, 2009.

Wright, Bradley. *Christians are Hate-Filled Hypocrites: and Other Lies You've Been Told*. Bloomington, Minnesota: Bethany House Publishers, 2010.

Yancey, George. *Hostile Environment: Understanding and Responding to Anti-Christian Bias*. Downers Grove, Illinois: InterVarsity Press, 2015.

Made in the USA
Monee, IL
08 September 2020